Concentration and Price

Concentration and Price

edited by
Leonard W. Weiss

The MIT Press
Cambridge, Massachusetts
London, England

This book was set in Palatino by Asco Trade Typesetting Ltd., Hong Kong and printed and bound in the United States of America.

Library of Congress Cataloging-in-Publication Data

Concentration and price / edited by Leonard W. Weiss.
    p.   cm.
  Includes index.
  ISBN 0-262-23143-3
  1. Industrial concentration. 2. Prices. 3. Pricing. I. Weiss, Leonard W.
HD2757.C66 1989
338.6′44—dc20   89-31997
                                       CIP

Contents

Contributors

The persons who have participated in this book fall into two categories. The first group are those who participated in extensive original research projects which are presented in part I. All but Yamawaki and Sleuwaegen had been graduate students at the University of Wisconsin-Madison, although most of them had received Ph.D.'s long before their participation in this project. The study by Belman derived from his thesis. The data for the chapter on auctions grew out of Brannman's and Klein's theses, though Klein's had been defended several years earlier. He used updated data from that thesis in the chapter. The participants in part I are presently affiliated as follows:

Dale Belman, University of Wisconsin, Milwaukee

Lance Brannman, University of Wisconsin, Milwaukee

Christina Kelton, University of Minnesota, Minneapolis

Douglass Klein, Union College, Schenectady, New York

Rolland Koller II, Brigham Young University, Provo, Utah

Leo Sleuwaegen, Catholic University of Leuven, Belgium

Hideki Yamawaki, Wissenschaftszentrum, Berlin, West Germany

The contributors who wrote sections of part II were for the most part responding to my request that they supply me with brief summaries of studies that had appeared elsewhere. Steven Berry, Hugh Briggs, Allen Berger, Timothy Hannon, Howard Marvel, Scott Milliman, and Robert Town did more. At my request Hugh Briggs wrote a brief summary of the extensive work that has been done on nineteenth-century rail cartels and ran some regressions based on the prices that dropped out of those studies. Allen Berger and Tim Hannon, also at my request, reran their data on MMDA interest rates to evaluate alternative functional forms. Howard

Marvel, in addition to summarizing his earlier work, ran a completely new set of regressions on gasoline retailing dating from the 1970s to evaluate a new hypothesis: that market forces determined gasoline prices during the price control period in the 1970s. The participants in part II and their affiliations are as follows:

Allen Berger, Board of Governors, Federal Reserve System, Washington, D.C.

Steven Berry, Yale University, New Haven, Connecticut

Harry Bloch, University of Tasmania, Hobart, Tasmania, Australia

Hugh Briggs, Marquette University, Milwaukee, Wisconsin

James Ferguson, Federal Trade Commission, Washington, D.C.

Timothy Hannan, Board of Governors, Federal Reserve System, Washington, D.C.

James MacDonald, U.S. Department of Agriculture, Washington, D.C.

Bruce Marion, University of Wisconsin, Madison

Howard Marvel, Ohio State University, Columbus

Scott Milliman, James Madison University, Harrisburg, Virginia

Robert Town, graduate student, University of Wisconsin, Madison

Preface

This project began in the late 1970s when I used to wind up my lecture on concentration, profits, and price cost margins and their difficulties with the proposal that we do a book with enough concentration price studies to be convincing. Early in 1981 one of the students (Scott Milliman) volunteered to do such a study (on airlines) as part of the project.

A few months later Lance Brannman defended his thesis on National Forest timber sales which contained the data needed for an auctions study. I knew that Douglass Klein had developed similar data on offshore oil in his thesis in 1977. George Stigler had already brought Kessel's massive study of underwriters' spreads on municipal bond issues to my attention. I called Doug that afternoon, and by close of business we had another project underway. Neither thesis carried auction theory nearly as far as we did in this book, nor had they fit number of bidder coefficients to order statistics.

After that start I set out to recruit a book from among others of our former students. Christina Kelton had been doing a study on change in concentration-change in price for Bruce Marion and Fritz Mueller, using one equation limited to food and tobacco products, having already defended her thesis on a wholly different topic. I suggested that she "expand her project," a process that took five years. In 1986, when I presented a preliminary summary of the project at a seminar, Professor Zwi Griliches pointed out that we hadn't really answered Peltzman. To do so, we decided that she should develop a fourth equation that made unit cost an endogenous variable. So there went another year of her life.

Rolland Koller had been a graduate student at Wisconsin more than a decade earlier. He expressed interest in doing one of the studies. I had worked with cement data in the 1960s and had always thought something was possible there. I set him on the trail and after about three years we had a chapter on cement also.

Dale Belman was a student in my graduate course in 1981–2. He was interested in labor and seemed the most likely candidate for a project I had begun in the early 1960s. I had already acquired the data he needed, and it was far better than what I had worked with. But it was his conception of the solution that won the day. It was an excellent thesis, and I feel he has settled the issue.

There is a part of one more thesis in the book, Steve Berry's on airlines. I was delighted to have him working in the field. Scott Milliman had decided to write his thesis on another topic, and his brief paper was not a chapter by itself. When he wrote it, we knew of no other concentration-price study on airlines, but there have been many since. Robert Town expanded the concentration concepts used and added to its usefulness, but we needed more. We decided that we should develop some data on revenue per passenger-mile and apply it to both Milliman's and Berry's papers. We bought the tapes from the Department of Transportation and struggled with them for several months without success. Almost a year later I paid a private firm to provide us with the 88 numbers per quarter needed for at least Milliman's study. The results showed that the underlying data from the tapes made little sense even with the code broken. Finally, in January 1989 I called a few of the others who had succeeded where we did not and learned that Boeing had been supplying cleaned up data from those tapes but was no longer doing so. At this late date, with about ten people working in the field, we can hardly claim to have made breakthroughs on price. So air fares are now, sadly, in the "other people's papers" category.

Finally, I was able to recruit Hideki Yamawaki for the EEC paper during a visit at the Wissenschaftzentrum in Berlin in the summer of 1984. He subsequently recruited Leo Sleuwaegen from Leuven. A major problem in this case was data. As far as we know, they have the only comparable data for concentration in the five original major EEC countries, and their EEC-wide concentration estimates are unique. This is why their chapter contains such a large amount of appendix material.

Although they could do a price change study somewhat like Kelton's for Germany, they had only price-cost margins for the other original EEC countries. I do not feel this is a disaster at all. The margins involved data from the 1960s and 1970s when the EEC was young. A correlation between concentration and margins within one of those countries might be explained as superior firms winning both high profits and high market shares, but that can hardly be convincing for the leaders in EEC industries in 1962 and 1976. They were large because their nations were large and/or had relatively concentrated markets in the industries in question. They could hardly have attained their large market shares by winning the European competitive race in those early, only partially integrated years of the EEC.

Over the six years that this project was under construction I received many papers from these participants, and sometimes after months of waiting, they received very long letters from me that often called for unconscionable changes in data, models, statistical procedures, and/or language. The process was repeated for most of them several times. Amazingly, none of them dropped out. I am enormously thankful to each of them.

The material in part II did not involve the same tension, but I again feel extremely thankful for the brief reports that many made, at my request, on research they have reported in full elsewhere. They could not possibly transmit the full content of their projects in three or four pages and a few tables. Interested readers should surely turn to the basic studies only summarized here. I thank my former student, Hugh Briggs, for his careful gleaning of concentration-price results from three other studies of nineteenth-century railroad freight rate data. I thank another former student, Tim Hannon, now at the Federal Reserve Board, whom I persuaded to apply a wide variety of concentration indexes in explaining a well-defined price in banking. This gave us another price capable of systematic analysis with respect to functional form. And, of course, I thank Scott Milliman and Steve Berry for their work on airlines.

By the time you, the reader, review the many results in this book, I hope you will agree with me that our work in part I and the large number whose work is summarized in part II have achieved the critical mass on the issues at hand.

And, beyond all of those whose names appear in the text, I wish to thank the many who are not authors but who performed devotedly. One was Reiko Gomi at Keio University in Tokyo who did an unbelievable job of typing chapter 12 and especially table 12.2 in English. Another was Jane McDonald who did an excellent and wholly believable job of typing much of the manuscript, often at unnatural hours. We owe a lot to many commentators over the years, but I am especially thankful to the six anonymous referees that The MIT Press found to comment on the manuscript.

Leonard W. Weiss

1 Why Study Concentration and Price?

Most oligopoly theory predicts that price will rise with concentration. Indeed, this is the oldest and most important prediction of that body of thought. The major purpose of this book is to test this hypothesis. The tests will deal with it more directly than has been commonly done before and altogether will offer more evidence on the subject.

The emphasis will be on price. We will not attempt to compare the prices of ships, shoes, and sugar, though one chapter will attempt to explain changes in prices of different goods by other changes in the same periods, including concentration change. In general, we will report on studies of markets separated by location (cement, airlines, banking services, retailing), by time (auctions), or on the prices of inputs (labor, beef). Except for the change-in-concentration–change-in-price studies, these will all be somewhat specialized, but we feel that the effect of all these studies taken together is greater than their simple sum.

The Theory of Concentration and Price

The relationship between concentration and price was the primary concern of classic oligopoly theory. The founder of the field was of course Augustin Cournot (1838). He assumed independent output decisions are made by oligopolists who expect other firms' outputs to remain fixed. Then, assuming no costs, the result is a price proportional to $1/N$, where N is the number of equal-sized firms. In the more likely world where N equal-sized firms have the same constant costs, Cournot's analysis yields a margin of $(P - C)/P = 1/EN$, where C is marginal cost and E is the elasticity of demand. Stigler (1968, 36–38) has shown that, with interfirm cost differences, the analysis yields an equilibrium with firms of unequal size. The Cournot model yields a profit prediction as well. With a straight line demand total industry profits decline as N rises.

Bertrand (1883) assumed that each firm expects the others' prices to remain fixed and adjusts to that. The price falls quickly to minimum average cost and stays there so long as more than one firm is in the market. Bertrand implicitly assumed an undifferentiated product. With product differentiation, price rises with concentration (Prescott and Visher 1977; Eaton and Lipsey 1978).

The Cournot and the Bertrand theories lead to what are often referred to as Nash equilibria. They are the result of recognized independence among a few firms who adjust to one another's positions acting independently. There are various other possibilities, for instance, an expectation that the rivals' output or price will change in some predetermined way rather than remain constant.

Another set of theories attempts to predict the presence or lack of successful collusion, tacit or explicit. In Chamberlin (1933, 1949) many small sellers act independently as purely or monopolistically competitive firms, but as their market shares rise, there comes a point where they recognize their interdependence and begin to act collusively. This means that at higher levels of concentration they will price in response to the industry's demand curve. In other words, Chamberlin believed in a critical level of concentration (pp. 48–50). He acknowledges that because of other variables or uncertainty, or both, the transition may not be abrupt, but he seems to have no doubt that beyond some point it will be complete and the firms will perform collusively (pp. 51–53).

Chamberlin's model has been expanded to make it more realistic. If costs, excess capacity, or judgments about the elasticity of demand differ among rivals, their optimal prices will differ. A major firm with lower costs, greater excess capacity, or an expectation of greater elasticity of demand among buyers than its rivals is apt to prefer a lower price and will probably win the argument (Boulding 1955, 639–645). As such differences increase, the collusive price will fall below the monopolistic profit-maximizing price. If within the oligopoly range the extent of such differences increases with the number of rival firms, then an increase in concentration should yield a higher price even above the critical concentration level.

Stigler (1964) developed another theory of collusive, oligopoly which is dependent on the ability of oligopolists to detect chiseling. His approach is a matter of statistical theory. Firms with large market shares can detect secret price cutting by rivals more readily than small firms, and the ability of leaders to identify secret price concessions increases at an increasing rate with concentration. He concludes that his theory implies than price will rise with the Herfindahl index.

There is more theory, but the purpose of this chapter is not to review all oligopoly theory. It is even possible to formulate a model where price declines when concentration rises (Salop 1979), though such theories seem to be few and based on unusual assumptions. In this book it will become clear that empirical cases where concentration significantly reduces price are also few.

Entry Conditions and Contestable Markets

In general, independent action by oligopolists seems to yield a positive effect of concentration on price, and the ability of the oligopolists to attain collusive prices also increases with concentration. But what determines the collusive optimal price that they attain? The classic answer seems to be the elasticity of demand for the industry's product. In fact, both elasticities and margins are so low that we are forced to conclude either that industries seldom attain optimal prices or that elasticities seldom if ever govern.

The obvious alternative is conditions of entry. In Bain (1956) these are the cumulative effect of a scale or displacement barrier, an absolute cost barrier (mainly special access to certain limited mineral deposits or very large capital requirements), and a product differentiation barrier. Although Bain did not emphasize them, barriers set by government such as patents, franchises, and import restrictions should surely be included. None of these barriers to entry involve concentration directly. However, since the scale or displacement barrier depends on the ratio of minimum efficient scale to demand, it apt to be related to concentration. In fact, all of the industries Bain characterizes as having "high" barriers to entry are very concentrated.

Bain's barriers do not play a central role in this book, but they do come up occasionally. One of the studies of airlines in chapter 3 provides a test of the effects of potential entrants on prices; another paper in the same chapter offers a new way of testing the effect of the scale or displacement barrier, and one of the banking papers reviewed in chapter 12 attempts a test of limit pricing. But we leave entry conditions generally to othe efforts.

Some mention should be made of contestable markets, however (Baumol 1982; Baumol et al. 1983). If a market can be entered and left quickly—which requires that no costs of entry are "sunk"—then it is not supposed to make any difference what the structure of the market is. A firm or an industry that sets its price in excess of the minimum average cost would attract prompt entry and quickly lose business. In a world of perfectly contestable markets, even a pure monopoly could yield competitive prices.

But does anything like perfect contestability exist in reality? In industries such as steel, oil refining, and cement where much of the investment is in specialized equipment, there are many long-lived sunk investments, and so their markets are far from perfectly contestable.

One of the industries covered by this book, airlines, was widely used as an example. Presumably airlines already flying in a region can readily offer service to a new city if flights to that city are overpriced. Entry requires virtually no sunk investment in aircraft. Airplanes can be shifted to other routes by simple rescheduling.

Another industry sometimes described as selling on contestable markets is banking. This is at least conceivable for loans to large and profitable corporations with access to the money markets. But it just has to be wildly off the mark for the local retail banking business in which complex and difficult legal and administrative regulations bar the establishment of new banks or even of new branches in many states and for the deep investments in individual business relationships needed to operate successfully in retail banking markets.

In any case we have a straightforward test of contestability. If price systematically rises with concentration, the market involved cannot be all that contestable. Our evidence and that of others in chapters 8 and 12 seems to rule out contestability in both industries.

It does not follow at all from a finding that few if any markets are perfectly contestable, that the barriers to entry are necessarily high. Bain, (1956, 179–180) found many markets where barriers to entry are "low" or "moderate," and Stigler (1950) believes that entry into most industries is "free." Industries with free entry or low or moderate barriers to entry are mostly far from being perfectly contestable because it takes time to enter them. Stigler says it well:

Free entry does not mean, as many infer, that a new firm can enter and immediately be as profitable as an established firm. We do not begrudge the firm a decent interval in which to build its factory; we should be equally willing to concede a period during which production is put on a smooth-running schedule, trade connections are developed, labor is recruited and trained, and the like. The costs of building up a going business are legitimate investment expenses ... (1950, 22–23).

Not only are such costs legitimate investment expenses, they are also sunk. We suspect that it is these human investments and similar time-consuming efforts to build up clientele that were overlooked when industries like airlines are pictured as selling on contestable markets.

Our general conclusion to this point is that almost all oligopoly theory makes predictions about price, and with few exceptions, those predictions are that price will rise with concentration. The differences among them on this point are matters of functional form, not direction.

Concentration and Profits

Most oligopoly theory also makes predictions about profits, and until the early 1970s the main emphasis in tests of the theory was on the concentration-profits relationship. It seemed to make sense to compare profit rates among industries rather than price.

Not all theory points to high profits in concentrated industries, however. Of course Bertrand does not, but he doesn't predict high prices either. Chamberlin also expects profits to disappear in oligopoly, even though he expects high prices to persist. Entry and excess capacity leave his oligopolists with only normal profits just as in monopolistic competition (1949, 104–105).

Posner (1975) offers yet another route. Oligopolists presented with price in excess of marginal cost will incur greater costs to attain higher sales. He expects this process to continue until marginal costs have risen to the level of price. His prime example was the excess capacity induced by the CAB's domestic air fare cartel. The notion has not yet received a great deal of attention. One suspects that the reason is that there are only limited cases where high prices can elicit large enough expenditures to eliminate profits. It seems quite probable, however, that *some* profits in oligopolistic industries are competed away by such a process: through construction of excess capacity or promotional effort that would not be worthwhile for a monopoly.

Finally, there is always X-inefficiency. Early in the life of this concept it was suggested that firms with monopoly power might find it easiest to let some X-inefficiency accumulate (Comanor and Leibenstein 1968). This concept is closely related to the organization theorist's slack.

Thus, although many theories point to a positive relationship between concentration and profits, some do not. It seems probable that even if profits do not fully disappear into excess capacity, nonprice competition, and slack, they will often erode profits in concentrated industries to some extent. A large proportion of the evidence supporting X-inefficiency depends on this tendency (Frantz 1988).

Measurement Problems

Our ability to observe economic profits is also limited by measurement difficulties. One clear problem occurs when the assets of a firm are recorded at their current market values. This is likely to occur if the firm or some large part of it is purchased for cash. The new owner may only receive a normal return on *his* investment, though profits have not disappeared in an economic sense. In addition assets are sometimes written down on the books to give the owner a better picture of the value of his firm. Either type of adjustment seems certain to bias the evidence with respect to profits, raising the value of profitable firms and lowering the values of unprofitable firms. As a result rates of return on investment are apt to be biased toward equality.

A second source of bias is the use of original cost valuation of assets in the presence of inflation. All long-term assets will be undervalued, but the error will be greater, the larger the proportion of old plant. This means that slowly growing industries will understate their assets more than rapidly growing industries. Since rapidly growing industries are usually more profitable, this factor will also tend to bias profit rates toward the mean.

The other very large source of bias is the expensing of intangibles, but the direction of bias is less clear. Expenditures on promotion and on R&D are usually written off as current expenses even though they may be investments that yield returns in future years. The expensing of such items commonly leads to the overstatement of rates of return—as is often the case with pharmaceutical houses whose main investments are R&D and promotion—but this is less clear as the growth rate of such expenditures increases. If the rate of growth is about equal to the reported rate of return, as is the case for IBM, then the expensing of intangibles does not distort rates of return at all. In other words, although this accounting practice normally overstates profit rates, the overstatement is less, the more rapidly the firm grows. A very rapidly growing firm may even understate profits as a result (Weiss 1969).

There are many other accounting procedures that affect firms' reported rates of return. The very profitable firm may prefer to select depreciation and inventory policies that understate profits. We suspect many unprofitable firms prefer to overstate their profits in their annual reports. So once more reported rates of return may tend to be biased toward the mean.

These errors affect mainly the reported rates of return on investment or equity. Price cost margins (usually value of shipments less payroll and cost of materials, all divided by value of shipments) are reasonably accurate (Collins and Preston 1968). But many things affect margins besides concentration. Virtually everyone who has used them has at least controlled for some sort of capital–output ratio. From its appearance in the Annual Survey of Manufactures in 1958 until its disappearance in 1982, the standard variable was gross fixed assests divided by value of shipments. Gross fixed assets avoids the obscurities of depreciation, though distortions due to inflation are still present and investments in intangibles are not included. The census reports another asset, inventory, but it was seldom used, perhaps because the ratio of inventory to shipments seldom has much effect on price—cost margins. As a result even price-cost margins, though a big improvement on reported profits divided by equity, are subject to many of the same defects.

Fisher and McGowan (1983) tell us that true economic profit is the internal rate of return, which can differ drastically from the reported rate of return on investment. Thomas Stauffer (1980) developed estimates of internal rates of return for quite a number of corporations. The results were quite plausible, though they were very different from the annual reports. The rates of return of the pharmaceutical houses were cut back to more ordinary levels, but IBM continued to earn a huge internal rate of return. When I introduced Stauffer's book into the IBM case (with Fisher sitting at the other, IBM side of the table), the attorney who was questioning me said, "Why, this is nothing but a Ph.D. thesis." I suspect that what Fisher and McGowan really meant is that there is no way that an outsider can know the appropriate rate of return.

Regression Results

There is some theory that points to no relationship between concentration and profits and many distortions in their measurement that at least weaken any observed relationships and probably bias rates of return toward equality. It follows that even if price does rise with concentration, there may be no measurable effect of concentration on profit rates.

Despite all this we produced 47 concentration-profits or concentration-price cost margin studies between 1951 and 1973 (Weiss 1974). They covered Britain, Canada, Japan, and the United States, and except for the inflationary years of the 1940s, they generally yielded significant positive effects for concentration. It certainly looked as if there was something there, and I believe that there were good reasons to expect it to be understated.

Then came a crucial criticism by Demsetz[1] (1974). He argued that a systematic positive relationship between concentration and profits mights be nothing more than superior firms winning both high profits and high market shares. Demsetz' empirical work on the subject was not convincing. He showed that IRS data for large firms classified by industry supported the conventional hypothesis, though data from the same source on small businesses did not. But IRS data contain many plants listed in the wrong industries and have all the problems of accounting profits mentioned earlier. Nevertheless, his simple and striking argument called for further testing. A few years later Peltzman (1977) developed a related argument that successful innovation increases both market share and profits and thus can lead to a related tendency over time. He also presented an empirical test, but it was extremely difficult to interpret.

What this clearly called for was studies that explained profitability in terms of both market shares and concentration. The first such study, which was really contemporary with Demsetz, was Shepherd's (1972). He had to use his own estimates of market share. Although he had not introduced them in the same regression with concentration, he concluded that market share had far more effect than concentration. He interpreted market share as a measure of monopoly power. This would clearly be correct for the leading firm. It would be the one firm concentration ratio. But Demsetz' argument and evidence had to do with large but not dominant firms. It is leading firms of lesser rank where a statistical test can be convincing.

A second test was run by Bradley and Gale (1982) using Harvard Business School's "PIMS" (profit impact of market strategy) data. The effect of concentration disappeared when market share was introduced. It was less convincing than it might have been because they used only concentration and market share in their analysis.

The clincher came when Ravenscraft (1983), using the FTC's Line of Business data, found in a convincing way that the effect of concentration disappeared when actual market shares were introduced. His results, however, were based on data from 1974, 1975, and 1976, all that was available in the LB data at the time. The concentration-profits relationship is strongest in years like 1963, and it is conceivable that some of it would still have been observable after market share was introduced in such a year even if it was not in the mid-1970s.

From Profits to Prices

What test of oligopoly theory can convince those who find Demsetz's argument persuasive or at least disturbing? What is clearly needed is a hypothesis that follows directly from oligopoly theory and will not succumb to his alternative interpretation.

The obvious hypothesis is that price will rise with concentration. Predictions about price are less equivocal results of oligopoly theory than those about profit. The trick is to formulate tests that are realistic enough to be believable and cover enough cases to suggest generality.

But before that, can prices play the same role here that profits did in Demsetz' argument? High prices certainly are goals, but they should not persist after the adjustment is complete *in competition*. Could high prices be read as an indication of superiority? Perhaps for wine in some sense, but surely not for cement. Even in a case like wine it is not necessarily the fact the vineyard with the highest price is the most successful economically. No variable will ever serve the function perfectly, but price seems a large improvement over profit for a test of the underlying hypotheses.

Our typical study will involve some sort of regression that explains price in terms of costs as well as concentration. Aren't we introducing price-cost margins through the back door? For the most part no. Usually we are not introducing unit costs in an industry but a variable that affects it. We don't use unit labor costs in cement in determining the costs of a region's cement plants but average hourly earnings in all manufacturing in that region. The cost standard in airlines is not based on wages and fuel costs on a particular route but on CAB standard fares that derive from industrywide wages and fuel interacting with distance. Gasoline costs in the first gas station study from the period of import quotes were proxied for by distance from Oklahoma, but the second part of the same paper covering years without import quotas used distance from nearest major refining centers. We feel that in the typical study we have to use cost, but costs in these forms are so far removed from those actually incurred by the firms involved that they are consistent with a huge range of profits.

The change-in-concentration–change-in-price study may appear on first reading to be an exception, but it is not. The variable ΔUC (change in unit cost) is not computed directly from the Census, but rather is an endogenous variable derived from capital intensity (derived from *Statistics of Income*), changes in average hourly wage (from the BLS), and in wholesale prices of the three most important material inputs (prices from BLS and importance from input-output matrix). The coefficients relating these to the unit cost are derived from a regression where the change in unit cost from the Census is dependent on these non-Census cost variables over the whole range of consumer goods, materials, or capital goods, depending on the class of the commodity involved. We feel it is at least as far removed from a reading of the costs of the industry directly measured as are the costs used in cement and airlines.

Finally, we have to acknowledge that one study does to some extent depend on conventional price-cost margins—chapter 6 on the effect of the coming of the Common Market. But in this case we feel that Demsetz' criticism does not apply, or at least not to the conclusion reached. The point to the study is to compare the relationship between concentration and margins when the Common Market was just starting with that in 1972 within each country and, again, concentration throughout the EEC with margins within each country. The 1966 figures are subject to Demsetz' criticism. High margins within France, say, may go mainly to the leaders there, which may be the most profitable and superior firms. You could claim the same in France in the first set of regressions in 1972, but surely not for French margins and the EEC concentration in 1972. Perhaps after a few decades of competition within the EEC the largest firms in the market really with have the highest margins because they have won the competitive race, but 1972 seems too soon.

Plan of Attack

The rest of the book consists of tests of the concentration-price hypothesis. It divides naturally into two parts. In part I appear the tests that were planned and undertaken for the purposes of this book; part II contains brief descriptions of other concentration-price studies. Most of these studies have been published already, so my goal is to convey only the approach and the main conclusions. In one area, banking the cases seem almost endless. More than with any of the other studies covered in the book, it seemed essential that those on banking be subject to review as well as to reports of results. I have therefore written as thorough and as searching a review of the literature as I could muster.

Chapter 2 covers an industry, cement, for which data on concentration and on price are available from different regional markets.

Chapter 3 presents a simultaneous equations model that explains changes in price, cost, output, and concentration for 135 five-digit consumer goods, 272 five-digit industrial materials, and 51 capital goods. It is by far the most general study in the book.

Chapter 4 has to do with auctions, most of which are really oligopolies in the sense that there are seldom more than a dozen bidders. But the theory is different. It emphasizes the importance of variety and how it increases as numbers of bidders rise. Using statistical theory, this study predicts that winning high bids will rise as numbers increase. It does so in a way that fits the predicted pattern with remarkable precision for "products" as different as the underwriting fees on municipal bond issues, oral and sealed bids for National Forest timber tracts, and offshore oil tracts. The results themselves seem important, but we are certain that they extend far beyond these auctions. There are many auction-type situations where alternative firms contend for the same contract to supply an industrial customer with sugar or electric motors or to build a power plant or an office building. We feel that what we have found should extend to those cases almost directly. Beyond that, we feel that diversity also affects the lowest cost or the greatest excess capacity on a market and should therefore produce a tendency for collusive prices to fall as the number of major sellers rises.

Chapter 5 deals with an important cost, labor, where concentration may raise cost, and therefore price. It turns out that rising concentration encourages unionism and therefore raises wages indirectly via the union or directly in nonunion firms.

Chapter 6 contains a price—cost-margin study that attempts to explain the effect of the Common Market. In addition it includes, for Germany only, a change-in-concentration—change-in-price study similar to that in chapter 3.

Part II is made up of many other studies of concentration and price. In some cases those who made the studies agreed to write brief summaries. In a few cases the authors revised their procedure or introduced more data. All of these are included. In one case, banking, their are dozens of studies, so I prepared a summary review.

Chapter 7, which begins this part, contains brief summaries of studies of charges for advertisting time and space, the area in which George Stigler began the study of concentration and price a quarter century ago. It also contains more current studies by Fergusson and by Bloch and Wirth.

Chapter 8 summarizes several recent studies of the effects of concentration on air fares on city pair routes. It also includes two studies done for this book. One tries a wide range of concentration measures in explaining fares on major routes. The other develops estimates of the displacement barrier.

Chapter 9 contains two studies from retailing—by Howard Marvel on gasoline and by Bruce Marion on food stores.

Chapter 10 turns to rail freight rates. The first paper there summarizes the work of MacAvoy, Ulen, and Porter on nineteenth-century grain freight rates from Chicago to the East Coast. This study is particularly interesting because we have detailed information about when the firms were pricing independently and when they were explicitly colluding. The second summary has a more modern cast—it gives a brief account of the determinants of freight rates on unit trains for grain for export once more, after the ICC lost its control over those rates.

Chapter 11 contains a study of concentration among buyers—this time slaughter houses buying beef cattle. Chapter 12 reviews many banking concentration-price studies. The authors of one of those studies tried many different concentration measures at my request and report their results in a brief section at the end of the chapter.

Finally, Chapter 13 summarizes and draws conclusions from all the studies in the book. It contains tables that attempt to evaluate the consistency of the results, the relative effectiveness of various functional forms, and the importance of the relationships.

Note

1. Lucille Keyes had presented Demsetz' argument in an earlier article (Keyes 1968). However, it was surely Demsetz who established this as the major issue with respect to concentration-profits studies.

References

Bailey, Elizabeth E., David R. Graham, and Daniel P. Kaplan. 1985. *Deregulating the Airlines*. Cambridge, MA: MIT Press.

Bain, Joe S. 1956. *Barriers to New Competition*. Cambridge, MA: Harvard University Press.

Baumol, William J., 1982. "Contestable Markets: An Uprising in the Theory of Industry Structure." *The American Economic Review* 72:1 (March), 1−15.

Baumol, William J., John C. Panzer, and Robert D. Willig. 1982. *Contestable Markets and the Theory of Industry Structure*. New York: Harcourt Brace, Jonovitch.

Bertrand, Jules. 1883. "Review of Cournot, Researches." *Journal des Savants*, 499−508.

Boulding, Kenneth. 1955. *Economic Analysis*. 3d ed. New York: Harper Bros.

Chamberlin, Edward H. 1933. *The Theory of Monopolistic Competition*. Cambridge, MA: Harvard University Press. Citations from 6th ed. (1949).

Collins, N. R., and L. E. Perston. 1970. *Concentration and Price Cost Margins in Manufacturing Industries*. Berkeley: University of California Press.

Comanor, William, and Harvey Leibenstein. 1969. "Allocative Efficiency, X-Inefficiency, and the Measurement of Welfare Losses." *Economica*, 36:143 (August), 304−309.

Cournot, Augustin. 1838. *Researches into the the Mathematical Principles of the Theory of Wealth.* Reprint 1963. Homewood, IL: Irwin.

Demsetz, Harold. 1974. "Two Systems of Belief about Monopoly." In Goldschmid et al., pp. 164–184.

Eaton, B. C., and R. G. Lipsey. 1976. "The Introduction of Space into the Neoclassical Model." In Arits and Nobay (eds.), *Studies in Modern Economics.* Oxford: Basil Blackwell.

Fisher, Franklin M., and John J. McGowan. 1983. "On the Misuse of Accounting Rates of Return to Infer Monopoly Profits." *American Economic Review* 73:1 (March), 82–97.

Frantz, Roger S., 1988. *X-Efficiency: Theory Evidence, and Applications.* Boston: Kluer Academic Publishers

Gale, B. T., and B. S. Branch. 1982. "Concentration versus Market Share: Which Determines Performance, and Why Does It Matter?" *Antitrust Bulletin* 23:1 (Spring), 83–105.

Goldschmid, Harvey S. H., Michael Mann, and J. Fred Weston. 1974. *Industrial Concentration: The New Learning.* Boston: Little, Brown.

Hannon, Timothy, "Limit Pricing and the Banking Industry." 1979. *Journal of Money, Credit and Banking* 11:4 (November), 438–446.

Keeler, Theodore E., and Michael Abrahams. 1981. "Market Structure, Pricing, and Service Quality in the Airline Industry under Deregulation." In Sichel and Gies (eds.) *Applications of Economic Principles in Public Utility Industries.* Ann Arbor: University of Michigan Graduate School of Business.

Keyes, Lucille S. 1968. "The Merger Guidelines of the Department of Justice." *Antitrust Law and Economic Review* 2 (Fall), 105–140.

Peltzman, Sam. 1977. "The Gains and Losses from Industrial Concentration." *Journal of Law and Economics* 20:2, 229–264.

Posner, Richard. 1975. "The Social Costs of Monopoly and Regulation." *Journal of Political Economy* 83:4 (August), 807–827.

Prescott, E. C., and M. Vischer. 1977. "Sequential Foresight among Firms with Foresight." *Bell Journal* 8:2 (Autumn), 378–393.

Ravenscraft, David. 1983. "Structure-Profit Relationships at the Line of Business and Industry Level." *Review of Economics and Statistics* 65:1 (February), 22–31.

Salop, Steven. 1979. "Monopolistic Competition with Outside Goods." *Bell Journal* 10:1 (Spring), 141–156.

Shepherd, W. G. 1972. "The Elements of Market Structure." *Review of Economics and Statistics* 54:1 (February), 25–27.

Stigler, George. 1964. "A Theory of Oligopoly." *Journal of Political Economy* 72 : 1 (February), 44–61.

Stigler, George. 1950. "Monopoly and Oligopoly by Merger." *American Economic Review* 40 : 2 (May), 23–34.

Stigler, George. 1968. *The Organization of Industry*. Homewood, IL: Irwin.

Stauffer, Thomas. 1980. *The Measurement of Corporate Rates of Return*. New York: Garland Publishing Company.

Weiss, Leonard W. 1969. "Advertising, Profits and Corporate Taxes." *Review of Economics and Statistics* 51 : 4 (November), 245–257.

Weiss, Leonard W. 1974. "The Concentration-Profits Relationship and Antitrust." In Goldschmid et al., 184–223.

I   Five Basic Studies

2   Price Levels and Seller Concentration: The Case of Portland Cement

Roland H. Koller II
and Leonard W. Weiss

In this chapter we will examine the relationship between price levels and seller concentration. Specifically, we will test the hypothesis that the degree of seller concentration, variously measured, is positively related to price. We have drawn the data for the test from the U.S. Portland cement industry. The cement industry is particularly well suited for this purpose for the following reasons:

First, markets in the industry are regional in scope. Due to the high weight to value ratio in cement, most output goes to customers relatively near the producing plant. In 1963, for example, near the midpoint of the study, 82.2 percent of cement in the United States was shipped less than 200 miles, 93.7 percent was shipped less than 300 miles, and 97.2 percent was shipped less than 400 miles.[1] Figures for other census years are comparable. This makes it possible to obtain a reasonably large set of separate market areas to use as observations in a cross-sectional study.

Second, the product is virtually homogeneous. This makes prices in the various markets quite comparable.

Third, data are available on transaction prices rather than list prices.

Fourth, data are available for a large number of years, making it possible to test the basic hypothesis in a variety of historical contexts.

Fifth, cement is an industrial input sold largely to commercial buyers and not the sort of product usually thought to be susceptible to collusive pricing. The cement industry thus presents a more demanding test of the relationship between price levels and seller concentration than would many other industries.

The Hypothesis to Be Tested

The basic hypothesis to be tested is that seller concentration exerts a positive influence on price levels in cement. More specifically, it is that price levels in cement can be explained by the function

$P = f(C, D, SC),$

Where P stands for price, C stands for cost, D stands for demand condition, and SC stands for seller concentration, and that in this function SC varies directly with P.

Cost is assumed in turn to be affected by wage levels, scale of productions, and the distance the product is shipped. We assume that demand conditions are reflected by rates of capacity utilization and that seller concentration can be adequately measured by concentration ratios, Herfindahl indexes, and similar measures.

The Data

Our test was conducted as follows:

We designated 24 regional markets for use as observations. Each market consisted of a major metropolitan market and all Portland cement plants located within approximately 250 air miles of this central city. The 24 central cities are listed in appendix A. We used only 21 markets in 1948, excluding Phoenix (which had no plants that year) and Los Angeles and San Francisco (data for which was not reported separately as in other years).

Price (P)   The U.S. Bureau of Mines publishes in its annual *Minerals Yearbook* data on shipments and value of shipments for each of the 30 Portland cement producing districts in the United States. Some of these districts include several states, while others consist of single states. California and Pennsylvania are divided into two districts each.

Since our designated market areas did not always correspond to either producing districts or groups of producing districts, it was necessary to assign both shipments and value of shipments to the market areas on some reasonable basis. This was done by assigning to each market a percentage of each district's shipments and value of shipments equal to the percentage of that district's production capacity which fell within the market's boundaries. We next obtained the total value of shipments and the total physical shipments within each market and divided the former by the latter to obtain "unit values," our price variable. This variable is a weighted average value per unit shipped (i.e., per 376-lb barrel) from anywhere within the market area, excluding cost of containers and of transportation from the plant.

Transport Cost (AD)   As our proxy for transport cost, we took the average distance from the cement plants in a market area to the area's central city weighted by the capacities of the individual plants. The distances are in air miles and do not necessarily reflect transport conditions in the actual areas.

Economies of Scale (AC)   Economies of scale are important in the cement industry. Our measure of this variable is simply the average capacity of all producing plants within a market area. Capacities for individual plants were obtained from *Pit and Quarry* magazine directories and maps, and we divided the total market capacity (in thousands of barrels) by the number of plants in the market to obtain our measure.

Wage Cost (AW)   For our wage cost variable, we used the average wage per production worker man-hour from the U.S. Department of Labor, *Handbook of Labor Statistics*, averaged over all states in a market area using our estimated cement shipments from each state as weights.[2]

Capacity Utilization (CU)   The *Minerals Yearbook* gives rates of capacity utilization (in decimals) by producing district, and these were averaged for each market area in a manner similar to that which we used to obtain the price variable.

Seller Concentration   Seller concentration was measured in a variety of ways for this study. Concentration ratios (CRi), Herfindahl indexes (H), and number of sellers (N) were all employed. Unlike most studies, however, our measures are not based on sales data but on firm capacities. These measures were all derived from the information found in *Pit and Quarry* directories and maps (which report locations and capacities for all Portland cement plants in the United States). Our concentration ratios thus measure the percentage of total market capacity accounted for by the largest one through six firms, and our Herfindahl indexes also reflect capacity concentration. The reason for this choice was the availability of data. Both of these measures were expressed in decimals when running the regressions. In addition to concentration ratios, Herfindahl indexes, and number of sellers, we include a variable that we refer to as "importers" (I). This is the number of firms without producing plants within a market area that operate distribution plants within roughly 150 miles of the market area's central city. This variable was taken as a proxy for intermarket competition. The importers variable was also combined with number of sellers to yield one other explanatory variable, $SLR = N + I$.

At this writing, there are real imports from abroad in certain coastal markets. The foreign suppliers ship clinker in and grind and sell it to domestic customers. These were not important in 1980 or before and are not considered in this study.

Theoretical Expectations

Our statistical tests were very straightforward. For each of the years 1948, 1953, 1959, 1961, 1965, 1973, and 1980 we ran a set of up to 23 ordinary least squares regressions in which price was regressed upon average distance, average wage, a variable reflecting the average capacity of cement plants, the rate of capacity utilization, and some combination of concentration variables. These regressions are specified in appendix B. The years chosen were determined primarily by the availability of data on plant capacities. The years 1948, 1953, 1959, 1965, and 1973 come during expansions, 1980 is a recession year, and 1961 is a year of sluggish growth following a recession.

We had no clear expectation regarding the effect of transport cost. On the one hand, it would seem that the greater this was, the lower would be mill-net price. On the other hand, it's possible that inasmuch as the marginal (most distant) plants must make profits over time to survive, the primary effect of high transport costs is to increase price f.o.b. destination. This would increase the mill-net price of all intramarginal plants and increase our price variable as well. Though the expected sign of the average distance variable is uncertain, it was felt that it could have some effect on price in this industry and should be included to control for this.

We expected cement prices to rise with average hourly wages, labor being a major cost in the industry.

Economies of scale imply that costs are lower, the larger the average scale of plant in a market. Our economies of scale variable is 1/(average capacity), so we expect cement prices to rise with it.[3] That is, we expect them to be higher when average capacity is small.

We thought of capacity utilization as a demand variable. A high level of capacity utilization was expected to indicate high demand and therefore high prices under either monopolistic or competitive market conditions.

The effect of concentration is the main concern of this chapter. Whether it is the work of Cournot (1838), Chamberlin (1932), or Stigler (1953), practically all static oligopoly theory predicts high prices when concentration is high. Some dynamic theory, notably that of Peltzman (1977), suggests that rising concentration might be associated with falling costs and, less certainly, falling prices. Our approach is to examine cross sections of the cement industry during seven separate periods. We thus propose to test the static model.

The number of "importers" in our study is the number of firms without plants in the 250-mile market radius that maintain distribution centers near the center of our markets. Since they are clearly in the market, they are surely an additional source of competition especially because they are almost always well established within their home markets and have thus already attained most economies of scale. We therefore expect them to have a depressing effect on price.

General Statistical Results

A set of representative regressions appears in table 2.1. We actually ran 125 regressions, 11 for each of the first three years when the number of "importers" was not available and 23 per year for the last four years when that variable could be included. The differences among these regressions were entirely in measures of concentration and the presence or absence of the importers variable. The control variables were the same throughout. (Again, see appendix B for the exact specifications of the regressions.) We will discuss the control variables here and the various concentration measures later. In table 2.1, and all subsequent tables, N denotes the number of observations in the regression, and a, b, and c designate statistical significance at the 1, 5, and 10 percent levels of significance, respectively.

Average distance from cement plants to our central cities appeared to have no consistent effect on price. As indicated in table 2.1, it had negative effects in 1948, 1953, 1959, and 1980 and positive effects in between. Referring to the other models (not shown) which differed only by the concentration and importers variables, the effect of distance to the mills was always significantly negative in 1953. In 1980 its effect was also always negative, but it was significant only once. It was always positive and almost always significantly so in 1961 and 1965. In 1973 it was positive in all but one case and significantly so four times. And its coefficient was sometimes positive, sometimes negative, and always close to zero in 1948 and 1959. We are unable to explain these results.

Production workers' average hourly earnings in manufacturing did have the expected positive effects in 1948 to 1965 and in 1980. They were usually highly significant. There was, however, an exception here as well, this time in 1973. The effect of wages on price in that year was significantly negative regardless of whether concentration or importers were in the

Table 2.1
OLS regressions explaining unit values in major cement markets, 1948–1980 (standard errors in parentheses, t ratios in brackets)

	1948	1953	1959	1961	1965	1973	1980
Constant	0.258 (0.496) [0.52]	1.10 (0.87) [1.26]	2.56 (0.343) [7.47]^a	1.98 (0.275) [7.19]^a	0.725 (0.533) [1.36]	5.80 (0.622) [9.32]^a	−0.716 (2.87) [−0.25]
Average distance	−0.0003 (0.0005) [−0.60]	−0.001 (0.0003) [−2.88]^a	−0.0002 (0.0006) [−0.35]	0.001 (0.0005) [1.98]^c	0.002 (0.0007) [2.97]^a	0.002 (0.001) [2.11]^b	−0.004 (0.005) [−0.82]
Average hourly earnings	0.712 (0.153) [4.65]^a	0.623 (0.103) [6.03]^a	0.426 (0.089) [4.77]^a	0.366 (0.063) [5.78]^a	0.364 (0.098) [3.73]^a	−0.325 (0.054) [−5.97]^a	0.274 (0.180) [1.52]
1/(average capacity)	774.8 (121.3) [6.39]^a	705.6 (165.2) [4.27]^a	422.2 (126.8) [3.33]^a	532.0 (116.7) [4.56]^a	724.8 (208.9) [3.47]^a	423.0 (345.6) [1.22]	−257.1 (1,998.0) [−0.13]
Capacity utilization	0.391 (0.395) [0.99]	0.112 (0.747) [0.15]	−0.274 (0.301) [−0.91]	0.339 (0.228) [1.49]	0.615 (0.535) [1.15]	−1.43 (0.607) [−2.35]^b	9.91 (2.67) [3.68]^a
Number of "importers"	na na na	na na na	na na na	0.024 (0.014) [1.74]	−0.051 (0.020) [−2.54]^b	−0.030 (0.020) [−1.51]	−0.136 (0.088) [−1.55]
Four-firm concentration ratio	0.468 (0.131) [3.56]^a	0.284 (0.134) [2.12]^b	−0.254 (0.098) [−2.59]^b	−0.196 (0.090) [−2.18]^b	0.604 (0.156) [3.87]^a	0.701 (0.146) [4.80]^a	2.99 (0.996) [3.00]^a
R^2	0.889	0.832	0.546	0.664	0.683	0.847	0.734
N	21	24	24	24	24	24	24

Note: Price has been adjusted to a per 376-lb barrel basis; na = not available.
a. Significant at the 1 percent level.
b. Significant at the 5 percent level.

equation and regardless of how concentration was measured. It is difficult to explain this. One possibility is that it has something to do with the fact that price controls were in effect in that year, but it is not clear how price controls could result in prices being higher the lower the wage within the industry.

We expected large plants to have lower costs, so 1/(average capacity) should have a positive coefficient. It generally does, but there is an exception again, this time in 1980. Looking at all the regressions run, all coefficients were significantly positive from 1948 through 1965. They were all positive in 1973 as well, but only one was significant. In 1980 they were positive 11 times and negative 12, and none of them was significant. A possible reason for this is that most of the very largest plants in operation in 1980 had higher costs than expected because they were "wet process" plants whose costs were elevated by the very high cost of fuel in that year.

Capacity utilization was expected to have a positive effect on cement prices, reflecting high levels of regional demand relative to regional capacity. What we found was the following: All coefficients were positive in 1961 and 1965, but none were significant. In 1980 all were positive and highly significant. In 1948, however, only eight out of 11 were positive, and in 1953 only seven out of 11. These 15 positive coefficients included all of the significant ones (four in each year). In 1959 and 1973 all coefficients were negative but nonsignificant.

Looking back on it now, it seems probable that capacity utilization reflects two interacting influences with opposite signs. Demand side effects should certainly be positive as we expected in advance, but higher levels of capacity utilization also involve lower average costs. A region with high capacity utilization would have lower average costs, reflecting less plant per barrel of cement shipped. If capacity utilization reflects both of these influences, it is not too surprising that it has little effect on price: to the extent that firms consider average cost in their pricing decisions, they tend to cancel each other out. The strong showing of capacity utilization in 1980 may reflect a dominance of demand considerations on pricing during a recession.

The effects of numbers of importers and of concentration will be dealt with in detail in the next section. Our comments here will be brief. We expected prices to be lower the greater the number of importers because they represent additional competition not reflected in our concentration measures. Their coefficients did have the expected negative signs in 1965, 1973, and 1980, but, as usual, there was an aberration, this time in 1961.

The same held for the pièce de résistance, concentration. It significantly increased price in 1948, 1953, 1965, 1973, and 1980, but it had a significant negative effect in 1959 and 1961.

At this point we wish only to defend the general exercise. A critic could say that something goes wrong in almost every equation. A few of these "wrong" coefficients probably reflect two or more influences working on one variable (e.g., average distance and capacity utilization). They are just control variables, however, and we do not analyze them more closely here. It is more troublesome that importers and concentration have "wrong" signs in some years. We explore these cases further in the next section.

But look at what we did get. These are cross-sectional regressions, not time series. None of the variables are definitionally related to each other. Some of the variables are not directly measured. (Average wage, for example, is for all manufacturing rather than for cement.) And we have as few as 15 degrees of freedom in the 1948 regressions, 18 for 1953 and 1959, and 17 for 1961, 1965, 1973, and 1980. To get expected signs on most coefficients and for a great many of those coefficients to differ significantly from zero is really quite remarkable. We feel that the general pattern of results in table 2.1, reflecting as it does the full 125 regressions run, deserves a good deal of credence.

The Effect of Concentration on Price

For five of the seven years shown in table 2.1, concentration had a strong positive effect on price. The relationship is statistically significant in every year, though two of the signs are negative.

Table 2.2 shows the coefficients of a variety of concentration indexes from some of the other regressions mentioned in connection with table 2.1. All the regressions also included average distance, average hourly earnings, 1/(average capacity), and capacity utilization as control variables.

Virtually all of the positive coefficients are significant. The only exceptions were $CR5$ and $CR6$ in 1953 and the Herfindahl index in 1961, and the last is, after all, the only positive coefficient in 1961.

Which measure yields the best fit? The answer differs from year to year. In 1948 and 1953 it is $CR1$, the market share of the leading firm. In both years that index fits better than any other concentration ratio and better even than H and $\sqrt{H}$, which summarize the entire concentration curve while $CR1$ uses only one point on it.[4]

The 1959 and 1961 figures[5] are hard to interpret in these terms because the best fit is farthest from the hypothesis. The best negative fit was for

Table 2.2
Regression coefficients for alternative concentration measures (standard errors in parentheses, t ratios in brackets)

Year	CR1	CR2	CR3	CR4	CR5	CR6	H	√H
1948	0.671	0.492	0.484	0.468	0.422	0.361	0.790	0.748
	(0.121)	(0.102)	(0.117)	(0.132)	(0.147)	(0.161)	(0.159)	(0.167)
	[5.52][a]	[4.81][a]	[4.15][a]	[3.56][a]	[2.86][b]	[2.24][b]	[4.96][a]	[4.48][a]
1953	0.507	0.460	0.347	0.284	0.229	0.170	0.467	0.598
	(0.091)	(0.107)	(0.122)	(0.134)	(0.141)	(0.142)	(0.091)	(0.115)
	[5.58][a]	[4.32][a]	[2.84][a]	[2.12][b]	[1.62]	[1.19]	[5.12][a]	[5.22][a]
1959	−0.117	−0.164	−0.220	−0.254	−0.277	−0.301	−0.060	−0.185
	(0.155)	(0.104)	(0.098)	(0.098)	(0.098)	(0.105)	(0.168)	(0.169)
	[−0.76]	[−1.58]	[−2.25][b]	[−2.59][b]	[−2.83][b]	[−2.86][b]	[−0.36]	[−1.10]
1961	−0.018	−0.139	−0.209	−0.254	−0.265	−0.278	0.010	−0.113
	(0.135)	(0.096)	(0.091)	(0.088)	(0.087)	(0.097)	(0.154)	(0.153)
	[−0.13]	[−1.45]	[−2.31][b]	[−2.89][a]	[−3.04][a]	[−2.87][b]	[0.06]	[−0.74]
1965	0.709	0.647	0.695	0.707	0.735	0.749	0.832	0.981
	(0.278)	(0.168)	(0.166)	(0.172)	(0.181)	(0.193)	(0.273)	(0.265)
	[2.55][b]	[3.85][a]	[4.18][a]	[4.11][a]	[4.06][a]	[3.87][a]	[3.05][a]	[3.71][a]
1973	0.869	0.583	0.572	0.624	0.628	0.664	1.06	1.03
	(0.278)	(0.160)	(0.147)	(0.141)	(0.139)	(0.149)	(0.306)	(0.267)
	[3.13][a]	[3.63][a]	[3.91][a]	[4.40][a]	[4.53][a]	[4.46][a]	[3.45][a]	[3.85][a]
1980	2.71	2.361	2.28	2.58	2.51	2.50	3.54	3.62
	(1.26)	(0.895)	(0.921)	(1.00)	(1.04)	(1.16)	1.49	(1.47)
	[2.15][b]	[2.64][b]	[2.48][b]	[2.58][b]	[2.41][b]	[2.16][b]	[2.38][b]	[2.46][b]

a. Significant at the 1 percent level.
b. Significant at the 5 percent level.

$CR6$ in 1959 and $CR5$ in 1961. In a sense these show where competition was greatest, or at least where prices were lowest. If we look for the largest positive coefficient, we see only a near-zero coefficient for the Herfindahl index in 1961. All of the 1959 coefficients have negative signs.

After these years the best fit occurs when concentration is measured at multiple firm levels: $CR3$ in 1965, $CR5$ in 1973, and $CR2$ in 1980.

The Herfindahl index plays an increasingly important role today in both policy and research. It has a number of advantages. It derives directly from Cournot's and Stigler's oligopoly theories (Stigler 1968), it summarizes the entire concentration curve, and it emphasizes the large firms and gives small firms little weight. By a simple arithmetic manipulation, we can calculate the effect of a merger on the index, and this same manipulation made it possible for the Justice Department to set a merger rule that would permit very large firms to merge with small ones rather than prohibit all mergers by such large firms.

One source of unease with respect to the Herfindahl index is the relatively great weight it gives to very large firms. Does going from monopoly to duopoly really cut monopoly power in half? And does the step from two to four firms halve it again? This is essentially an empirical issue.

One transformation of the Herfindahl index that still summarizes the concentration curve but reduces the very sharp declines from one- to four-firm markets is $\sqrt{H}$. The last column of table 2.2 contains coefficients for $\sqrt{H}$.

Not surprisingly, H fits better than $\sqrt{H}$ in 1948, a year when $CR1$ offers the best fit, although this is not true in 1953. In 1959 and 1961, neither offers any information. In the last three years, however, $\sqrt{H}$ yields the higher t ratio. In each of the years studied, there is at least one ordinary CR that does better than either H or $\sqrt{H}$. In no case does the coefficient of H differ significantly from that of $\sqrt{H}$. We moderately prefer $\sqrt{H}$ because the conditions in 1965 to 1980 seem more nearly normal than in 1948, when the share of the leader in the most concentrated market was most important, and certainly more normal than 1959 to 1961. We would like to see more comparisons between the two.

Critical Concentration Ratios

Another transformation of concentration that has received some attention in research and quite a lot in policy is the critical concentration ratio (CCR). It also derives from theory, this time Chamberlin's (Chamberlin 1932, 46–51).

The policy appeal of the CCR is plain. If such a level can be identified, the antitrust agencies could quickly decide which mergers were likely to lessen competition. A more appealing point is that if we could say that a merger in an industry where concentration was no more than X will not lessen competition, we could set standards of concentration below which suits would not be filed. There can be no doubt that a large majority of mergers are not anticompetitive and that at least the participants in the mergers believe them to be useful.

We hope we can throw some light on this question too. There have been a number of estimates of CCR made on an all-manufacturing basis and using profits or price-cost margins as a criterion (Bain 1951; Dalton and Ford 1976; Kwoka 1979; Meehan and Dechesneau 1973; Rhoades and Cleaver 1973; White 1976). Although some of these studies would be criticized today, they did yield quite consistent results—a four-firm CCR of about 50.

Table 2.3 shows coefficients for dummy variables having values of one when $CR2$ exceeds the numbers at the tops of the columns and zero otherwise. For instance, the first number in the first row of coefficients shows the effect of two-firm concentration ratios of 30 or more in 1948 compared with markets where $CR2$ was less than 30. Table 2.4 does the same for dummies with values of one if $CR4$ exceeds the numbers at the tops of the columns. Table 2.5 does the same for alternative critical values of the Herfindahl index. In interpreting these tables, it may be useful to note that the lowest $CR2$ in our data set is 16.7. The lowest $CR4$ is 31.8, and the lowest H is 519. The first of these was in the Pittsburgh market in 1973, and the other two were in that same market in 1961.

The first two years yield very high critical levels for $CR2$, $CR4$, and H. A two-firm CCR of 90, as in 1953, implies that two or fewer firms must make up most of the market to sustain a higher price. A $CCR4$ of 90 implies the same for four or fewer large firms. And Herfindahl indexes of 2,000 and 2,500 are roughly equivalent to five or four equal-sized firms. At least the results were consistent. The only markets in our sample where there were only two or three firms in 1953 were Phoenix (1 firm), Denver (2), Salt Lake City (3), and New Orleans (3). Phoenix had no cement producer within 250 miles in 1948 and was therefore not in our sample in that year. That may account for the increase in $CCR2$ between 1948 and 1953. A comparison between the t ratios of the three types of CCR's and those of the continuous concentration variables in table 2.2 reveals that none of the best fits among the CCR's and CH's in 1948 or 1953 come close to explaining as much of the variability in price as do $CR1$ or H.

Table 2.3
Coefficients of dummy variables with values of one if the two-firm concentration ratio exceeds the indicated number ($CCR2$) (standard errors in parentheses, t ratios in brackets, $\bar{R}^2$ on fourth lines)

Year	0.30	0.40	0.50	0.60	0.70	0.80	0.90
1948	0.065	0.100	0.153	0.354			0.195
	(0.067)	(0.042)	(0.037)	(0.100)	—	—	(0.082)
	[0.98]	[2.36]^b	[4.10]^a	[3.53]^a			[2.38]^b
	0.808	0.851	0.904	0.888			0.851
1953	0.017	0.070	0.095	0.158	0.215		0.242
	(0.054)	(0.049)	(0.087)	(0.068)	(0.060)	—	(0.067)
	[0.31]	[1.45]	[1.08]	[2.31]^b	[3.56]^a		[3.61]^a
	0.791	0.811	0.802	0.838	0.876		0.878
1959	−0.114	−0.124		−0.104	0.010	0.086	0.111
	(0.044)	(0.040)	—	(0.056)	(0.073)	(0.087)	(0.081)
	[2.59]^b	[3.11]^a		[1.84]^c	[0.13]	[0.98]	[1.37]
	0.546	0.595		0.476	0.378	0.409	0.436
1961	−0.092	−0.107	−0.096	−0.091	0.022	0.024	0.116
	(0.039)	(0.032)	(0.039)	(0.047)	(0.065)	(0.059)	(0.068)
	[2.35]^b	[3.31]^a	[2.45]^b	[1.94]^c	[0.34]	[0.41]	[1.70]
	0.581	0.660	0.589	0.547	0.456	0.458	0.528
1965	0.201	0.129	0.257	0.194	0.195	0.278	
	(0.077)	(0.099)	(0.099)	(0.121)	(0.121)	(0.138)	—
	[2.60]^b	[1.30]	[2.59]^b	[1.61]	[1.61]	[2.01]^c	
	0.417	0.267	0.416	0.299	0.299	0.345	
1973	0.166	0.265	0.318	0.135		0.087	0.434
	(0.071)	(0.072)	(0.114)	(0.103)	—	(0.109)	(0.197)
	[2.34]^b	[3.68]^a	[2.79]^b	[1.31]		[0.79]	[2.20]^b
	0.739	0.806	0.762	0.689		0.671	0.732
1980	0.697	0.438	1.43	0.741		0.799	1.80
	(0.402)	(0.451)	(0.487)	(0.566)	—	(0.615)	(0.876)
	[1.73]	[0.97]	[2.94]^a	[1.30]		[1.30]	[2.06]^c
	0.664	0.627	0.735	0.641		0.641	0.682

a. Significant at 1 percent level.
b. Significant at 5 percent level.
c. Significant at 10 percent level.

Table 2.4
Coefficients of dummy variables with values of one if the four-firm concentration ratio exceeds the indicated number ($CCR4$) (standard errors in parentheses, t ratios in brackets, $\bar{R}^2$ on fourth line)

Year	0.30	0.40	0.50	0.60	0.70	0.80	0.90
1948			0.086	0.091	0.108	0.224	0.354
	—	—	(0.052)	(0.041)	(0.053)	(0.067)	(0.100)
			[1.65]	[2.23]^b	[2.06]^c	[3.36]^a	[3.53]^a
			0.827	0.846	0.841	0.883	0.888
1953		−0.071	0.045	0.047	0.064	0.118	0.280
	—	(0.097)	(0.050)	(0.045)	(0.069)	(0.064)	(0.056)
		[0.73]	[0.90]	[1.06]	[0.92]	[1.84]^c	[5.01]^a
		0.796	0.799	0.802	0.799	0.823	0.912
1959		−0.125	−0.078	−0.068	−0.124	−0.117	−0.100
	—	(0.074)	(0.041)	(0.041)	(0.040)	(0.047)	(0.080)
		[1.68]	[1.90]^c	[1.66]	[3.11]^a	[2.50]^b	[1.25]
		0.462	0.481	0.460	0.595	0.538	0.427
1961		−0.005	−0.092	−0.085	−0.096		−0.126
	—	(0.091)	(0.039)	(0.034)	(0.039)	—	(0.064)
		[0.05]	[2.35]^b	[2.46]^b	[2.45]^b		[1.95]^c
		0.453	0.581	0.591	0.589		0.548
1965		0.241	0.235	0.123	0.213	0.367	0.278
	—	(0.126)	(0.073)	(0.082)	(0.074)	(0.135)	(0.137)
		[1.92]^c	[3.24]^a	[1.49]	[2.90]^a	[2.72]^b	[2.02]^c
		0.334	0.494	0.287	0.454	0.431	0.346
1973		0.209	0.150	0.229	0.265	0.318	0.135
	—	(0.071)	(0.067)	(0.064)	(0.072)	(0.114)	(0.103)
		[2.95]^a	[2.24]^b	[3.56]^a	[3.68]^a	[2.79]^b	[1.31]
		0.770	0.734	0.800	0.806	0.762	0.689
1980		0.688	0.622	0.438		1.43	0.758
	—	(0.487)	(0.391)	(0.451)	—	(0.487)	(0.649)
		[1.42]	[1.59]	[0.97]		[2.94]^a	[1.17]
		0.647	0.656	0.627		0.735	0.635

a. Significant at 1 percent level.
b. Significant at 5 percent level.
c. Significant at 10 percent level.

Table 2.5
Coefficients of dummy variables with values of one if the Herfindahl index has a value greater than the indicated number (CH) (standard errors in parentheses, t ratios in brackets, $\bar{R}^2$ on fourth line)

Year	1,000	1,500	2,000	2,500	3,000	3,500	4,000
1948	0.050	0.092	0.190	0.354			
	(0.059)	(0.045)	(0.050)	(0.100)	—	—	—
	[0.85]	[2.04]c	[3.82]a	[3.53]a			
	0.805	0.840	0.896	0.888			
1953	0.045	0.051	0.095	0.280	0.212	2.15	0.266
	(0.050)	(0.049)	(0.087)	(0.056)	(0.045)	(0.060)	(0.074)
	[0.90]	[1.03]	[1.08]	[5.01]a	[4.67]a	[3.56]a	[3.58]a
	0.799	0.801	0.802	0.912	0.905	0.876	0.877
1959	−0.085	−0.100	−0.117	0.021		0.086	
	(0.043)	(0.039)	(0.047)	(0.078)	—	(0.087)	—
	[1.99]c	[2.54]b	[2.50]b	[0.27]		[0.98]	
	0.490	0.542	0.538	0.380		0.409	
1961	−0.111	−0.096	−0.096	−0.010		0.126	0.116
	(0.038)	(0.031)	(0.039)	(0.068)	—	(0.074)	(0.068)
	[2.92]a	[3.06]a	[2.45]b	[0.15]		[1.69]	[1.70]
	0.629	0.640	0.589	0.453		0.528	0.528
1965	0.190	0.213	0.367	0.194	0.242		0.278
	(0.078)	(0.074)	(0.135)	(0.121)	(0.137)	—	(0.138)
	[2.43]b	[2.90]a	[2.72]b	[1.61]	[1.77]c		[2.01]c
	0.396	0.454	0.431	0.299	0.317		0.345
1973	0.150	0.265	0.318	0.135			0.434
	(0.067)	(0.072)	(0.114)	(0.103)	—	—	(0.197)
	[2.24]b	[3.68]a	[2.79]b	[1.31]			[2.20]b
	0.734	0.806	0.762	0.689			0.732
1980	0.575	0.438	1.43	0.741			1.42
	(0.414)	(0.451)	(0.487)	(0.566)	—	—	(0.602)
	[1.39]	[0.97]	[2.94]a	[1.31]			[2.35]b
	0.645	0.627	0.735	0.641			0.700

a. Significant at 1 percent level.
b. Significant at 5 percent level.
c. Significant at 10 percent level.

The results for 1959 and 1961 were even stranger than those for the continuous concentration variables. $CCR2$ and CH had both positive and negative ranges. Prices seem to take a clear step down at $CCR2$ of 40 and to step back up again at $CCR2$ of 90 in both years. The best negative fit for CH was at 1,500 in both years, and the best positive fit was at 3,500 to 4,000. $CCR4$ has nothing but negative coefficients in either year. It had its clearest negative effect at $CCR4$ of 70 in 1959 and 60 or 70 in 1961. The maxima appear in the very concentrated markets of the mountain West, which seems plausible, but why the low prices in markets where $CCR2$ was 40, $CCR4$ was 70, and H was 1,500?

$CCR2$ and CH yielded better fits than any unconstrained CR or H in 1961, and $CCR2$ did so in 1959 as well. This makes some sense. The CCR's and CH separate out the positive and negative segments. But the continuous variables merge the two together and so the variables have a single coefficient summarizing the relationship over the entire range of experience. $CCR4$, whose coefficient is always negative, yields a weaker fit than $CR5$ in 1961, though a $CCR4$ of 70 fits better than $CR6$, the best-fitting unconstrained CR in 1959.

In 1965, 1973, and 1980 CCR and CH had coefficients of the sort we had expected in advance. $CCR2$ was 30 or 50 in 1965, 40 in 1973, and 50 in 1980. $CCR4$ yielded its best fits at 50 in 1965, 70 in 1973, and 80 in 1980. And the closest fits for CH were at 1,500 in the first two years and 2,000 in the last. None of the dummy variables fit as well as unconstrained $CR3$ in 1965 or as unconstrained $CR5$ in 1973. In 1980, however, $CCR2$, $CCR4$, and CH all fit better than any unconstrained concentration variables.

CH may be of some interest because it was the criterion used in the merger guidelines of the Antitrust Division of the Justice Department. The Antitrust Division was to investigate any merger whose effect was to increase H by 100 or more if H exceeded 1,000, and it would probably challenge the merger if H exceeded 1,800. These numbers would have been in the right range in years when our regressions yielded positive coefficients. But the cement industry sells almost exclusively to business customers. It was not clear in advance that concentration would have any effect at all on price in such an industry. We would expect tacit collusion to have an effect at lower levels of concentration in branded consumer goods than for producer materials like cement.

Merger guidelines can of course be justified, even if there is no evidence of critical concentration ratios in studies like the present. If the true relationship is one of steadily increasing effect as concentration rises, as in Cournot, Stigler, or auction theory (see chapter 5), then there will be some level of concentration below which mergers can do little harm. But it is crucial to select the proper guidelines.

We are doubtful about how much, if any, weight should be given to any of our estimates of CCR's and CH's, not just those with negative price effects. But the evidence from these data tells a story which we suspect goes far beyond cement. CCR's were tremendously high in 1948 to 1953 and so were those with positive effects in 1959 to 1961. They then moved down to levels closer to those that dropped out of the general cross-sectional studies. We suspect that such shifts reflect changes in structure and conduct in the industry, and that similar shifts could be found in other industries. Based on the bit of evidence we have from this and a few other industries (e.g., Geithman, Marvel, and Weiss 1981), we suspect that some industries have CCRs and others do not, and that in those that have them, they often change over time.

The Critical Number of Leading Firms

There is one more aspect of the critical concentration ratio that we may be able to cast light on. Kwoka (1979) made an heroic effort to test whether the market shares of the second-largest, third-largest, fourth-largest, etc., firm made any difference in explaining price-cost margins over a wide range of heterogeneous manufacturing industries. He found that the first two firms' market shares had significant positive effects on margins, the third firm's share had a negative effect, and the shares of the fourth and smaller firms had no significant effects. As he pointed out, the inherent collinearity involved in his estimation procedure made it almost impossible for these smaller firms to show any significant effect one way or another. Later Mueller and Rogers (1982) ran similar regressions using the shares of the first, second, and fourth firms to explain price-cost margins and found a negative effect for the fourth firm. They were able to get similar results by substituting the shares of the fifth and smaller firms (Kwoka's Reply, 1984). In this chapter we offer an alternative approach that may enhance our knowledge on this issue. In doing so, we wish to imply no criticism of Kwoka who pioneered in this important area.

Table 2.6 illustrates our approach. For each year we regress price on the control variables, a concentration ratio CRi and the market share of the next largest firm $MS(i + 1)$. On the first line, for instance, we show the coefficients of the one-firm concentration ratio ($CR1$) and the market share of the second-largest firm ($MS2$). On the second line we show the coefficients of the two-firm concentration ratio and the third firm's market share, and so forth.[6]

Table 2.6
Coefficients of CR_i and MS_{i+1} in standard regression in years when CR had a positive effect (standard errors in parentheses, t ratios in brackets)

	1948			1953			1965			1973			1980		
	CR_i	MS_{i+1}	N	CR_i	MS_{i+1}	N	CR_i	MS_{i+1}	N	CR_i	MS_{i+1}	N	CR_i	MS_{i+1}	N
$CR_1 MS_2$	0.686 (0.152) [4.51][a]	−0.060 (0.349) [−0.17]	21	0.584 (0.118) [4.97][a]	−0.093 (0.246) [−0.38]	23	0.445 (0.259) [1.72]	0.981 (0.366) [2.68][b]	24	−0.264 (0.585) [−0.45]	1.870 (0.871) [2.15][b]	24	0.923 (1.56) [0.59]	6.039 (3.404) [1.77]	24
$CR_2 MS_3$	0.701 (0.136) [5.16][a]	−0.315 (0.404) [−0.78]	19	0.345 (0.108) [3.19][a]	0.062 (0.374) [0.17]	22	0.475 (0.256) [1.85]	1.437 (0.886) [1.62]	22	0.137 (0.192) [0.71]	2.510 (0.798) [3.14][a]	23	1.802 (1.276) [1.41]	0.969 (6.456) [0.15]	23
$CR_3 MS_4$	0.386 (0.102) [3.79][a]	−0.645 (0.545) [−1.18]	18	0.288 (0.127) [2.27][b]	0.132 (0.534) [0.25]	20	0.624 (0.228) [2.74][b]	0.763 (1.411) [0.54]	21	0.369 (0.162) [2.27][b]	2.317 (0.840) [2.76][b]	21	3.161 (3.029) [1.04]	−5.298 (16.979) [−0.31]	20
$CR_4 MS_5$	0.350 (0.108) [3.25][a]	−0.623 (0.616) [−1.01]	18	0.246 (0.156) [1.57]	−0.419 (0.687) [−0.61]	19	0.663 (0.221) [3.00][a]	1.312 (2.330) [0.56]	20	0.842 (0.222) [3.80][a]	−1.589 (1.478) [−1.07]	20	3.627 (2.118) [1.71]	−17.164 (17.112) [−1.003]	20
$CR_5 MS_6$	0.355 (0.106) [3.36][a]	−1.340 (0.802) [−1.67]	18	0.100 (0.17) [0.58]	−0.480 (0.825) [−0.58]	18	0.573 (0.283) [2.02][c]	−2.828 (3.896) [−0.73]	18	0.613 (0.171) [3.59][a]	0.749 (1.842) [0.41]	19	3.641 (2.249) [1.62]	−35.545 (21.296) [−1.67]	18

a. Significant at 1 percent level.
b. Significant at 5 percent level.
c. Significant at 10 percent level.

Our results are less emphatic than Kwoka's. In the years shown (which exclude 1959 and 1961), CRi usually has a positive coefficient, and it is commonly significantly so. $MS(i + 1)$ often does have a negative coefficient, but only those of $MS6$ in 1948 and 1980 approach significance. $MS(i + 1)$ also has significant positive effects, such as $MS2$ in 1965, $MS2$, $MS3$, and $MS4$ in 1973, and (marginally) $MS2$ in 1980. Since these seem to us the more nearly "normal" years, we feel the effect of the marginal firm's market share is more likely to be positive when it ranks second, third, or fourth. If a negative effect exists, it is most likely when the marginal firm ranks fifth or sixth. Encouraging mergers among marginal firms to promote competition is not supported by our findings, though mergers to remove suboptimal firms may still be useful. It should be noted that the regressions toward the bottom of table 2.6 have fewer degrees of freedom than those near the top because we dropped all cases where $MS(i + 1)$ was zero. Finally, we acknowledge that this is based on only one industry, cement. We would like to see results for other industries.

The Institutions of Postwar cement pricing

Perhaps the most puzzling finding of this study is the significant negative effect of concentration on price during 1959 and 1961. What caused this to occur? The following are our thoughts on this question.

The most important change in cement pricing in the postwar era was the *Cement Institute* decision of 1948 [FTC v. Cement Institute 333 US 683 (1948)]. From that year on, the industry sold at f.o.b. mill prices or delivered prices as the customer chose. Most sales were at delivered prices at first with delivery by rail, but as time passed, more and more sales were made f.o.b. mill with the customer taking the shipment away by truck. A hybrid system developed about 1960 in which producers shipped clinker to a distribution facility near a major consumption center (usually by rail or barge), sold it there, and delivered it from there by truck. Quite a lot of sales still occur on a delivered price basis, however, especially where firms absorb freight to meet or beat the prices of sellers having plants closer to the customers.

It is our view that the basing point system served mainly as an aid to tacit collusion. It did not end overnight, but gradually. As long as it remained, collusive prices may well have prevailed in all markets with sufficient concentration to make use of this aid. As time passed, however, the basing point system became increasingly difficult to maintain, and by 1959 the collusive solution had broken down in many markets. Not surprisingly, prices were maintained in some of the very concentrated markets ($CR2 > 70$ and $H > 3,000$), but they fell more in markets where $CR2 > 40$ or $CR4 > 60$ or 70 than in the less-concentrated markets where they had never been too far above competitive levels in the first place. Since the least concentrated markets (Pittsburgh, Philadelphia, New York, and Baltimore) also had the oldest plants, they may have had higher production costs as well. If so, then when prices declined in the moderately concentrated markets, they may have fallen to reflect cost levels below those in the unconcentrated markets, thereby producing the negative correlations.

The contents of the preceding paragraph is after-the-fact conjecture. When we presented earlier versions of this chapter, we were always asked to explain what happened in 1959 to 1961, and this is our reply. The following explanation of what happened after that is quite different. It is based on an hypothesis formulated by one of the authors two decades ago on the basis of extensive interviews and correspondence in the industry from 1965 to 1967 (in connection with research leading to Weiss 1976).

In April 1962, Atlantic Cement, a new corporation then owned by Cerro Corporation, opened a cement plant at Ravenna, New York, (25 miles south of Albany); its main facility was a cement kiln with 8,500,000 barrels per year capacity. It was by far the largest kiln in the United States. At the time the usual cement kiln had 1,500,000 or 2,300,000 barrels capacity. The huge new kiln yielded large economies of scale. During 1965 to 1967 Weiss was told repeatedly by persons from eastern cement companies that they were shipping more cement than ever before but making no profits on it. They always explained this by the low prices set by the Ravenna plant. A comparison between eastern state unit values and those in the Midwest showed much lower prices in the East in the mid-1960s. The Ravenna plant's cement was shipped by water down the Hudson and down the East Coast as far as Florida where the firm had set up distribution centers.

Subsequently, several more very large kilns were built, two at new plants on the Mississippi (at Clarksville, Missouri, by Dundee Cement, and at Festus, Missouri, by River Cement) and two on the Great Lakes (at Detroit by Peerless Cement and at Charlevoix, Michigan, by Medusa Cement). None of these were as large as that at Ravenna, but all were very large by previous standards. And they all depended on dispersed distribution facilities to sell part of their output. They had the effect of spreading prices in line with those in the East to parts of the Midwest and South reachable from the Great Lakes and the Mississippi system.

The immediate effect of the Ravenna plant was to reduce price sharply, and concentration some, in four large and relatively unconcentrated markets (New York, Philadelphia, Pittsburgh, and Baltimore) and to reduce price but increase concentration in the Boston market which is smaller and more concentrated ($CR4 = 60.5$ in 1961). It is only natural that this should strengthen the positive correlation between concentration and price found in 1965.

By 1973, however, when the new large kilns were in place on the Great Lakes and the Mississippi River, the relationship no longer depended on one plant, and the effect of concentration on price probably came closer to deriving from the variables economists tend to emphasize.

Most of the new kilns were wet process. Both wet and dry process kilns were built widely in the 1960s, but the run-up of energy prices in late 1973 and in 1974 changed this. The cost of operating wet process kilns was so high thereafter, that no new wet process kilns were built after 1973. High fuel costs greatly reduced the advantage of most large kilns installed from 1962 to 1973.

By 1980 the industry had lost most of the old basing-point system characteristics, and its prices were no longer dominated by a few new and very large units. That year may yield somewhat more general results than the others, although it was also a time of sharp recession which may explain the unusual explanatory power of capacity utilization.

Conclusions

Cement offers cleaner evidence on the effects of concentration on price than most industries because of its many geographic markets, its standardized product, and its data on firm market share and price, none of which depend on the census. We feel the evidence gives strong support to the concentration-price hypothesis.

It does not give a great deal of support to the concept of a critical concentration ratio, and if there was one during our period, it moved around from year to year. In the later years, when the story came closest to the picture envisioned by most oligopoly theory, it settled near a $CCR2$ of 40–50, a $CCR4$ of 60–80, and a CH of 1,500–2,000. All of these are within the range of concentration levels that would have brought at least investigation by the Antitrust Division, but, as noted earlier, since cement is an industrial input often sold in large lots, it seems likely that branded consumer goods would have lower CCR's.

Our main conclusion is broader. In this study, and several others in this book, it is clear that concentration does raise price. The basic hypothesis of oligopoly theory has lots of support. Our two-decade digression on concentration and profits and our subsequent 13 years of doubt were unnecessary.

Finally, we owe a comment on the cement industry. Although our goal was not to examine its performance but to use its remarkable data, the evidence is overwhelming that it has become much more competitive in recent decades. The *Cement Institute* decision did indeed change the industry, though not overnight. Moreover the new distribution facilities created in consumption centers far from the mills have unquestionably increased competition, both in our period of interest (which ends in 1980) by extending the regional markets and since then by the introduction of international imports. And the construction of kilns at Ravenna, Clarksville, Festus, Charlevoix, and Detroit was exactly what one would expect in a competitive environment, and the new kilns had the normal effect on price. The fact that even large cement markets are inevitably oligopolies is due to the very great economies of scale in cement kilns and the limited geographic markets of the industry. Despite these structural conditions we have no doubt that the industry has become more competitive than it was a few decades ago.

Appendix A: Central Cities of the Market Areas

Cities marked with an asterisk were excluded from the 1948 sample because of data problems.

Atlanta	Minneapolis
Baltimore	New Orleans
Birmingham	New York
Boston	Oklahoma City
Chicago	Philadelphia
Cincinnati	Phoenix*
Cleveland	Pittsburgh
Dallas	St. Louis
Denver	Salt Lake City
Detroit	San Antonio
Kansas City	San Francisco*
Los Angeles*	Seattle

Appendix B: Specification of Regression Equations

Equations marked with an asterisk were not run for 1948, 1953, and 1959 due to lack of information on I.

$$P = \beta_0 + \beta_1 AD + \beta_2 AW + \beta_3 (1/AC) + \beta_4 CU + U$$
$$P = \beta_0 + \beta_1 AD + \beta_2 AW + \beta_3 (1/AC) + \beta_4 CU + \beta_5 CR1 + U$$
$$P = \beta_0 + \beta_1 AD + \beta_2 AW + \beta_3 (1/AC) + \beta_4 CU + \beta_5 CR2 + U$$
$$P = \beta_0 + \beta_1 AD + \beta_2 AW + \beta_3 (1/AC) + \beta_4 CU + \beta_5 CR3 + U$$
$$P = \beta_0 + \beta_1 AD + \beta_2 AW + \beta_3 (1/AC) + \beta_4 CU + \beta_5 CR4 + U$$
$$P = \beta_0 + \beta_1 AD + \beta_2 AW + \beta_3 (1/AC) + \beta_4 CU + \beta_5 CR5 + U$$
$$P = \beta_0 + \beta_1 AD + \beta_2 AW + \beta_3 (1/AC) + \beta_4 CU + \beta_5 CR6 + U$$
$$P = \beta_0 + \beta_1 AD + \beta_2 AW + \beta_3 (1/AC) + \beta_4 CU + \beta_5 N + U$$
$$P = \beta_0 + \beta_1 AD + \beta_2 AW + \beta_3 (1/AC) + \beta_4 CU + \beta_5 (1/N) + U$$
$$P = \beta_0 + \beta_1 AD + \beta_2 AW + \beta_3 (1/AC) + \beta_4 CU + \beta_5 H + U$$
$$P = \beta_0 + \beta_1 AD + \beta_2 AW + \beta_3 (1/AC) + \beta_4 CU + \beta_5 \sqrt{H} + U$$
$${}^*P = \beta_0 + \beta_1 AD + \beta_2 AW + \beta_3 (1/AC) + \beta_4 CU + \beta_5 SLR + U$$
$${}^*P = \beta_0 + \beta_1 AD + \beta_2 AW + \beta_3 (1/AC) + \beta_4 CU + \beta_5 (1/SLR) + U$$
$${}^*P = \beta_0 + \beta_1 AD + \beta_2 AW + \beta_3 (1/AC) + \beta_4 CU + \beta_5 I + \beta_6 CR1 + U$$
$${}^*P = \beta_0 + \beta_1 AD + \beta_2 AW + \beta_3 (1/AC) + \beta_4 CU + \beta_5 I + \beta_6 CR2 + U$$
$${}^*P = \beta_0 + \beta_1 AD + \beta_2 AW + \beta_3 (1/AC) + \beta_4 CU + \beta_5 I + \beta_6 CR3 + U$$
$${}^*P = \beta_0 + \beta_1 AD + \beta_2 AW + \beta_3 (1/AC) + \beta_4 CU + \beta_5 I + \beta_6 CR4 + U$$
$${}^*P = \beta_0 + \beta_1 AD + \beta_2 AW + \beta_3 (1/AC) + \beta_4 CU + \beta_5 I + \beta_6 CR5 + U$$
$${}^*P = \beta_0 + \beta_1 AD + \beta_2 AW + \beta_3 (1/AC) + \beta_4 CU + \beta_5 I + \beta_6 CR6 + U$$
$${}^*P = \beta_0 + \beta_1 AD + \beta_2 AW + \beta_3 (1/AC) + \beta_4 CU + \beta_5 I + \beta_6 N + U$$
$${}^*P = \beta_0 + \beta_1 AD + \beta_2 AW + \beta_3 (1/AC) + \beta_4 CU + \beta_5 I + \beta_6 (1/N) + U$$
$${}^*P = \beta_0 + \beta_1 AD + \beta_2 AW + \beta_3 (1/AC) + \beta_4 CU + \beta_5 I + \beta_6 H + U$$
$${}^*P = \beta_0 + \beta_1 AD + \beta_2 AW + \beta_3 (1/AC) + \beta_4 CU + \beta_5 I + \beta_6 \sqrt{H} + U$$

Notes

1. U.S. Bureau of the Census, *Census of Transportation, 1963. Volume III. Commodity Transportation Survey, Parts 1 and 2* (U.S. Government Printing Office, Washington, D.C., 1966), pp. 64–65.

2. Wage data for 1948 was inadequate in the *Handbook of Labor Statistics*. As a result we obtained our 1948 wage variable from the 1947 Census of Manufactures.

3. This functional form is the result of experimentation. We tried average capacity, the natural logarithm of average capacity, and 1/(average capacity) and found that the last yielded the best fit. This does not violate the conventional LAC curve of industrial organization where average cost falls out to minimum efficient scale and becomes flat beyond that because most U.S. cement capacity is probably sub-optimal (ignoring transport costs). Using estimates of MES from the mid-1960s by Scherer and Weiss, 86 percent of U.S. capacity in 1967 was suboptimal, and using an estimate by Pratten from the same period, all of it was (Weiss 1976).

4. The concentration measures are constrained to fall between 0 and 1.00. As 1.00 was approached, it seemed that we could be misled by the results. So we did the regressions in tables 2.1 and 2.2 over using $CR1$, $CR2$, ..., $CR6$ for each year, transforming CRi to $CRi/(1 - CRi)$ after changing CR's of 1.00 to 0.99. The results were almost exactly what they were before the transformations.

5. Originally we ran these regressions for only six years, including 1961 but not 1959. Five of the years fit our expectations, but of course 1961 did not. We searched for numerical errors and found none. Finally, we tried another nearby year, 1959, to see if 1961 was unique. It was not, so we clearly had to search for an explanation. Our search has not been entirely successful, but we will present some hopefully useful comments later.

6. Blank cells in tables 2.3, 2.4, and 2.5 indicate that the data were such that the observations on the dummy variable involved were identical with those on the dummy variable involved in the first entry to the left of it in the table, so there was no new information to report. In Table 2.4 there are some blank cells having no entries to the left. The reason for this is that there were no markets with $CR4$ below the indicated level, so the dummy variable had a value of 1.00 for all observations.

References

Bain, Joe S. 1951. "Relation of Profit Rate to Industry Concentration: American Manufacturing, 1936–1940." *Quarterly Journal of Economics* 65 (August), 293–324.

Branmann, Lance J., Douglas Klein, and Leonard W. Weiss. 1988. "The Price Effects of Increased Competition on Auction Markets." *Review of Economics and Statistics*, forthcoming.

Chamberlin, Edward H. 1949. *The Theory of Monopolistic Competition*. Sixth edition. Cambridge; MA: Harvard University Press.

Cournot, Augustin. 1838. *Researches into the Mathematical Principles of the Theory of Wealth*. Trans. by Nathaniel Bacon. New York: Macmillan.

Dalton, James E., and David W. Penn. 1976. "The Concentration-Profitability Relationship: Is There a Critical Concentration Ratio?" *Journal of Industrial Economics* 25 (December); 133–42.

Federal Trade Commission v. Cement Institute. 1948. 333 U.S. 683.

Geithman, Frederick E., Howard P. Marvel, and Leonard W. Weiss. 1981. "Concentration, Price, and Critical Concentration Ratios." *Review of Economics and Statistics* 63 (August), 346–353.

Kwoka, John E. Jr. 1979. "The Effect of Market Share Distribution on Industry Performance." *Review of Economics and Statistics* 61 (February), 101–109.

Kwoka, John E. Jr. 1984. "The Effect of Market Share Distribution on Industry Performance: Reply." *Review of Economics and Statistics* 66 (May), 358–361.

Meehan, James W., Jr., and Thomas Duchesneau. 1973. "The Critical Level of Concentration." *Journal of Industrial Economics* 22 (September), 21–36.

Mueller, Willard F., and Douglas F. Greer. 1984. "The Effect of Market Share Distribution on Industry Performance Reexamined." *Review of Economics and Statistics* 66 (May), 353–358.

Peltzman, Sam. 1977. "The Gains and Losses from Industrial Concentration." *Journal of Law and Economics* 20 (October), 229–263.

Pit and Quarry maps and directories for various years. Chicago: Pit and Quarry Publications.

Rhoades, Stephen A., and Joe M. Cleaver. 1973. "The Nature of the Concentration-Price/Cost Margin Relationship for 352 Manufacturing Industries: 1967." *Southern Economic Journal* 40 (July), 90–102.

Stigler, George J. 1964. "A Theory of Oligopoly." *Journal of Political Economy* 72 (February), 44–61.

U.S. Bureau of Labor Statistics. Various years. *Handbook of Labor Statistics.* Washington, DC: Government Printing Office.

U.S. Bureau of Mines. 1948, 1953, 1959, 1961, 1965, 1973, 1980. *Minerals Yearbook.* Washington, D.C.: Government Printing Office.

U.S. Bureau of the Census. 1966. *Census of Transportation. 1963: Commodity Transportation Survey, Parts 1 and 2.* Vol. 3. Washington, D.C.: Government Printing Office.

Weiss, Leonard W. 1976. "Optimal Plant Size and the Extent of Sub-optimal Capacity." In Robert T. Masson and P. David Qualls (eds.), *Essays on Industrial Organization in Honor of Joe S. Bain.* Cambridge, MA: Ballinger, pp. 123–141.

White, Lawrence J. 1976. "Searching for the Critical Industrial Concentration Ratio: An Application of the 'Switching of Regimes' Technique." In Stephen Goldfeld and Richard E. Quandt (eds.), *Studies in Non-linear Estimation.* Cambridge, MA: Ballinger, pp. 61–75.

3

Change in Concentration, Change in Cost, Change in Demand, and Change in Price

Christina M. L. Kelton and Leonard W. Weiss

Projects described elsewhere in this book study the relationship between concentration and price in certain industries such as airlines, banking, and cement across different geographic markets, in markets for important inputs used by many industries such as labor, and for multiple transactions in a market (six groups of auctions). It does not seem feasible, however, to compare prices across distinct markets such as steel and paper in the same way one compares profits or margins there. But we find that by examining the effects of change in concentration (and in cost and demand) on the change in price across different products, we are able to conduct a more general analysis of the classic concentration-price hypothesis than that possible in individual industry studies.

We propose to test the basic hypothesis—that concentration raises price—directly (not indirectly with profits data), and we propose to test Peltzman's hypothesis (1977) as well. We consider more narrowly defined markets (five-digit product classes rather than four-digit industries) and use a model that determines price change and cost change simultaneously so that any trade-off for society can be evaluated directly.

The Model

We propose a simultaneous equations model for several reasons. We believe that the relationships between demand and supply as determinants of price are inherently simultaneous in nature. Beyond that, a full exploration of Peltzman's trade-off requires that we look not only at the effect of change in concentration on cost but also at the effects of change in both concentration and cost on the change in price, using the same data and the same model. Finally, many factors affect change in concentration besides the innovations of leaders or of other firms. For example, growth in output is commonly expected to have a negative effect. Rapid growth in demand is expected to attract entry that usually reduces the shares of industry leaders.

We specify a four-equation model, with change in price, change in average cost, change in real output, and change in concentration as the endogenous variables:

$$\Delta P = a_1 + a_2 \Delta UC + a_3 \Delta Q + a_4 \Delta CR + e, \tag{1}$$

$$\Delta UC = b_1 + b_2 KI + b_3 \Delta W + b_4 \Delta P' + b_5 \Delta P''$$
$$+ b_6 \Delta P''' + b_7 \Delta CR + e', \tag{2}$$

$$\Delta Q = c_1 + c_2 \Delta P + c_3 A + c_4 \Delta Q' + c_5 \Delta Q'' + c_6 \Delta Q''' + e'', \tag{3}$$

$$\Delta CR = d_1 + d_2 A + d_3 \Delta Q + d_4 CR(58) + d_5 S + e''', \tag{4}$$

where all variables are as defined in table 3.1, a_i, b_i, c_i, and d_i are unknown parameters to be estimated, and e, e', e'', and e''' are additive error terms, though not necessarily with zero cross-equation correlations.[1] All equa-

Table 3.1
Notation and data source summary

Symbol	Variable	Source
ΔP	Change in price	*Census of Manufactures*, Vol. 4
ΔUC	Change in unit cost	*Census of Manufactures*, Vols. 2, 4
ΔQ	Change in output	*Census of Manufactures*, Vols. 2, 4
ΔCR	Change in concentration	*Census of Manufactures*, Vol. 1
KI	Capital intensity	IRS *Statistics of Income, Census of Manufactures*, Vol. 2
ΔW	Change in average hourly earnings	BLS *Employment and Earnings*
$\Delta P'$, $\Delta P''$, $\Delta P'''$	Price changes of top three suppliers	*Input-Output Structure of the U.S. Economy: 1967, Census of Manufactures*, Vol. 4
A	Advertising-to-sales ratio	*Input-Output Structure of the U.S. Economy: 1967*
$\Delta Q'$, $\Delta Q''$, $\Delta Q'''$	Output changes of top three buyers	*Input-Output Structure of the U.S. Economy: 1967, Census of Manufactures*, Vols. 2, 4
E	Long-run income elasticity of demand	Houthakker and Taylor (1970)
$CR(58)$	Initial concentration	*Census of Manufactures*, Vol. 1
S	Product class size	*Census of Manufactures*, Vol. 2

tions are overidentified, and a three-stage least squares procedure is used.[2] [For consumer goods, $\Delta Q'$, $\Delta Q''$ and $\Delta Q'''$ are not included in the model. Rather, E, or the long-run income elasticity of demand, replaces them as the variable of interest in equation (3).] We discuss our measures of change (Δ) below for each of the variables separately.

Specification of Equations

The price equation is meant to characterize the supply side variables that affect price. In unconcentrated markets like soybean oil, it is surely a literal supply equation. For tight oligopolies, such as cigarettes, this concept is moderately misleading, and yet economic analysis of monopoly and oligopoly leaves no doubt that the levels of demand and of costs are important determinants of price. If so, we can reasonably expect change in cost and change in demand to be important determinants of change in price. In a supply function we would, of course, expect a positive relationship between ΔP and ΔQ, although our indirect measurement of ΔQ (partially from ΔP) establishes a "natural" negative relationship in equation (1). Change in concentration forms part of the price determination equation because one of the two primary hypotheses of this study examines whether increases in concentration are associated with increases in price. We expect ΔCR to exert a positive impact on ΔP, especially for consumer goods where collusion among sellers is potentially easiest.[3]

The cost equation is an essential part of our pricing function and one of our main performance indicators. Its specification is straightforward. Change in unit cost is assumed to be affected by input price changes and market structure. We use hourly earnings change ΔW derived by the Bureau of Labor Statistics (BLS) as our labor price variable. We also include the price changes of a sector's top three suppliers $\Delta P'$, $\Delta P''$, and $\Delta P'''$ for suppliers one, two, and three, respectively. We expect that both labor price change and materials price change will directly affect ΔUC and that the material price effects will decline in importance from $\Delta P'$ to $\Delta P'''$. Capital intensity, KI (or capital's cost share essentially), appears in the cost relation also, along with long-term change in concentration. Thus, with this cost-change model, we are able to test Peltzman's (1977) hypothesis that increases in concentration carry with them decreases in unit costs.

Equation (3) simply specifies physical output change as a function of price change and level of advertising intensity. We think of this as a demand relationship, so we would expect a negative coefficient on the price change variable. We also expect the extent of advertising effort on the part of firms to affect demand directly. For materials and capital goods. we postulate a derived-demand effect on output change in supplier industries, where $\Delta Q'$, $\Delta Q''$, and $\Delta Q'''$ represent output or demand changes of the product class's top buyer, second-largest buyer, and third-largest buyer, respectively. We expect that $\Delta Q'$, $\Delta Q''$, and $\Delta Q'''$ will have positive effects on ΔQ, with the effects declining in importance from the primary to the tertiary buyer.

For consumer goods, we include E, rather than $\Delta Q'$, $\Delta Q''$, and $\Delta Q'''$, in the model, where E is estimated long-run income elasticity of demand from Houthakker and Taylor (1970).[4] Since consumer personal income change from 1958 to 1977 is the same for each consumer good in our sample, we expect that ΔQ increases with elasticity.

We include a structural change relationship in our model as well, since growth or output change (itself already an endogenous variable in the system) is assumed to exert downward pressure on concentration as new firms enter the market, and existing (small) firms expand their production. We also include initial concentration $CR(58)$, with the expectation that leading firms in concentrated markets are more likely to lose market share over time than those in more competitive markets. We thus expect a negative effect of initial concentration on structural change. To some extent this would occur naturally due to the "regression effect." Beyond that, the upper limit on concentration of 100 ensures that the top four firms in highly concentrated markets cannot increase their shares by much, and vice versa. We expect large market size to indicate potential absence of large (Bain-Sylos Labini type scale) entry barriers, so we anticipate a negative effect of size on change in concentration. However, as Mueller and Rogers (1980) point out, an initial equilibrium would argue that size itself should have no particular effect on structural change. Mueller's and Rogers' strong results point to a positive effect of advertising on concentration change for consumer goods and a weaker such relationship for producer goods. The latter arises because many producer goods have some sales to consumers (e.g., sugar and flour).

The second through fifth columns of table 3.2 show the expected coefficient signs for each variable in each equation.

Variable Measurement

Price Change
The dependent variable in our supply equation is measured as the natural logarithm of the ratio of 1977 and 1958 cross-weighted unit values (divided

Table 3.2
Expected coefficient signs and levels of aggregation of explanatory variables

Explanatory variable	Expected signs				Level of aggregation
	Price-change equation	Cost-change equation	Quantity-change equation	Concentration-change equation	
ΔP	LHS[a]		−		5-digit
ΔUC	+	LHS[a]			5-digit
ΔQ	+		LHS[a]	−	5-digit
ΔCR	+	−		LHS[a]	5-digit
KI		+			About 3-digit
ΔW		+			4-digit
$\Delta P', \Delta P'', \Delta P'''$		+, +, +			About 4-digit
A			+	+	About 4-digit
$\Delta Q', \Delta Q'', \Delta Q'''$			+, +, +		About 4-digit
E			+		About 3-digit
$CR(58)$				−	5-digit
S				−	5-digit

a. LHS = left-hand side.

by 100) calculated as follows from available information:[5]

$$\Delta P = \log[P(77)P(72)P(67)P(63)] = \log[P(77)_{58}],$$

where $P(t)$ is a price ratio of price in year t relative to the previous census (base) year, and $P(77)_{58}$ is the ratio of 1977 to 1958 prices, or 1977 price "base 58." For our study, the implicit, realized price index $P(t)$ enjoys several advantages over its explicit BLS counterpart. $P(t)$ is a five-digit unit value, and hence it is more representative of the buyer transaction price, especially since it captures rebates, special allowances, and discounts offered buyers. Further, the census unit values are generally more available for precisely defined five-digit manufacturing product classes than BLS price indexes. Of course, neither BLS prices nor census data avoid the problem of quality change. If change in quality is related systematically to structural change, the empirical results may be biased.

Table 3.3 presents unweighted average implicit price ratios by product type for various time periods. The three general product types in our study (defined precisely below) did not show identical price trends. Capital goods showed the highest increases in price, with prices more than doubling from 1958 to 1977. The materials and consumer goods showed lower overall price indexes of 196 and 190, respectively. This ranking developed only from the most recent period, 1972 to 1977, however, with consumer goods showing at least as high price rises as the materials for all prior years.

Table 3.3
Average price indexes for various time periods (initial year = 100)

Product class type	1958–1963	1963–1967	1967–1972	1972–1977	1958–1977
Consumer	101.8	107.7	117.0	147.0	190.3
Producer	100.7	105.5	118.2	160.8	202.8
Material	100.0	104.4	117.5	159.6	196.0
Capital	104.6	111.1	122.0	167.2	239.0
All products	101.1	106.2	117.8	156.8	199.1

Unit Cost Change

Three major components of production cost were obtained from census figures: material cost $CM(t)$, which includes purchase of intermediate products, packaging materials, and fuels; the production worker wage bill $WB(t)$; and annual capital costs, which are equal to an estimated 10 percent of the value of gross fixed assets $GFA(t)$ plus year-end inventory $INV(t)$. Thus

$$\Delta UC = \log\left\{\frac{CM(77) + WB(77) + 0.1 \times [GFA(77) + INV(77)]}{[CM(58) + WB(58) + 0.1 \times (GFA(58) + INV(58))] \times Q(77)_{58}}\right\},$$

where $Q(77)_{58}$ is change in physical output from 1958 to 1977 and is defined below.[6] With this cost change formulation, the labor, material, and capital components are implicitly weighted for each product class, and potential multicollinearity among separate cost change variables is avoided.

Table 3.4 shows unweighted average major industry group long-term implicit price and unit cost changes (1958 to 1977). Relative to base 1958 (1958 = 100), prices doubled on average by 1977, with range from 156.8 for rubber and plastics to 254.5 for petroleum products. Unit cost rise averaged 183.3 over this same time period, ranging from 134.3 for transportation equipment to 223.5 for primary metals.

Quantity Change

Change in physical quantity shipped is measured as the log ratio of 1977 to 1958 deflated shipments values and is calculated as follows:

$$\Delta Q = \log[Q(77)Q(72)Q(67)Q(63)] = \log[Q(77)_{58}],$$

where $Q(t) = [VS(t)/VS(t-1)]/P(t)$, $VS(t)$ refers to value of shipments at time t, $t-1$ refers to the previous census year, and $Q(77)_{58}$ is the ratio of 1977 to 1958 quantity, or 1977 quantity base 58.[7]

Table 3.4
Average industry group price indexes and unit cost indexes, 1958–1977 (1958 = 100)

Industry group	Number of classes	1977 Price index	1977 Cost index
Food and kindred products	56	203.5	198.5
Tobacco manufactures	3	194.5	170.0
Textile mill products	36	168.8	166.2
Apparel and other textile products	33	188.9	174.0
Lumber and wood products	11	238.8	199.8
Furniture and fixtures	12	182.2	163.0
Paper and allied products	29	184.2	171.1
Printing and publishing	22	216.0	191.5
Chemicals and allied products	28	181.5	168.9
Petroleum and coal products	5	254.5	197.9
Rubber and plastics products	11	156.8	171.9
Leather and leather products	15	217.1	222.4
Stone, clay, and glass products	22	212.1	222.7
Primary metal industries	12	218.8	223.5
Fabricated metal products	37	212.7	191.4
Machinery, except electrical	56	236.7	201.3
Electric and electronic equipment	37	163.8	141.4
Transportation equipment	7	186.1	134.3
Instruments and related products	18	174.5	176.5
Miscellaneous manufacturing	24	190.2	179.8

Change in Concentration

Percentage change in concentration is measured as

$$\Delta CR = CR(77) - CR(58),$$

where $CR(t)$ is the four-firm seller concentration ratio in year t. Notice that since CR is already measured in percentage terms, ΔCR is computed simply as the difference in concentration levels. (Our other change variables are calculated in ratio form since this is required to capture percentage change in these cases.) We feel that this makes intuitive sense. Going from a concentration ratio of 10 to 20 seems much more similar to moving from 50 to 60 than from 50 to 100.

Capital Intensity

Also included in our cost change equation is the ratio of capital to value

$$KI(t) = \frac{TA(t)}{VS(t)},$$

where $TA(t)$ represents total assets at time t. 1967 values are used since they are midway in our study period. As opposed to our other independent variables in the cost change relationship, KI is essentially a cost share, with capital price change data unavailable and assumed to be constant across our sample.

Wage Rate Change
We compute

$$\Delta W = \log\left[\frac{W(77)}{W(58)}\right],$$

where $W(77)$ and $W(58)$ are average hourly earnings and are taken from the March 1978 and March 1959 issues of *Employment and Earnings*, respectively, a source distinct from the *Census of Manufactures* used in the construction of our endogenous cost change variable ΔUC.

Seller Price Change
Material price changes also appear in the model. These variables are based on the three sectors that constitute a given sector's top three suppliers, according to the 1967 input–output table. For each of the three sellers, a weighted average price change was calculated. For example,

$$\Delta P' = \frac{\sum_{i=1}^{n} VS_i \log[P(77)_i P(72)_i P(67)_i P(63)_i]}{\sum_{i=1}^{n} VS_i},$$

where n is the number of product classes in the seller sector (commonly industry, but in some cases, minor or major industry group), $VS_i = [VS(77)_i + VS(58)_i]/2$, and $\Delta P'$ refers to the price change of the top input. Likewise $\Delta P''$ and $\Delta P'''$ were computed for the second- and third-most-important supplying sectors.

Advertising Intensity
$A = AD(67)/VS(67)$, where $AD(67)$ is advertising expenditure from the 1967 input–output table. We use level of advertising effort rather than change. We feel that heavy advertising has as its main purpose to increase demand for the advertised product. This seems especially appropriate for a period such as 1958 to 1977 when a major new advertising medium, television, had just been introduced.

Buyer Quantity Change (Derived Demand)
From the 1967 input–output table it could be determined which industries were the three primary manufacturing sector purchasers of any given

(material or capital-good) sector's output.[8] For each of these three buyers, we calculated a weighted (by mean shipments value for 1958 and 1977) average of that buyer's product classes' 1958 to 1977 quantity ratios, rather analogously to our seller price change computations. Thus

$$\Delta Q' = \frac{\sum_{i=1}^{n} VS_i \log[Q(77)_i Q(72)_i Q(67)_i Q(63)_i]}{\sum_{i=1}^{n} VS_i},$$

where n is now the number of product classes in the buyer sector, and $\Delta Q'$ refers to the output change of the top buyer. $\Delta Q''$ and $\Delta Q'''$ were calculated in a similar fashion for the second- and third-largest buyers, respectively.

Market Size
Finally, average product class size is measured as

$$S = \tfrac{1}{2}\{\log[VS(77) - CM(77)] + \log[VS(58) - CM(58)]\},$$

where $[VS(t) - CM(t)]$ is simply value added. We believe that, in general, larger industries are characterized by lower entry barriers. As a result we expect lower increases in concentration than in smaller industries. However, as explained by Mueller and Rogers (1980), the effect of size on structural change may diminish as size increases, hence the logarithmic transformation.

Levels of Aggregation

Our basic endogenous variables—changes in price, cost, output, and concentration—are all measured at the five-digit level. We feel that product classes are generally more realistic economic markets and that there are far fewer noncompeting subproducts there than at the four-digit level. Unit cost refers only to plants that specialize in the product in question. In a few cases (e.g., lubricants) such plants account for far less than half of total output. We, in effect, assume that the diversified plants have costs similar to those of the specialists.

$\Delta P'$, $\Delta P''$, $\Delta P'''$, $\Delta Q'$, $\Delta Q''$, and $\Delta Q'''$ are measured at essentially the four-digit level, but their interrelationship with the product in question is based on the input–output matrix, where a few sectors are broader than that. We feel that this is usually a minor matter. We ascribe sector values to our product classes in the manner described and evaluated statistically in Haworth and Reuther (1978) and followed in much of the empirical literature. The BLS average hourly earnings data and the advertising expenditures from the input–output matrix are usually four-digit in char-

Table 3.5
Three-stage least squares regression results for 135 consumer goods (standard errors in parentheses, t ratios in brackets)

Explanatory variable	Left-hand-side variable			
	ΔP	ΔUC	ΔQ	ΔCR
Intercept	0.1017 (0.1741) [0.5843]	0.0916 (0.1857) [0.4932]	0.6220^c (0.3727) [1.6690]	16.7820^a (4.2872) [3.9144]
ΔP	—		−0.6094 (0.5243) [−1.1624]	
ΔUC	0.7980^a (0.2294) [3.5095]	—		
ΔQ	−0.0508 (0.0842) [−0.6033]		—	−0.9314 (5.9367) [−0.1579]
ΔCR	0.0142^a (0.0183) [2.7759]	−0.0119^c (0.0064) [−1.8507]		—
KI		−0.2857^b (0.1157) [−2.4700]		
ΔW		0.3815^c (0.1972) [1.9345]		
$\Delta P'$		0.2624^b (0.1096) [2.3952]		
$\Delta P''$		0.2003^c (0.1028) [1.9489]		
$\Delta P'''$		0.1176 (0.1010) [1.1647]		
A			2.8508^b (1.3217) [2.1570]	28.5644 (32.3823) [0.8821]
E			0.1026^c (0.0604) [1.6977]	
$CR(58)$				−0.1769^a (0.0465) [−3.8066]

Table 3.5 (continued)

Explanatory variable	Left-hand-side variable			
	ΔP	ΔUC	ΔQ	ΔCR
S				-0.8194
				(0.9722)
				$[-0.8428]$
F^{d}	7.96^{a}	2.46^{b}	7.37^{a}	4.55^{a}

a. Significant at the 0.01 level of significance.
b. Significant at the 0.05 level of significance.
c. Significant at the 0.10 level of significance.
d. F statistic from second stage for a test of the null hypothesis that all nonintercept coefficients $= 0$.

In the structural change equation, advertising effort does not seem to have such a strong positive influence, in contrast with the single-equation findings of Mueller and Hamm (1974) and Mueller and Rogers (1980). Growth, as measured by change in real output, product class size, and initial concentration are seen to have their theoretically expected negative effects, although the former two variables' estimated coefficients are not significant at the 10 percent level.[14]

Materials

Based on 272 product classes considered as materials in our sample, we obtained the results reported in table 3.6. In this case every coefficient has the expected sign except for advertising in the change in concentration equation. We had expected a weakened but not a negative effect here. We read the negative effect as zero. All variables have estimated positive and significant effects on ΔP. The estimated coefficient values of ΔCR for the two product groups, consumer goods and materials, are very close.

For materials, which contain the largest number of product classes in our sample, ΔCR has a nonsignificant effect on ΔUC. This time, at least, capital intensity raises unit cost, though the relationship could have occurred by chance. Wage rate change had a nonsignificant effect also. For materials, the top supplier's price change significantly effects unit cost change, and there is a declining impact as expected from $\Delta P'$ to $\Delta P'''$.

As is only right for a demand relationship, ΔP has a negative, though nonsignificant, effect on ΔQ. Advertising effort has a positive but again nonsignificant impact, as one might expect for intermediate goods whose

Table 3.6
Three-stage least squares regression results for 272 materials (standard errors in parentheses, t ratios in brackets)

Explanatory variable	Left-hand-side variable			
	ΔP	ΔUC	ΔQ	ΔCR
Intercept	−0.1287 (0.1400) [−0.9196]	0.0082 (0.1676) [0.0489]	−0.0133 (3.6842) [−0.0490]	21.7639[a] (4.2642) [5.1039]
ΔP	—		−0.1543 (0.3330) [−0.4634]	
ΔUC	1.1777[a] (0.1743) [6.7584]	—		
ΔQ	0.2809[a] (0.1083) [2.5932]		—	−8.0406[a] (2.6561) [−3.0272]
ΔCR	0.0135[b] (0.0059) [2.3827]	−0.0019 (0.0044) [−0.4291]		—
KI		0.0429 (0.0454) [0.9457]		
ΔW		0.1913 (0.1648) [1.1610]		
$\Delta P'$		0.3101[a] (0.0912) [3.4008]		
$\Delta P''$		0.1117 (0.0683) [1.6364]		
$\Delta P'''$		0.0432 (0.0693) [0.6232]		
A			2.9498 (3.9446) [0.7478]	−39.6769 (60.1165) [−0.6600]
$\Delta Q'$			0.1756[b] (0.0687) [2.5545]	
$\Delta Q''$			0.4381[a] (0.0922) [4.7548]	

Table 3.6 (continued)

Explanatory variable	Left-hand-side variable			
	ΔP	ΔUC	ΔQ	ΔCR
$\Delta Q'''$			0.2215[a]	
			(0.0791)	
			[2.8015]	
$CR(58)$				-0.1386[a]
				(0.0347)
				$[-3.9947]$
S				-1.8403[b]
				(0.8270)
				$[-2.2253]$
F[d]	8.79[a]	2.85[b]	12.21[a]	14.24[a]

a. Significant at the 0.01 level of significance.
b. Significant at the 0.05 level of significance.
c. Significant at the 0.10 level of significance.
d. F statistic from second stage for a test of the null hypothesis that all nonintercept coefficients = 0.

primary purchasers are other producers. The output changes of the three major purchasers of each material positively affect intermediate output change. $\Delta Q''$ and $\Delta Q'''$ show higher estimated coefficients than the primary buyer does, but all derived demand coefficients are significant at at least the 5 percent level.

The structural change results for materials show significant and expected effects of all independent variables except advertising effort. The coefficient for size has the theoretically predicted negative sign found in other, single-equation models. For materials, then, the results suggest lower entry barriers for larger industries, all else the same. Initial concentration and growth both have significantly negative effects on concentration change.

Capital Goods

For our (much smaller) sample of 51 product classes used more for private domestic investment than as either a consumer good or intermediate product, we show the estimated relationships in table 3.7. The number of individual significant relationships in the model has dropped considerably, and there are four unexpected signs, all characterized, however, by very small t statistics. ΔUC still strongly affects ΔP. As predicted, our structural change theory is given weaker support for capital goods than for materials and consumer products. The estimated effect of ΔCR on ΔP is positive,

Table 3.7
Three-stage least squares regression results for 51 capital goods (standard errors in parentheses, t ratios in brackets)

Explanatory variable	Left-hand-side variable			
	ΔP	ΔUC	ΔQ	ΔCR
Intercept	0.3045[c]	−0.4313	−0.2135	−4.0674
	(0.1654)	(0.4432)	(0.5903)	(8.2253)
	[1.8414]	[−0.9731]	[−0.3617]	[−0.4945]
ΔP	—		−0.3332	
			(0.4950)	
			[−0.6731]	
ΔUC	0.8433[a]	—		
	(0.1994)			
	[4.2293]			
ΔQ	−0.0649		—	4.4029
	(0.0856)			(4.9400)
	[−0.7584]			[0.8913]
ΔCR	0.0039	−0.0177[c]		—
	(0.0075)	(0.0097)		
	[0.5223]	[−1.8159]		
KI		0.1139		
		(0.1356)		
		[0.8399]		
ΔW		−0.1051		
		(0.3922)		
		[−0.2680]		
$\Delta P'$		0.8844[a]		
		(0.2531)		
		[3.4940]		
$\Delta P''$		0.1661		
		(0.2339)		
		[0.7101]		
$\Delta P'''$		0.3912[b]		
		(0.1889)		
		[2.0705]		
A			26.7612[b]	484.8583
			(13.2185)	(311.6456)
			[2.0208]	[1.5558]
$\Delta Q'$			0.5436[a]	
			(0.1848)	
			[2.9409]	
$\Delta Q''$			0.3851[b]	
			(0.1820)	
			[2.1159]	

Table 3.7 (continued)

Explanatory variable	Left-hand-side variable			
	ΔP	ΔUC	ΔQ	ΔCR
$\Delta Q'''$			0.2168 (0.2688) [0.8066]	
$CR(58)$				−0.0897 (0.0769) [−1.1658]
S				0.9359 (1.4241) (0.6572)
F^{d}	8.25[a]	2.43	4.80[a]	1.20

a. Significant at the 0.01 level of significance.
b. Significant at the 0.05 level of significance.
c. Significant at the 0.10 level of significance.
d. F statistic from second stage for a test of the null hypothesis that all nonintercept coefficients = 0.

though nonsignificant, and this time the price supply curve has a slightly negative slope.

ΔUC is seen to have a negative relationship with ΔCR. Otherwise, only $\Delta P'$ and $\Delta P'''$ have significant effects on change in unit costs. In this case rapidly rising wages seem to reduce cost increases, if anything, though the effect is tiny.

Advertising intensity has a surprisingly strong effect on output change. As with materials, derived demand is seen to be an important factor. The changes in output of the top three buyers seem all to lead to output change of the seller. For capital goods, moreover, the results "rank" the buyers as postulated. The top buyer's demand has the largest impact, followed by the second buyer's and then the third's. The coefficient of ΔP has the right sign, but it does not amount to much.

Change in concentration does not seem to be explained very well. Two of the coefficient signs are as expected, but no coefficient is significant, even at the 10 percent level. The estimated coefficient for growth is actually positive (though nonsignificant).

Producer Goods

We look finally at our entire producer-goods sample of 323 product classes and note the estimates in table 3.8. These results are very similar to the

Table 3.8
Three-stage least squares regression results for 323 producer goods (standard errors in parentheses, t ratios in brackets)

Explanatory variable	Left-hand-side variable			
	ΔP	ΔUC	ΔQ	ΔCR
Intercept	−0.0525	−0.0276	−0.0804	21.5466[a]
	(0.1192)	(0.1374)	(0.2236)	(3.5617)
	[−0.4404]	[−0.2008]	[−0.3595]	[6.0495]
ΔP	—		−0.0821	
			(0.2583)	
			[−0.3179]	
ΔUC	1.1950[a]	—		
	(0.1489)			
	[8.0248]			
ΔQ	0.1329		—	−6.3155[b]
	(0.0845)			(2.4788)
	[1.5725]			[−2.5478]
ΔCR	0.0088[c]	−0.0031		
	(0.0049)	(0.0042)		
	[1.8074]	[−0.7378]		
KI		0.0335		
		(0.0368)		
		[0.9079]		
ΔW		0.1967		
		0.1280		
		[1.5367]		
$\Delta P'$		0.3415[a]		
		(0.0773)		
		[4.4191]		
$\Delta P''$		0.1228[b]		
		(0.0584)		
		[2.1028]		
$\Delta P'''$		0.0860		
		(0.0554)		
		[1.5536]		
A			3.8850	−9.1559
			(3.6773)	(62.3274)
			[1.0585]	[−0.1469]
$\Delta Q'$			0.2213[a]	
			(0.0626)	
			[3.5355]	
$\Delta Q''$			0.4112[a]	
			(0.0807)	
			[5.0951]	

Table 3.8 (continued)

Explanatory variable	Left-hand-side variable			
	ΔP	ΔUC	ΔQ	ΔCR
$\Delta Q'''$			0.2197[a]	
			(0.0730)	
			[3.0088]	
$CR(58)$				-0.1510[a]
				(0.0308)
				$[-4.8955]$
S				-1.9221[a]
				(0.6788)
				$[-2.8316]$
F[d]	14.87[a]	4.41[a]	14.20[a]	13.35[a]

a. Significant at the 0.01 level of significance.
b. Significant at the 0.05 level of significance.
c. Significant at the 0.10 level of significance.
d. F statistic from second stage for a test of the null hypothesis that all nonintercept coefficients = 0.

estimated equations for materials. Almost every coefficient has the expected sign, and many of them are significant. ΔP does rise with ΔCR too, and the effect is roughly an average of those found for materials and capital goods. It is marginally significant.[15]

Subperiod Analysis

Table 3.9 shows the estimated effects of ΔCR on ΔP, based on ordinary least squares, for various subperiods in our study, for our four product subgroups plus all groups combined. We note that for consumer goods, our structural change hypothesis finds strongest support through 1967, with producer goods showing the opposite trend, after 1967 there is evidence that ΔP and ΔCR are positively related for them. Since structural change generally occurs gradually over a long period of time, it is interesting that we observe any strong, significant effects at all over these shorter time spans. For the two separate ten-year time periods reported at the bottom of table 4.9, all estimated effects are positive, although only the consumer goods show a strong positive relationship.[16] A similar table cannot be constructed for ΔUC since we do not have sufficient data for capital intensity, labor cost change, and material cost changes for the various subperiods.

Table 3.9
The estimated effects of ΔCR on ΔP for various time periods (standard errors in parentheses, t ratios in brackets, number of observations on fourth line)

Time period	Consumer goods	Materials	Capital goods	Producer goods	All goods
1958–1963	0.0021[c]	−0.0001	0.0024	0.0006	0.0010
	(0.0012)	(0.0010)	(0.0016)	(0.0008)	(0.0006)
	[1.7419]	[−0.0973]	[1.5016]	[0.7402]	[1.5611]
	140	285	59	344	484
1963–1967	0.0038[a]	−0.0007	−0.0007	−0.0008	0.0005
	(0.0013)	(0.0009)	(0.0014)	(0.0007)	(0.0007)
	[2.9453]	[−0.7805]	[−0.5074]	[−1.0814]	[0.6790]
	150	315	60	375	525
1967–1972	0.0014	0.0011	−0.0002	0.0008	0.0008
	(0.0015)	(0.0010)	(0.0017)	(0.0009)	(0.0008)
	[0.9488]	[1.1164]	[−0.1156]	[0.8812]	[1.0222]
	159	325	56	381	540
1972–1977	−0.0002	0.0022[b]	0.0037[c]	0.0023[b]	0.0017[b]
	(0.0014)	(0.0011)	(0.0021)	(0.0010)	(0.0009)
	[−0.1434]	[1.9900]	[1.7624]	[2.3109]	[1.9753]
	167	318	56	374	541
1958–1967	0.0029[b]	0.0001	0.0011	0.0004	0.0012[c]
	(0.0012)	(0.0007)	(0.0018)	(0.0009)	(0.0007)
	[2.4212]	[0.1472]	[0.6266]	[0.4313]	[1.7455]
	136	287	60	347	483
1967–1977	0.0028[c]	0.0006	0.0018	0.0007	0.0005
	(0.0017)	(0.0012)	(0.0024)	(0.0011)	(0.0010)
	[1.6582]	[0.4947]	[0.7480]	[0.6468]	[0.4885]
	158	316	58	374	532

Note: Estimates are based on the model: $\Delta P = f_1 + f_2 \Delta VS + f_3 \Delta UVC + f_4 \Delta CR + u$, where ΔVS replaces ΔQ in a single-equation model, and ΔUVC does not include estimated capital cost change.
a. Significant at the 0.01 level of significance.
b. Significant at the 0.05 level of significance.
c. Significant at the 0.10 level of significance.

Conclusions

In this chapter we have developed a simultaneous model to explain both price and output changes by shifts in cost and demand, while also estimating effects of various factors on structural change and unit cost change. We find strong evidence that rising concentration does tend to lead to long-term price rises. Although this effect is strongest for consumer goods as we would have expected, it is also strong for materials as well. We find some evidence, for consumer goods and capital goods, that rising concentration is also associated with falling unit costs over time, consistent with Peltzman's (1977) results. However, for materials that constitute the clear majority of our sample, there is no such "offsetting" performance result.[17]

Appendixes listing the product classes in each sample and reporting simple correlation coefficients among the variables used in our regressions are available from the authors on request.

Notes

1. We do not test specifically for simultaneity nor for optimal estimation procedure (e.g., using the Hausman test).

2. In an earlier version of this chapter (March 1985), unit cost change variables were exogenous to the system rather than determined endogenously in the model. The effect of concentration change on price change proved to be strongly positive in the earlier model for consumer goods but not so for either materials or producer goods in general. With the addition of the unit cost change equation and other model modifications, including an accounting for income elasticity of demand in the quantity change equation, the empirical results are generally stronger and more robust against minor model respecifications.

3. The data themselves are not used to select the functional forms in our model. See Layson and Seaks (1984) for a description of such an approach. Following Peltzman's (1977) and Vita's (1984) derivations, we logarithmically transform all nonstructural change variables.

4. Values for E are themselves derived from separate regression analyses for product groups in their study. Pagan (1984) and Hoffman and Schlagenhauf (1985) address the problem of using regressors obtained from other regressions and find that, unless all regressions are estimated jointly, statistical inference based on the final results may be invalid. We clearly cannot correct for this potential problem in our study, however, and our empirical situation, in any case, differs from that studied by Pagan. E in our quantity-change equation is derived from separate regressions (one for each product group) rather than from a single estimated model.

5. By multiplying these four price ratios, we obtain essentially 1977 prices, 1958 base, since each individual price index is based on the previous census year's prices. When cross-weighted census unit value indexes were missing for a product class, we imputed, in order of preference, its corresponding four-digit, three-digit, or two-digit value. The following observations had one or several of these imputations: 20179, 20471, 20515, 20517, 20661, 20670, 20871, 22415, 22822, 22953, 23710, 23860, 23940, 23970, 24266, 24351, 24354, 24361, 24362, 24364, 24495, 24991, 26318, 26462, 27411, 27511, 27512, 27513, 27514, 27515, 27516, 27519, 27522, 27523, 27524, 27525, 27530, 27712, 27821, 27822, 27891, 27892, 27930, 27940, 28198, 28315, 28349, 28423, 28651, 28652, 28653, 28655, 28694, 28695, 28742, 28994, 29510, 29521, 30694, 31115, 31497, 32640, 32929, 32932, 34292, 34423, 34425, 34446, 34661, 34662, 35199, 35231, 35327, 35421, 35424, 35453, 35494, 35591, 35595, 35624, 35629, 35681, 35893, 36292, 36462, 36463, 36470, 36485, 36623, 37327, 37328, 38111, 38251, 38291, 38423, 38737, 39141, 39313, 39522, 39530, 39620, 39931, 39932, 39933, 39991, and 39992.

6. Actually, *GFA* and *INV* are measured at the four-digit level and are taken for the years 1963 and 1976, due to numerous missing values (for *GFA*) for both 1958 and 1977. For several observations, data for either gross fixed asset or inventory value were missing; in these cases ΔUC was approximated by change in unit variable cost instead:

$$\Delta UC = \log \left\{ \frac{CM(77) + WB(77)}{[CM(58) + WB(58)] \times Q(77)_{58}} \right\}.$$

7. *VS*, depending on its context in our empirical analyses, is taken either from the *Census of Manufactures* (five-digit) or the input–output table (commonly four-digit). In its role in the computation of capital intensity, it is measured commonly at the three-digit level for consistency with the assets data.

8. The rankings of the top three buyers of capital goods are based on the parts and supplies sold by capital goods producers.

9. Even when perfect definitional "splits" or "mergers" were encountered, we omitted those observations. The empirical results do not change substantially when additional observations with minor definitional changes are reintroduced into the sample. We note that several (about 5 percent) of our products are really sold in local or regional markets, thus rendering national concentration values from the census inappropriate. See Weiss (1972). However, since our focus in this chapter is on ΔCR, rather than on the level of concentration per se, we do not attempt to correct for this potential bias.

10. The following observations were reclassified from their classification based on the input–output table: 20179, 20234, 20261, 20661, 20830, and 20851 were classified as materials; 20430, 20471, 22531, 22532, 22533, 22541, 38424, 39522, and 39620 as consumer goods; and 35327, 35331, 35332, 35333, 35361, and 35362 as capital goods.

11. We do not test statistically for differences across product types. Since, theoretically, we expect ease of collusion to vary considerably, and since we must

employ different quantity-change (demand-change) equation specifications for meaningful relationships in any case, we simply treat consumer goods and producer goods separately. In note 12 we report results for our entire sample of product classes, although with an abbreviated "demand curve" specification.

12. We obtain the following three-stage least squares results for our entire sample of 474 product classes (including 16 observations with missing data either for $\Delta Q'''$ or E, hence not included in the regressions reported in the text), omitting $\Delta Q'$, $\Delta Q''$, and $\Delta Q'''$ (producer goods only) and E (consumer goods only):

$$\Delta P = 0.0751 \; - \; 0.0983\Delta Q \; + \; 1.1151^a\Delta UC \; + \; 0.0082^b\Delta CR$$
$$(0.1008) \quad\;\; (0.0601) \qquad\quad\; (0.1509) \qquad\qquad (0.0035)$$
$$[0.74] \quad\;\; [-1.62] \qquad\qquad [7.39] \qquad\qquad\;\; [2.36]$$

$$\Delta UC = -0.0103 \; - \; 0.0031\text{KI} \; + \; 0.2175^b\Delta W \; + \; 0.2520^a\Delta P'$$
$$(0.0935) \qquad (0.0256) \qquad\; (0.0858) \qquad\;\; (0.0624)$$
$$[-0.11] \qquad [-0.12] \qquad\;\; [2.53] \qquad\qquad [4.04]$$

$$+ \; 0.1979^a\Delta P'' \; + \; 0.1265^a\Delta P''' \; - \; 0.0057^c\Delta CR$$
$$(0.0423) \qquad\qquad (0.0392) \qquad\qquad (0.0034)$$
$$[4.67] \qquad\qquad\; [3.23] \qquad\qquad\; [-1.69]$$

$$\Delta Q = 0.5788^a \; - \; 0.2351\Delta P \; + \; 4.0003^a A$$
$$(0.1794) \qquad (0.2221) \qquad\;\; (1.0626)$$
$$[3.77] \qquad\;\; [-1.06] \qquad\;\;\; [3.77]$$

$$\Delta CR = 22.1189^a \; + \; 97.0687^b A \; - \; 13.3081\Delta Q \; - \; 0.167^a CR(58) \; - \; 1.349S$$
$$(4.5667) \qquad\;\; (40.4740) \qquad\;\; (9.4237) \qquad\quad (0.043) \qquad\quad\;\; (1.462)$$
$$[4.84] \qquad\qquad [2.40] \qquad\quad\;\; [-1.41] \qquad\quad\; [-3.89] \qquad\;\; [-0.95]$$

Again, our price change hypothesis is given support. The estimated coefficient for ΔCR in equation (1) is statistically significant at the 5 percent level. In keeping with Peltzman's (1977) results, moreover, ΔCR is seen to have a (modestly significant) downward influence on average costs. Directional effects are generally as expected from the preceding section.

13. All hypothesis tests in this study are two-tailed. Two-stage least squares results do not differ importantly from the three-stage estimates for any of our relationships. However, ΔCR never has a significant effect in any of the ΔUC relationships in the second stage. It actually has a positive coefficient for materials and producer goods. What does 0.0142 mean in this nonlinear model? From $\Delta P = 0.1017 - 0.0508\Delta Q + 0.7980\Delta UC + 0.0142\Delta CR$, we know that $P(77)_{58} = \exp(0.1017)\exp(-0.0508\Delta Q)\exp(0.798\Delta UC)\exp(0.0142\Delta CR) = X$. Thus $\partial P(77)_{58}/\partial\Delta CR = 0.0142X$. Setting ΔQ, ΔUC, and ΔCR at their respective average values for the consumer products in the sample, we calculate $\partial P(77)_{58}/\partial\Delta CR = 2.62$ percent, suggesting that a 1 percentage point rise in ΔCR leads to a 2.62 percentage point rise in the 1977 price index (base $1958 = 100$). This result compares with 2.57 percent for materials and 0.91 percent for capital goods (derived from the regression estimates later in this chapter) and with 1.29 percent from Kelton (1982) for food and tobacco products.

14. The traditional administered-price hypothesis is not supported. When $[CR(77) + CR(58)]/2$ is included as an additional variable in equations (1) and (2), it has generally nonsignificant effects in both relationships. For materials, the level of concentration actually has a significantly negative effect on price change for the period studied, consistent with results from Qualls (1978), among others. We do not include average concentration level in the relationships reported in the text due to suspected severe (though possibly subtle) multicollinearity problems with respect to $CR(58)$ and ΔCR. Due to the simultaneous nature of our model, we cannot conveniently calculate the "total effect" of ΔCR on ΔP. When we considered a 20 percent, rather than 10 percent, capital cost, and when we considered advertising expenditures as part of total cost, results were very similar, but there were fewer strongly significant effects, and several nonintuitive coefficient signs.

15. Vita (1984) developed a similar simultaneous model to explain changes in price, total factor productivity, real output, and concentration, and the level of investment relative to output. He used the Census-SRI-Penn Industry Profiles panel data set and tracked 297 four-digit manufacturing industries over approximately our same time period of interest, 1958 to 1977. Our study differs from his in model specification (e.g., our real output growth equation contains a derived demand component), in data sources (we used primarily census data), and in level of aggregation (we used five-digit, instead of four-digit, observations). Vita's results differ markedly from ours, moreover, in that he does not find evidence of a strong positive relationship between price change and concentration change. He attributes this finding to the possibly poor quality of his price data. Consistent with our results, Vita did find a positive link between concentration change and productivity change (in our case, a negative relationship between concentration change and unit cost change) for consumer goods but none for the much larger sample of producer goods (in our case, materials—for capital goods, we found some support for the efficiency argument that rising concentration reduces unit costs).

16. For the entire 1958 to 1977 period we report the following ordinary least squares estimation results for consumer goods, materials, capital goods, producer goods, and the complete sample, respectively (with ΔVS, ΔUC including capital cost change, and ΔCR as independent variables, and N as the number of observations):

Consumer goods, $N = 143$

$$\Delta P = 0.2108^a + 0.0941^a \Delta VS + 0.4907^a \Delta UC + 0.0039^a \Delta CR, \quad R^2 = 0.52,$$
$$\quad\quad (0.0439) \quad (0.0233) \quad\quad (0.0402) \quad\quad\quad (0.0014) \quad\quad\quad\quad F = 49.85^a$$
$$\quad\quad [4.80] \quad\quad [4.04] \quad\quad\quad [12.20] \quad\quad\quad\quad [2.88]$$

Materials, $N = 279$

$$\Delta P = 0.3326^a + 0.0960^a \Delta VS + 0.3982^a \Delta UC + 0.0004 \Delta CR, \quad R^2 = 0.40,$$
$$\quad\quad (0.0334) \quad (0.0205) \quad\quad (0.0296) \quad\quad\quad (0.0296) \quad\quad\quad\quad F = 60.63^a$$
$$\quad\quad [9.97] \quad\quad [4.68] \quad\quad\quad [13.44] \quad\quad\quad\quad [0.41]$$

Capital goods, $N = 58$

$$\Delta P = 0.4347^a + 0.0556\Delta VS + 0.4722^a\Delta UC + 0.00004\Delta CR, \quad R^2 = 0.43,$$
$$\quad (0.0978) \quad (0.0534) \quad\quad (0.0740) \quad\quad\quad (0.00214) \quad\quad\quad F = 13.59^a$$
$$\quad [4.44] \quad\quad [1.04] \quad\quad\quad [6.38] \quad\quad\quad\quad [0.02]$$

Producer goods, $N = 337$

$$\Delta P = 0.0311^a + 0.0187^a\Delta VS + 0.0272^a\Delta UC + 0.0001\Delta CR, \quad R^2 = 0.42,$$
$$\quad (0.0311) \quad (0.0187) \quad\quad (0.0272) \quad\quad\quad (0.0012) \quad\quad\quad F = 81.58^a$$
$$\quad [10.58] \quad\quad [5.50] \quad\quad\quad [15.54] \quad\quad\quad\quad [0.80]$$

Total sample, $N = 489$

$$\Delta P = 0.3068^a + 0.0982^a\Delta VS + 0.4347^a\Delta UC + 0.0006\Delta CR \quad R^2 = 0.43,$$
$$\quad (0.0256) \quad (0.0150) \quad\quad (0.0229) \quad\quad\quad (0.0008) \quad\quad\quad F = 121.53^a$$
$$\quad [11.98] \quad\quad [6.55] \quad\quad\quad [19.00] \quad\quad\quad\quad [0.73]$$

with t statistics in brackets. We expect ΔVS (the 1977 to 1958 log shipments ratio) to be a better measure than ΔQ of demand change in a single-equation model.

17. Since we expect changing import concentration, relative to domestic production, to be inversely related to price change, we include

$$\Delta M = \left\{ \frac{IM(77)}{IM(77) + VS(77) - EX(77)} - \frac{IM(65)}{IM(65) + VS(65) - EX(65)} \right\}$$

in the price-change equation, where IM and EX are imports and exports, respectively, and where IM, EX, and VS (in this case) were taken from tapes prepared by Robert Baldwin, University of Wisconsin, Madison, based on original census import and export reports by TSUSA and Schedule B classifications, respectively. The data were reclassified to four-digit SIC classifications using a concordance developed at Wisconsin. Unfortunately, we had data for only a third of our observations in the text (and for these back only to 1965). For the 51 consumer goods and the 91 materials for which we did have data, ΔM's estimated coefficient was negative, but nonsignificant. Its effect was nonsignificantly positive for 17 capital goods. For this smaller sample, change in concentration still had a significantly positive effect on price change for consumer goods but a nonsignificant effect on ΔUC. For materials, however, we observed the opposite. We observed a significantly positive effect of concentration change on unit cost change, coupled with a modestly significant negative effect on price change.

References

Haworth, Charles T., and Reuther, Carol Jean. 1978. "Industrial Concentration and Interindustry Wage Determination." *Review of Economics and Statistics* 60, 85–95.

Hoffman, Dennis L., and Schlagenhauf, Don E. 1985. "Real Interest Rates, Anticipated Inflation, and Unanticipated Money: A Multi-Country Study." *Review of Economics and Statistics* 77, 284–296.

Houthakker, Hendrik S., and Taylor, Lester D. 1970. *Consumer Demand in the U.S.: Analyses and Projections.* Cambridge, MA: Harvard University Press.

Kelton, Christina M. L. 1982. "The Effect of Market Structure on Price Change for Food Manufacturing Product Classes." North Central Project 117 Working Paper 60. Madison: University of Wisconsin.

Layson, Stephen K., and Seaks, Terry G. 1984. "Estimation and Testing for Functional Form in First Difference Models." *Review of Economics and Statistics 66,* 338–343.

Mueller, Willard F., and Hamm, Larry G. 1974. "Trends in Industrial Market Concentration, 1947 to 1970." *Review of Economics and Statistics 56,* 511–520.

Mueller, Willard F., and Rogers, Richard T. 1980. "The Role of Advertising in Changing Concentration of Manufacturing Industries." *Review of Economics and Statistics 62,* 89–96.

Pagan, Adrian. 1984. "Econometric Issues in the Analysis of Regressions with Generated Regressors." *International Economic Review 25,* 221–247.

Peltzman, Sam. 1977. "The Gains and Losses from Industrial Concentration." *Journal of Law and Economics 20,* 229–250.

Qualls, P. David. 1978. "Market Structure and Price Behavior in U.S. Manufacturing, 1967–72." *Quarterly Review of Economics and Business 18,* 35–57.

Vita, M. G. 1984. "Profits, Concentration, and the Collusion-Efficiency Debate: A Simultaneous Equations Model." Ph.D. dissertation. Madison: University of Wisconsin.

Weiss, Leonard W. 1972. "The Geographic Size of Markets in Manufacturing." *The Review of Economics and Statistics 54,* 245–257.

4

The Price Effects of
Increased Competition
in Auction Markets

Lance Brannman,
J. Douglass Klein, and
Leonard W. Weiss

Chapters 2 through 4 offered tests that dealt fairly directly with the standard predictions of oligopoly theory, but there are other reasons to expect a positive effect of concentration on price. One is diversity among firms. Here we must turn to an entirely different body of "oligopoly theory," the theory of auctions. Admittedly, the relative fewness of bidders (generally less than 12) and the practice of the seller (usually the government) in honestly reporting all bids seem likely to facilitate collusion. Yet our emphasis is not on collusion but rather on how the increased diversity among larger numbers of firms affects auction prices.

When bidders compete to sell a good or service, as the number of sellers increases, the expected value of costs for the low cost producer gets lower and lower. Conversely, when bidders compete to buy, the level of optimism of the highest buying bidder gets higher and higher. That is the argument explored in this chapter.

Those who picture the bidders as dealers operating in many markets with little commitment to any of them may question the economic significance of our findings. In fact, however, many of the bidders in each of the markets considered have substantial sunk costs that tie them to the markets in which they did. We have no doubt that if half of the top 20 oil companies were to merge with the other half, then the number of bidders for offshore oil tracts would be reduced importantly. And if half the lumber mills within 50 miles of Eugene, Oregon, close or merge with the other half, we would certainly expect the number of bidders in National Forest timber auctions there to fall in the process. The underwriting of municipal bonds certainly must include some brokers with little commitment to the particular market, but many of the underwriters are local banks. They have plenty of sunk costs that tie them to the local market, once more.

Originally published in *Review of Economics and Statistics* 69:1 (February 1987), 24–32. Reprinted with permission.

Beyond that, we feel that the many private "auctions" where contractors submit bids sometimes formally, sometimes through salesmen, to build plant or to install equipment are similarly affected by the number of bidders. Even where formal auction theory might be strained, increasing numbers of sellers should carry with it increasing variety. When this happens, the low cost supplier or most optimistic buyer is apt to call the shots.

Altogether, we feel that auction theory offers much that is relevant to many oligopolistic markets and deserves a prominent place in this book.

Auction Theory

Auction theory predicts that an increased number of bidders increases winning bids.[1] The particular pattern of this increase depends on the type of auction, characteristics of the good being sold, and firm and industry characteristics. For certain types of auctions, there are clear theoretical predictions regarding the relationship between the average level of winning bids and the number of bidders. In other types of auctions the relationship is less predictable. Such influences as risk aversion, uncertainty about the true value of the item at auction, and interdependence in the individual bidders' estimates of the item's value affect the pattern of winning bids.

In this chapter we test theoretical predictions about the effects of increased competition on winning bids in five different auction settings: (1) underwriters' spreads on tax-exempt general obligation bonds, (2) underwriters' spreads on tax-exempt revenue bonds, (3) U.S. Department of Interior's offshore oil lease auctions, (4) oral ascending, and (5) sealed-bid auctions of National Forest Service timber in the Pacific Northwest. All these auctions are conducted on a first-price sealed-bid basis, except for the oral timber sales. Our results can be used to suggest which auction models best represent those various markets. A fuller understanding of the actual relationship between an auction's winning bid and the degree of competition in that auction is important, not only for auction design, but also in the formation of anti-merger and other antitrust policies.

We begin with a brief review of the theory of auctions. Next we discuss determinants of winning bids in our different auction settings and present estimates of the price effects caused by additional competition. Finally, we consider the specific form of the relationship between winning bid (price) and the number of bidders.

The pattern of dependence between winning bids and the number of bidders is determined by the rules of the auction and its surrounding environment. Relevant environmental factors include the type of good being sold, attributes of the bidders, and overall industry characteristics.

Two frameworks developed to deal with different combinations of these factors under different auction rules are known as the independent private values (IPV) and common values (CV) models. Milgrom and Weber (1982) have shown that the IPV and CV models can be treated as special cases of a more general auction theory which we call the Milgrom-Weber (MW) model.

In the IPV model, a known number of bidders, N, place different (independent) subjective values on an object being offered for sale. These values may be treated as a random sample from some underlying value distribution that is assumed known to all auction participants. Each individual firm knows its own valuation with certainty, but not those of its competitors. In this model, when firms are bidding for inputs, differences in the good's subjective values may be due to differences in the opportunity costs of the firm's resources. Value differences to ultimate consumers arise due to different tastes.

In the IPV model, if bidders are risk neutral, the expected winning bid is equal to the expected second-order statistic of the sample made up of all bidders' independent private valuations of the object for sale. This result is apparent in oral auctions where the winner pays only slightly more than the second-highest bidder. It also holds in a wide variety of other auction settings, including our sealed-bid first-price auctions (Riley and Samuelson 1981). Larger samples (i.e., more bidders) in this model increase the expected value of winning bid (the expected second-order statistic) as it then lies farther and farther in the right-hand tail of the underlying distribution. Thus the IPV auction's price (winning bid) should follow the pattern of the second-highest value drawing and increase with the number of bidders.

The pattern of winning bids in the IPV model when firms are risk averse depends on the type of auction conducted. In an oral auction the number of bidders and all bids are directly observed by all participants. Hence the winning bid will be slightly higher than the second-highest bidder's valuation. In a sealed-bid first-price auction the expected winning bid is greater than the second-order statistic when firms are risk averse (Riley and Samuelson 1981), but the winning bid pattern that results from increased competition depends on the form of each firm's risk aversion. The maximum order statistic is an upper limit to winning bids. In IPV settings we therefore expect oral auctions to fit second-order statistics better than sealed-bid auctions.

The common value (CV) model assumes that the object offered for sale has some "true" value that is common but unknown to all bidders. Each bidder independently estimates the true value of the object for sale. In the symmetric version of the CV model, if bidders' estimates of the good's true value are unbiased, then those estimates represent independent drawings from a probability distribution with mean equal to the true value.

Many authors have noted that winners in CV auctions are subject to a "winner's curse,".[2] If firms simply bid their estimates of the good's value and there is more than one bidder, the winner will, on average, pay more than the true value, and price should rise with this highest value estimate (maximum-order statistic) as the number of bidders increases.

Wilson (1977), Milgrom (1979), Cox and Isaac (1984), and Thiel (1988) have shown how optimal bids in a CV auction depend on both the number of competing bidders and the accuracy of each bidder's estimation procedure. More bidders suggests that a higher bid will be required to win. But more bidders or greater variance in the estimation process call for more cautious (i.e., lower) bids in order to avoid the winner's curse. We call this the pure CV strategy. Rothkopf (1969) derives specific bid strategies that show that optimal bids decline as competition increases with three or more bidders, assuming that all firms' value estimates are drawn from a Weibull distribution. Capen et al. (1971) reach similar results by simulating auctions with values drawn from a lognormal distribution.

Despite this decline in optimal bids as the number of bidders increases, the expected winning bid rises toward the good's true value in the CV model when bidders use a multiplicative bid strategy and act to avoid the winner's curse. Wilson (1977) and Milgrom (1979) show that the expected winning bid converges in probability to the unknown true value as competition increases. Rothkopf (1969), Wilson (1977), and Thiel (1988) show that the expected payoff to the winning bidder (the difference between the unknown true value and the winning bid) is proportional to $1/N$, where N is the number of bidders. Since the true value is constant, this implies that the expected winning bid increases in proportion to $1/N$ in the CV model when firms act to avoid the winner's curse.

Milgrom and Weber (1982) argue that the IPV and CV assumptions are overly restrictive. In particular, the IPV model does not allow for uncertainty about the good's true value or interdependence in the value drawings. On the other hand, the CV model does not allow for differences in tastes. The MW model relaxes these restrictions, allowing room for elements of both independent private and common values. As far as we know, the specific nature of the relationship between winning bids and the number of bidders in such a model has not been determined. However, it seems reasonable that in the presence of any degree of independent private valuations, the expected winning bid will not be bounded above by a common true value (as in the pure CV model when bidders seek to avoid the winner's curse). Hence, as competition increases, the increases in winning bids in the MW model should lie between the IPV and pure CV predictions. Winning bids should fit expected second-order statistics best when IPV elements dominate an auction and firms are risk neutral. Winning bids should fit $1/N$ best when CV elements dominate an auction and firms bid optimally to avoid the winner's curse.

Other aspects of real auctions further confound the relationships between winning bids and the number of bidders. Oren and Rothkopf (1975) consider sequential auctions where competitors may learn about (and retaliate against) one bidder's strategy in subsequent auctions. Rothkopf (1977), Gilley and Karels (1981), and Klein (1982) consider simultaneous auctions with firm-specific capital constraints. Gilley and Karels deal with the distinction between the number of potential auction participants and the actual number of nonzero price bidders on a particular item.[3] Other complications include joint venture bids, after markets in which the auctioned goods may be resold, sequential auctions, and the possibility of tacit or overt collusion in auction sales.

In sum, auction models predict that expected winning bids will rise as the number of bidders increases. The simplest case arises when firms are risk neutral, the assumptions of the IPV model hold, and the underlying distribution of bidder values follows a well-defined distribution function. Then the winning bid should increase with the expected second-order statistic from the value distribution as the number of bidders increases. Winning bids in the CV sealed-bid first-price model, when bidders fail to adjust to the winner's curse, should increase with the expected maximum-order statistic of the sample of value estimates. When firms adjust for the winner's curse, winning bids should increase with the number of bidders toward the true value as $1/N$ approaches zero. The MW model offers no clear predictions about the pattern of changes in winning bids caused by changes in competition. Price patterns in the MW model should depend on the relative strengths of each auction's IPV and CV components.

Predicting Winning Bids

Estimates of the price effects resulting from increased competition are needed in order to compare predicted winning bid patterns with reality. These estimates are obtained by explaining winning bids as a function of the number of bidders. A series of dummy variables, $D_1, \ldots, D_{11}$ are included as explanatory variables to account for any nonlinearity in the price-competition relationship ($D_i = 1$ if there are i bidders, and $D_i = 0$ otherwise). The coefficients of D_i will allow us to compare the winning bids corresponding to various levels of competition with those when there are 12 or more bidders (the excluded category).

In many auctions winning bids and the number of bidders may increase together because they are both correlated to a third variable—the value, or quality, of the object offered for sale (i.e., valuable objects attract both more bidders and higher bids). We adjust for this correlation by including variables that control for variations in the quality of objects offered for sale.[4] The quality variables expected to be important in each auction market are discussed below.[5]

Tax-Exempt Bond Underwriting

Our analysis of municipal bond underwriters' spreads is based on Kessel (1971) who studied 9,420 issues submitted to competitive sealed bids in 1959 to 1967. About one-quarter of Kessel's sample were revenue bonds; the rest were general obligation bonds (Kessel, p. 708). We assume that underwriters independently sample the bonds' value from a normal distribution. Kessel controlled for variations in bond quality across issues by including as explanatory variables issue size, quality of bonds by Standard and Poor's rating dummies, volume of bonds already outstanding by the issuer, trend in underwriting costs for bonds of the same ratings, long-term interest rates in the week of issue and their change since the previous week, call date, and average maturity (Kessel, p. 718). The coefficients of these number-of-bidder dummies and their standard errors appear in the first two columns of table 4.1. There is a systematic tendency for the winning bid to decline as the number of bidders increases.

Offshore Oil Auctions

The next set of auction data comes from the Lease, Production, and Revenue (LPR) data tapes maintained by the U.S. Geological Survey (1979), and cover 2,221 offshore oil leases auctioned by the Department of the Interior during the years 1954 to 1975.[6] All tracts were auctioned using the bonus bid system of sealed bidding, with the high bid winning. The distribution of bids in these auctions is skewed upward, but the natural logs of the bids are approximately normally distributed (Arps 1976; Klein 1983). Because of this, the logs of bids are analyzed.

Table 4.1
Number-of-bidder coefficients (standard errors in parentheses, t ratios in brackets)

Number of bids	Bonds		Oil		Timber	
	General obligation	Revenue	1954–1971	1972–1975	Sealed bids	Oral bids
1	5.09[a]	6.32[a]	−3.03[a]	−2.02[a]	−106.64[a]	−94.64[a]
	(0.32)	(0.63)	(0.17)	(0.17)	(14.69)	(15.62)
	[15.90]	[10.03]	[−17.82]	[−11.88]	[−7.25]	[−6.06]
2	2.50[a]	2.73[a]	−2.46[a]	−1.31[a]	−70.48[a]	−81.30[a]
	(0.18)	(0.53)	(0.18)	(0.17)	(13.66)	(12.64)
	[13.89]	[5.15]	[−13.67]	[−7.71]	[−5.16]	[−6.43]
3	2.33[a]	2.38[a]	−1.99[a]	−1.22[a]	−44.83[a]	−60.90[a]
	(0.15)	(0.51)	(0.20)	(0.18)	(12.45)	(11.87)
	[15.53]	[4.67]	[−9.95]	[−6.78]	[−3.60]	[−5.13]
4	1.69[a]	1.38[a]	−1.63[a]	−0.69[a]	−46.49[a]	−48.45[a]
	(0.14)	(0.51)	(0.20)	(0.18)	(13.88)	(11.99)
	[12.07]	[2.71]	[−8.15]	[−3.83]	[−3.35]	[−4.04]
5	0.95[a]	1.12[a]	−1.16[a]	−0.81[a]	−11.38	−59.39[a]
	(0.13)	(0.51)	(0.21)	(0.20)	(12.79)	(12.20)
	[7.31]	[2.20]	[−5.52]	[−4.05]	[−0.89]	[−4.87]
6	0.72[a]	0.58	−0.95[a]	−0.63[a]	−14.59	−21.51
	(0.13)	(0.53)	(0.22)	(0.19)	(12.58)	(12.58)
	[5.53]	[1.09]	[−4.32]	[−3.32]	[−1.16]	[−1.71]
7	0.51[a]	0.49	−0.87[a]	−0.37[a]	−3.82	−50.45[a]
	(0.13)	(0.54)	(0.22)	(0.20)	(13.64)	(13.10)
	[3.92]	[0.91]	[−3.95]	[−1.85]	[−0.28]	[−3.85]
8	0.29[a]	0.60	−0.42[a]	0.06	14.49	−32.18[a]
	(0.14)	(0.55)	(0.24)	(0.21)	(14.07)	(12.87)
	[2.07]	[1.09]	[−1.75]	[0.29]	[1.03]	[−2.50]
9	0.13	0.10	−0.53[a]	−0.04	3.93	−17.49
	(0.15)	(0.50)	(0.23)	(0.24)	(15.12)	(13.88)
	[0.87]	[0.20]	[−2.30]	[−0.17]	[0.25]	[−1.26]
10	0.18	0.54	−0.20	−0.01	11.53	−10.90
	(0.17)	(0.60)	(0.24)	(0.27)	(16.01)	(14.73)
	[1.06]	[0.89]	[−0.83]	[−0.04]	[0.72]	[−0.74]
11	0.13	−0.21	−0.09	−0.04	−5.60	−17.71
	(0.18)	(0.70)	(0.26)	(0.39)	(18.67)	(19.25)
	[0.72]	[−0.31]	[−0.35]	[−0.10]	[−0.30]	[−0.92]

a. Significant at the 0.05 confidence level.

The leases were divided into two subsets, consisting of leases sold from 1954 to 1971 and those sold from 1972 to July of 1975. One important explanatory variable, the USGS pre-sale estimate of tract value, was only available for the latter period. In addition events surrounding the dramatic rise in the price of oil in 1973 and 1974 might have significantly altered bidding behavior. Data were included only through mid-1975 in order to be able to control for tract quality by including variables indicating actual production of the leases over the subsequent five years.

Tract quality was controlled for by including variables affecting revenues, costs, and the government's pre-sale expectation of the value of the lease. Revenue variables, which are expected to positively affect winning bids, include the price of oil (upper tier oil, when relevant), the number of barrels of oil produced from the lease in the first five years of production, a dummy variable indicating whether the lease was ever drilled and another indicating whether it ever produced oil or gas, and the number of acres in the lease. Our only cost variable is depth, which was expected to have a negative effect on the winning bid. Finally, the government's pre-sale expectation is indicated by the USGS pre-sale estimate of lease value (available only for 1972 to 1975), which was expected to have a positive coefficient.[7]

All estimated quality coefficients for the 1954–1971 period had the expected signs, and nearly all were significant. For 1972 to 1975, the coefficients on the quality variables were less consistent with expectations, although the two measures of pre-sale expectations continued to perform well, as did the first five years' output and the dummies for tracts that ever produced oil and gas or were ever drilled.

The middle two columns in table 4.1 show the estimated coefficients and their standard errors for the number-of-bidder dummies. In both periods the coefficients increase successively; that is, leases with greater competition command higher prices, holding tract quality constant.

National Forest Service Timber Sales

The fourth and fifth data sets cover National Forest Service timber auctions in the Pacific Northwest during 1977. Our sample of 243 oral auctions and 396 sealed-bid auctions represents all commercial sale auctions in the western parts Washington, Oregon, and northern California (an area known as the Douglas fir region) for which the award and contract execution was expected to proceed without difficulty.[8] We assume that, for a single auction, timber values are normally distributed among firms.

There is much less uncertainty involved in National Forest Service auctions than in offshore oil, but it is still important to control for the quality characteristics likely to affect stumpage prices (Brannman, Buongiorno, and Fight 1981). Relevant quality variables include National Forest Service estimates of permanent and temporary road construction costs, whether the sale is a salvage sale, the number of acres in the tract, estimated hauling distance from the sale site to local mills, the percentage of "pre acre material" (PAM consisting of deadwood and other scrap) relative to total volume, the National Forest Service appraisal price, and the length of time allowed winners to harvest the timber. We expect the pre-auction appraisal price and harvesting horizon to have a positive effect on winning bids. Temporary road construction costs, salvage sale, hauling distance, acreage, and PAM should have negative effects. We had no a priori expectation about the sign of permanent road construction costs (for which the buyer is compensated based on National Forest Service estimates).

The estimated quality coefficients generally fit our sign expectations. Salvage sales, however, had a significant positive influence on winning sealed bids and a nonsignificant positive influence of winning oral bids. We are unable to explain this result. In addition estimated hauling distance at oral auctions had a significant positive effect, possibly because of preclusive bidding by firms close to the sale site (Mead 1966, 148–150).

The last two columns of table 4.1 show the estimated number of bidder coefficients for oral and sealed bidding, respectively. Winning bids increase with the number of bidders in both cases.

The Relation of Number-of-Bid Coefficients to Order Statistics

In all types of auctions covered in this chapter, prices rose with the number of bidders (fell in bond underwriting where the low bid won the auction) after controlling for differences in the quality of the object auctioned. This section investigates the predicted form of this relationship, which depends on the relative strengths of each auction's IPV and CV elements. Previous literature guides the assessment of these relative strengths somewhat, but each reader may have a different idea about each auction's IPV and CV elements.

Municipal bond underwriting is characterized by a mix of strong IPV and some CV elements. Underwriters have different customers with differing preferences. Municipal bond interest is often exempt from state income tax in the issuing state, but not elsewhere. In-state banks and brokers probably have more knowledge of local bond issues than other underwriters and are apt to have access to the most likely customers. Moreover the bank's own trust department is often one of the major customers; ultimate consumers often have little knowledge of underwriting actions and overall financial markets. On the other hand, future national credit conditions determine a bond's present value.

Common value components probably dominate in oil auctions. In reviewing the CV model, Milgrom and Weber (1982) refer to it as the "Oil, Gas and Mineral Rights model." Oil lease auctions are characterized by a large degree of uncertainty about the amount of recoverable oil. This common value component, along with competitively determined product market prices, should dominate any private value elements in offshore oil lease auctions. Offshore oil winning bids should therefore fit expected maximum-order statistics best when firms do not bid optimally to avoid the winner's curse, they should fit and $1/N$ best when firms do bid optimally.

Timber auctions are the most difficult to categorize. Previous authors (Hansen 1985, 1986; Johnson 1977, 1979) have used the IPV model in their analyses of government timber sales. Value differences among bidders are caused in part by product mix differences, varying tract and mill locations, the high costs of transporting logs, capacity and inventory considerations, and the opportunity costs of the firm's resources.[9] A CV component is injected into timber auctions through uncertainty about the volume of timber offered for sale. Mead, Schniepp, and Watson (1981) find that Forest Service appraised volumes on a sale by sale basis differ considerably from the amount actually cut. If uncertainty about timber volume is small, then predictions from the IPV model should best fit timber sales. On the other hand, the general MW model becomes more appropriate as uncertainty over a tract's value grows relative to the auction's IPV elements.

In this section we test the following: (1) The expected winning bid equals the expected second-order statistic from the underlying value distribution when bidders are risk neutral. This pure IPV prediction is most likely to be upheld in oral auctions where uncertainty about rival bids disappears. (2) The expected winning bid equals the expected maximum-order statistic (MOS). This is the CV prediction, when bidders fail to avoid the winner's curse. (3) The expected bids rise in proportion to $1/N$. This is the CV prediction when firms bid optimally and avoid the winner's curse.

If the underlying value or value estimate distributions are normal (lognormal for offshore oil) then hypothesis 1 implies that there is linear relationship between the number-of-bidder coefficients in table 4.1 and the expected second-order statistic of a sample drawn from a standard normal distribution.[10] Hypothesis 2 implies a linear relationship between the number-of-bidder coefficients and the expected maximum-order statistic of a sample from a standard normal distribution. Hypothesis 3 implies that there is a linear relationship between the number-of-bidder coefficients and $1/N$.

Two subsets of the 11 number-of-bidders coefficients shown in table 4.1 were used to test these hypotheses. First, the coefficients corresponding to $N = 2, 3, \ldots, 11$ bidders were regressed on our three predictors of winning bids. $N = 1$ is omitted in order to include the expected second-order statistic as an explanatory variable. Table 4.2 shows the results. Table 4.3 shows the results of regressing all 11 number-of-bidders coefficients on first the expected maximum-order statistics and then on $1/N$.

Tests of our hypotheses involve comparing error variances among the regressions in tables 4.2 and 4.3. The null hypothesis is that MOS explains the same amount of the variance among the coefficients as do the alternatives, taken one at a time. The alternative hypothesis is that MOS explains more of the variance among the number-of-bidder coefficients than the other indexes. These are one-tailed tests with distributions $F(8, 8)$ for comparisons from table 4.2 and $F(9, 9)$ for those from table 4.3. There are 12 such comparisons in table 4.2 , and 6 in table 4.3. In table 4.2 the fit with MOS is significantly ($\alpha = 0.05$) better than with another index in only one case: $1/N$ in offshore oil in 1954 to 1971. In table 4.3 MOS fit significantly better than $1/N$ for only oral timber auctions.

A difficulty in finding one index statistically superior to the others is the close correlation among all three. The correlations between MOS and $1/N$ ($N = 1, \ldots, 11$) and MOS and SOS ($N = 2, \ldots, 11$) are -0.968 and 0.996, respectively. The correlation between SOS and $1/N$ is -0.995.

Despite this collinearity, the F tests reported above understate the relative "success" of MOS. In table 4.2 MOS and SOS yield better fits than $1/N$ for all six comparisons. If the null hypothesis is that MOS (or SOS) and $1/N$ are equally good predictors of the coefficient pattern, then the probability of one providing a better fit in all six cases is 0.016. MOS fit better than $1/N$ in five cases in table 4.3 and better than SOS in five of the six cases in table 4.2. This would occur by chance a little less than 10 percent of the time ($p = 0.094$).

Conclusions

In this chapter we have examined the theoretical and empirical relationships between price and the number of bidders in a variety of auction markets. An obvious and important result is the very significant positive effect of

Table 4.2
Three alternative functional forms relating number of bidders to winning bids, $N = 2, \ldots, 11$ (standard errors in parentheses, t ratios in brackets)

Type of auction	Functional form		
	Maximum-order statistics (MOS)	1/N	Second-order statistic (SOS)
Underwriting general obligation bonds	$4.26 - 2.70$ MOS[a] (0.21) [−12.86] $r^2 = 0.955$	$-0.41 + 6.70(1/N)$[a] (0.77) [8.70] $r^2 = 0.906$	$1.88 - 1.72$ SOS[a] (0.16) [−10.75] $r^2 = 0.935$
Underwriting revenue bonds	$4.39 - 2.79$ MOS[a] (0.26) [−10.73] $r^2 = 0.936$	$-0.45 + 7.02(1/N)$[a] (0.78) [9.0] $r^2 = 0.910$	$1.95 - 1.79$ SOS[a] (0.17) [−10.53] $r^2 = 0.929$
Offshore oil (1954–1971)	$-3.93 + 2.37$ MOS[a] (0.11) [21.55] $r^2 = 0.980$	$0.148 - 5.83(1/N)$[a] (0.59) [−9.88] $r^2 + 0.915$	$-1.85 + 1.50$ SOS[a] (0.10) [15.0] $r^2 = 0.958$
Offshore oil (1972–1975)	$-2.30 + 1.46$ MOS[a] (0.17) [8.59] $r^2 = 0.898$	$0.211 - 3.55(1/N)$[b] (0.59) [−6.02] $r^2 = 0.817$	$-1.01 + 0.92$ SOS[a] (0.13) [7.08] $r^2 = 0.866$
National forest timber oral bids	$-118.0 + 63.60$ MOS[b] (11.33) [5.61] $r^2 = 0.798$	$-8.3 - 157.00(1/N)$[b] (32.37) [−4.85] $r^2 = 0.746$	$-62.2 + 40.5$ SOS[b] (7.54) [5.37] $r^2 = 0.783$
National forest timber sealed bids	$-114.5 + 79.75$ MOS[a] (10.62) [7.51] $r^2 = 0.876$	$24.2 - 202.60(1/N)$[a] (27.91) [−7.30] $r^2 = 0.868$	$-44.8 + 51.3$ SOS[a] (6.80) [7.54] $r^2 = 0.877$

a. Significant at the 0.0001 confidence level.
b. Significant at the 0.001 confidence level.

Table 4.3
Two alternative functional forms relating number of bidders to winning bids,
$N = 1, 2, \ldots, 11$ (standard errors in parentheses, t ratios in brackets)

Type of auction	Functional form	
	Maximum-order statistics (MOS)	1/N
Underwriting general obligation bonds	$4.77 - 3.1$ MOS[a] (0.17) [-18.24] $r^2 = 0.974$	$-19.5 + 5.51(1/N)$[a] (0.39) [14.13] $r^2 = 0.958$
Underwriting Revenue bonds	$5.59 - 3.7$ MOS[a] (0.30) [-12.33] $r^2 = 0.943$	$-0.40 + 6.77(1/N)$[a] (0.34) [19.91] $r^2 = 0.978$
Offshore oil (1954–1971)	$-3.48 + 2.02$ MOS[a] (0.12) [16.83] $r^2 = 0.969$	$-0.30 - 3.37(1/N)$[a] (0.48) [-7.02] $r^2 = 0.836$
Offshore oil (1972–1975)	$-2.12 + 1.33$ MOS[a] (0.11) [-12.09] $r^2 = 0.939$	$-0.03 - 2.24(1/N)$[a] (0.34) [-6.59] $r^2 = 0.829$
National forest timber oral bids	$-103.5 + 52.51$ MOS[a] (7.57) [6.94] $r^2 = 0.842$	$-21.2 - 86.70(1/N)$[a] (18.27) [-4.75] $r^2 = 0.714$
National forest timber sealed bids	$-109.6 + 76.02$ MOS[a] (6.55) [11.61] $r^2 = 0.937$	$11.1 - 131.17(1/N)$[a] (17.01) [7.71] $r^2 = 0.869$

a. Significant at the 0.0001 confidence level.

the number of bidders on buying price (negative effect on selling price), regardless of the specific index used. Here is a place where concentration clearly leads to higher selling prices (lower buying prices) in both theory and practice. The specific predicted pattern of this price increase depends on the model employed.[11]

When risk-neutral bidders independently and with certainty decide on the value of an object for sale (the pure IPV model), then regardless of the auction method, expected winning bid equals the second-highest valuation. We expected this pattern in oral timber sales but found that the maximum-order statistic fit slightly better even there. This clearly may have been due to random data variation. Other explanations are greater chances for collusion (Mead 1966) or bidders learning from each other while bidding. The second-order statistic was the best index for predicting the patterns of winning bids in only one of our six cases (timber sealed bids, and then only barely).

For sales involving objects of fixed but unknown value (the CV model), firms form their bids based on estimates of that value. If bidders simply bid their value estimates (and suffer the winner's curse), then winning bids should rise with the maximum-order statistic. On the other hand, if firms adopt optimal strategies to avoid the winner's curse, then winning bids should rise toward the true value in proportion to $1/N$.

The relative strength of the maximum-order statistic in explaining winning bid patterns in all our auctions suggests that the pure CV model with optimal strategies to avoid the winner's curse does not apply as well in these cases as some alternatives. What seems most likely is that in addition to making different value *estimates*, firms also differ in the subjective *values* which they place on the object being sold. This mix of common and private values is the central feature of the MW model.

An alternative explanation of the superior explanatory power of the maximum-order statistic is that the CV assumptions do apply, but firms are not avoiding the winner's curse. This alternative is supported by Mead, Moseidjord, and Sorenson (1983) who examined discounted aftertax oil lease values in the Gulf of Mexico from 1954 to 1969. They found that winners overbid an average of $192,000 per lease when a discount rate of 12.5 percent is used and $335,000 per lease when a discount rate of 15 percent is used. Firms underbid slightly when the discount rate is 10 percent.[12]

Our analysis shows that expected maximum- and second-order statistics and, to a lesser extent $1/N$, fit very closely the increase in winning bids that occurs as competition increases, despite few degrees of freedom. The superiority of expected maximum order statistics is remarkable. These were cross-sectional rather than time series regressions with only eight or nine degrees of freedom and the relationship was in no way definitional. We considered auctions involving three very different types of objects, ranging from timber, where uncertainty is probably quite small, to offshore oil tracts, where it is huge. The fits obtained would occur by chance only once in 1,000 times in all cases and only once in 10,000 times in most cases and were computed with precise functional forms that derive from theory.

Our conclusions surely apply to other markets besides those that involve formal auctions. Wherever sellers compete for contracts to supply products or services with unique specifications, we expect a tendency for winning bid to fall as number of competing contractors rises. This characterizes much of construction and many types of industrial equipment. In such cases prices should fall as the number of potential sellers increases. The probability that collusion (tacit or explicit) will become more difficult as numbers increase reinforce this tendency. The public surely has an interest in preserving a number of competitors in such markets.

Notes

1. Comprehensive bibliographies of auctions and bidding may be found in Stark and Rothkopf (1979), Engelbrecht-Wiggans (1980), and McAfee and McMillan (1987).

2. For examples of the winner's curse in a number of different markets see Capen, Clapp and Campbell (1971), Mead, Moseidjord and Sorenson (1983), Brown (1974, 1985), Hill (1985), Klein (1987), Hendricks, Porter and Boudreau (1987) and Thaler (1988). Some, including Cox and Issac (1984) and Thiel (1988) question whether the winner's curse is a significant problem.

3. Gilley and Karels (1981) find this an important distinction in their analysis of individual bids (not winning bids) for offshore oil. Hansen (1985, 1986) finds that controlling for the number of potential bidders makes little difference in forestry auction prices.

4. Multicollinearity between quality and the number of bidders may lessen the significance of the a number-of-bidder coefficient estimates. This is only a minor problem, however, since our primary concern is with unbiased estimates.

5. The quality coefficient estimates and corresponding summary statistics are available from the authors upon request.

6. The government rejected high bids for being unnecessarily low on about 10 percent of the tracts offered between 1954 and 1975. We have no reason to suspect any difference in the relationship between the high bid and the number-of-bidders to differ between the rejected tracts and the tracts actually leased.

7. In another attempt to control for quality, we introduced the geometric mean bid as an explanatory variable. The coefficients of our other quality variables mostly became nonsignificant, but the number-of-bidder dummies still had significant coefficients that followed the pattern in table 4.1.

8. Difficulties are encountered when the winner has insufficient financial resources to harvest the timber.

9. If these differences are known by all firms prior to bidding, then there should be less competition at oral auctions. For our data set, the mean number of bidders was 5.6 (standard deviation = 3.2) in sealed bid auctions and 5.5 (standard deviation = 3.1) in oral auctions, suggesting that known value differences do not substantially affect bid strategies in the Pacific Northwest.

10. If $V_i \sim N(\mu, \sigma^2)$, then $V_i = \sigma Z_i + \mu$, where $Z_i \sim N(0, 1)$. Expected values of the maximum- and second-order statistics from samples of a standard normal distribution are given in the CRC statistical tables.

11. Actually one of the authors proposed maximum-order statistics as the relevant variable and used them in a very limited test based on four number-of-bidder classes (Geithman, Marvel, and Weiss 1981).

12. If winning bidders pay more than the object is worth, then resource allocation is not efficient. Although Cox and Isaac (1984) argue that no rational bidder would fall prey to the winner's curse, the references given in note 2 indicate some dissatisfaction among auction winners. This area clearly needs more empirical research.

References

Arps, J. 1965. "A Strategy for Sealed Bidding." *Journal of Petroleum Technology* 17 (September), 1033−1039.

Brannman, Lance, Joseph Buongiorno, and R. Fight. 1981. "Quality Adjusted Douglas-Fir Price Indices." *Western Journal of Agricultural Economics* 20.

Brown, Keith C. 1974. "A Note on the Apparent Bias of Net Revenue Estimates for Capital Investment Projects." *Journal of Finance* 29 (September), 1215−1216.

Brown, Keith C. 1985. "The Winner's Curse: What It Is and Why It Matters." Krannert School of Management Institute Paper No. 888 Purdue University November.

Capen, E. C., R. V. Clapp, and W. M. Campbell. (1971). "Competitive Bidding in High Risk Situations." *Journal of Petroleum Technology* 23 (June), 641−653.

Cox, James C., and R. Mark Isaac. 1984. "In Search of the Winner's Curse." *Economic Inquiry* 22 (October), 579−592.

Engelbrecht-Wiggans, Richard. 1980. "Auctions and Bidding Models: A Survey," *Management Science* 26, 119−142.

Geithman, F., H. Marvel, and L. Weiss. 1981. "Concentration, Prices, and Critical Concentration Ratios." *Review of Economics and Statistics* 63 (August), 346–353.

Gilley, Otis W., and Gorden V. Karels. 1981. "The Competitive Effect in Bonus Bidding: New Evidence." *Bell Journal of Economics* 12:2 (August), 637–648.

Hansen, Robert G. 1985. "Empirical Testing of Auction Theory." *American Economic Review* 75:2 (May), 156–159.

Hansen, Robert G. 1986. "Sealed-Bid vs. Open Auctions: The Evidence." *Economic Inquiry* 24:1 (January), 125–142.

Hendricks, Kenneth, Robert H. Porter, and Bryan Boudreau. 1987. "Information, Returns and Bidding Behavior in OCS Auctions: 1954–1969." *Journal of Industrial Economics* 35 (June), 517–542.

Hill, James R. 1985. "The Threat of Free Agency and Exploitation in Professional Baseball: 1976–1979." *Quarterly Review of Economics and Business* 25 (Winter), 68–82.

Johnson, Ronald N. 1977. "Competitive Bidding for Federally Owned Timber." Ph.D. Dissertation. Seattle: University of Washington.

Johnson, Ronald N. 1979. "Oral Auction versus Sealed Bids: An Empirical Investigation." *Natural Resources Journal* 19 (April), 315–335.

Kessel, Reuben 1971. "A Study of the Effects of Competition in the Tax-Exempt Bond Market." *Journal of Political Economy* 79 (July), 706–738.

Klein, J. Douglass. 1982. "Some Determinants of Money Exposed and Spent in Outer Continental Shelf Oil and Gas Auction." Paper presented to the 8th Annual Convention of the Eastern Economics Association (April 20–May 1). Washington, D.C.

Klein, J. Douglass. 1983. *The Impact of Joint Ventures on Bidding for Offshore Oil.* New York: Garland Publishing, Inc.

Klein, J. Douglass. 1987. "Avoiding the Winner's Curse: Are Bidders Rational?" Union College Department of Economics Working Paper Series August.

McAfee, R. Preston, and John McMillan. 1987. "Auctions and Bidding." *Journal of Economic Literature* 25 (June), 699–754.

Mead, Walter J. 1966. *Competition and Oligopsony in the Douglas-Fir Lumber Industry.* Berkeley: University of California Press.

Mead, Walter J., Absjorn Moseidjord, and Philip E. Sorenson. 1983. "The Rate of Return Earned by Lessees under Cash Bonus Bidding for OCS Oil and Gas Leases. *Energy Journal* 99 (October), 37–52.

Mead, Walter J., Schniepp, M., and Watson, R. B. "The Effectiveness of Competition in the Auction Markets for National Forest Timber in the Pacific Northwest." USDA Forest Service Contract No. 53-3187-1-43 and PSW G-34.

Milgrom, Paul R. 1979. "A Convergence Theorem for Competitive Bidding with Differential Information." *Econometrica* 47, 879–888.

Milgrom, Paul R., and Robert J. Weber. 1982. "A Theory of Auctions and Competitive Bidding." *Econometrica* 50:5 (September), 1089–1122.

Oren, Shmuel, and Michael B. Rothkopf. 1975. "Optimal Bidding Sequential Auctions." *Operations Research* 23:6 (November–December), 1080–90.

Riley, James G., and William F. Samuelson. 1981. "Optimal Auctions." *American Economic Review* 71 (June), 381–392.

Rothkopf, Michael. 1969. A Model of Rational Competitive Bidding." *Management Science* 15, 362–373.

Rothkopf, Michael H. 1977. "Bidding in Simultaneous Auctions with a Constraint on Exposure." *Operations Research* 25:4 (July–August), 620–629.

Stark, Robert M., and Michael H. Rothkopf. 1979. "Competitive Bidding: A Comprehensive Bibliography." *Operations Research* 27, 364–390.

Thaler, Richard H. 1988. "Anomalies: The Winner's Curse." *Journal of Economic Perspectives* 2 (Winter), 191–202.

Thiel, Stuart E. 1988. "Some Evidence on the Winner's Curse." *American Economic Review* 78 (December), 884–895.

U.S. Geological Survey, Lease, Production and Revenue (LPR) Data Base. Available from Minerals Management Services, U.S. Department of the Interior, M.S. 643, National Center, Reston, VA 22091.

Wilson, Robert. 1977. "A Bidding Model of Perfect Competition." *Review of Economic Studies* 44 (October), 511–518.

5

Concentration and Wages: Direct and Indirect Effects

Dale Belman and Leonard W. Weiss

Research on the welfare implications of market concentration has focused on the relation between concentration and profits or price-cost margins. Concentration may also affect the economic efficiency of firm operation if it causes technological inefficiency in production or increases the cost of inputs. Indeed, the effect of concentration on the latter factors may have greater consequences than the effect on profits. The cost of inputs are far larger than profits. In 1982 manufacturers spent $1,516 billion on production inputs and reported $108 billion in profits. It would take a very large rise in profits to equal the price increase caused by a small rise in input prices. Although there is disagreement, many economists believe labor costs are influenced by market structure. The work of Dunlop (1948), Segal (1964), and Galbraith (1952), among others, has suggested that concentration may influence wages directly, or indirectly through institutions such as unions. Empirical research has failed to substantiate or reject these theories. Results have varied from positive and significant to nonsignificant, depending on the universe used for the study, the level of aggregation of the data, the specification of the control variables, the measure of concentration, and the type of model. Attempts to measure the indirect effect of concentration have had persistent problems with sample size and measurement error.

We report new results on the wage effect of concentration. Using both simultaneous and nonsimultaneous models of wages and union membership, it is shown that the elasticity of the wage with respect to concentration ranges between 0.07 and 0.20. We also demonstrate that concentration's effect on wages through unions is as large as its direct effect.

Adapted from "Concentration, Unionism, and Labor Earnings: A Sample Selection Approach," *Review of Economics and Statistics* 70:3 (August 1988), 391–397. Reprinted with permission.

Theories Concerning the Wage Effects of Concentration

Contemporary theory indicates that concentration may affect wages directly or indirectly. There is a direct effect if there is an immediate relation between concentration and the wage. There is an indirect effect if the relation is mediated through another factor, notably unionization. Commonly cited arguments for a direct effect are:[1]

1. Concentrated industries pay higher than average wages as a shield against public opinion.

2. Firms in concentrated industries face relatively inelastic demand curves. Since the effect of high wages on profits is small, firms will have less incentive to resist union wage demands or restrain nonunion wage increases.

3. Unions have less difficulty coordinating wage policies when there are few firms in a market. Firms face similar economic conditions, reducing the pressure for concessions to less well-off firms. Firms also have little incentive to expend resources to break wage patterns, because success would lead to union concessions to their competitors.

4. Threat effects are stronger in concentrated industries. Wage comparisons between union and nonunion firms are easier where there are few firms. The wage in the nonunion sector will not be able to lag far behind the union wage without employee dissatisfaction. Union wages will spill over into the nonunion sector, attenuating the drag on wages from nonunion competition.

5. Concentrated industries have higher labor productivity, allowing payment of a higher wage.[2]

An indirect effect through unionization occurs if increases in concentration lead to higher levels of unionization, enabling the union to better extract concessions from firms. The arguments for this relation between union strength and the wage are well known. A positive relation may exist if:

1. Large firms are hesitant to fight unions as fiercely as competitive firms because of public opprobrium.

2. Unions are attracted to industries where there are monopoly rents because of the relative ease in raising wages.

3. Concentration and related aspects of industry structure increase the likelihood of union success in organizing. The small number of firms in concentrated markets reduces the number of victorious organizing campaigns required to establish union power. This reduces the cost of achieving successful collective bargaining and encourages union organizing efforts.

The multiplant firm common in concentrated industries is also conducive to organizing. Partial organization gives the union some leverage over management when efforts to organize are made at new locations. Finally, firms in concentrated industries tend to have large plants, further facilitating organization.

4. Unions are easier to maintain in concentrated markets. In competitive markets, the escalation of the costs of organized firms provide incentives for entry to nonunion firms. Barriers to entry exist in many concentrated markets. This prevents or slows the drift toward disorganization which occurs in competitive markets. The longer life of firms in concentrated industries also serves to maintain organization.[3]

Not all economists accept these arguments for a positive relation between market concentration and the wage. Rees (1962) has pointed out that monopolized industries operate in a more elastic portion of the industry demand curve than competitive industries. Facing a less favorable trade-off between employment and the wage, unions in monopoly industries may bargain lower wages than under competitive conditions. Levinson (1967) has argued that the large resources of firms in concentrated industries better equips them to resist union wage demands. Lewis (1963) suggests that under "competitive unionism," competitive industries will be more readily unionized than monopoly industries.

Previous Empirical Research

The effect of concentration on unionism and on wages clearly differs with the sociopolitical climate. In the first third of this century large firms in concentrated industries were harder to organize than others. Our analysis applies mainly to American industries since the New Deal.

There have been a number of empirical studies of the effect of market concentration on the wage. Most have considered only the direct effect. Lewis's (1963) research is often cited as the first modern study of this subject. Using a small data set and a limited number of controls, Lewis found that concentration and union penetration had a positive effect on wage change, while the interaction of these variables had a negative effect. The net effect of concentration and union penetration was strictly positive. Weiss (1966) replicated Lewis's study with data on individual's wage levels and with controls for human capital as well as industry structure. Although concentration had a positive effect on the wage in the absence of controls for personal characteristics, addition of controls such as age, education, and race caused the coefficient on concentration to become statistically nonsignificant. Weiss concluded that concentrated industries pay higher wages that attract better-qualified employees. The coefficient on union penetration remained significantly positive, however. Similar results have been found by Masters (1969), Haworth and Rasmussen (1971), and Haworth and Reuther (1978). Using industry data, these studies found that concentration did not have a statistically significant effect on the wage in the presence of controls for plant size, education levels, and unionization. The last study indicated that macroeconomic conditions had an important influence on the direct effect of concentration. In contrast, Kwoka (1983), Hendricks (1975), Heywood (1986), and Dalton and Ford (1978) have found a positive relation between concentration and the wage. Although evidence for a direct relation between concentration and the wage is ambiguous, five of the latter seven studies have found a positive relation between union penetration and the wage. None of these studies provides a full test of the indirect effects hypothesis, but the findings on union penetration, along with those of Lewis, Weiss, and most of the others are consistent with the indirect effects hypothesis.

There has been substantially less research on indirect effects. Although the existence of an indirect effect does not require simultaneity between union membership and the wage, all relevant research has been done with simultaneous equation models. Ashenfelter and Johnson's (1972) study uses three equations to determine union penetration (average union membership by industry), the wage, and worker's educational attainment. Although their results indicate a positive relation between concentration and union penetration, the results do not support the direct or indirect effects hypotheses because the effect of unionism on wages was nonsignificant. Because of the small size of their data set (two-digit industries), the authors caution against reliance on these estimates. Kahn (1979) has obtained similar results with less aggregate industry data.

More favorable results have been obtained in studies using individuals as the elementary level of observation. Although these studies have not been intended to measure concentration's wage effects, several have included concentration among the explanatory variables. The models have an equation to determine individual union membership, and separate wage equations for union members and nonmembers. Lee's (1978) study found an indirect effect for union members; concentration had a positive effect on union status and union penetration had a positive effect on the wage of union members. As concentration was omitted from the wage equations and penetrations was omitted from the nonunion wage equation, the direct effect and the indirect effect for nonmembers were not measured. Hirsch and Berger (1975) have also found a positive relation between market concentration and union membership.[4] Using a specification that did not include concentration, Duncan and Leigh (1980) found that aggregate union membership had a positive effect on the wage. Although none of these studies provides a complete measure of concentration's indirect effect on the wage, each provides partial evidence for the existence of this effect.

The Current Project

Measurement of the direct effect of concentration on wages is straightforward, requiring only the inclusion of a measure of market concentration among the explanatory variables in the wage equation. Measurement of the indirect effect is more complex because it is embedded in the relationship between unionization and the wage. The conceptualization of this relationship, whether or not it is simultaneous, will determine how the system used to measure indirect effects is modeled and estimated. There are a number of theoretic arguments for simultaneity between wages and union membership. Simultaneity will exist if union wage premiums attract superior workers (Johnson 1975) or if workers consider the differential between union and nonunion wages in their membership decision (Ashenfelter and Johnson 1972). While these arguments have been influential in the economics profession, they have not met universal acceptance. For example, Mitchell (1980) argues against simultaneity because, despite substantial changes in union-nonunion wage differentials over the past 40 years, the level of unionization by industry has remained stable. Because of this lack of consensus, this research uses both types of models to measure concentration's wage effect. The nonsimultaneous model and results will be discussed first.

A Nonsimultaneous Model

The measurement of indirect effect requires two equations: one to measure the effect of concentration on union membership, the second to measure the effect of union membership on the wage. The system is estimated in two stages. The membership equation is estimated first and used to generate estimates of the membership variable. This estimate, along with a measure of market concentration and control variables, is used for estimation of the wage equation. The measure of the indirect effect is the product of the concentration's coefficient from the membership equation and union membership's coefficient from the wage equation. Both coefficients must be positive and significant to be consistent with the indirect effect hypothesis. As stated previously, the direct effect is measured by the coefficient of concentration in the wage equation. This coefficient must also be positive and significant to support the hypothesis.

The union membership equation, referred to as the union penetration equation, is used to measure the relationship between concentration and unionization and to generate estimates of unionization for use in the wage equation. The dependent variable was the proportion of employees in an industry belonging to a labor organization. The data for this variable was constructed from employee responses to a question on union membership in the May 1978 *Current Population Survey*. It is aggregated by Population Industry Codes (PIC), a system of classification that is somewhat broader than three-digit SIC codes. The explanatory variablels in this equation are used to control for differences in the value of union membership to workers and tastes. These differences are associated with differences in workers job attachment (%MALE, %WHITE), in the conditions of work (INJURY RATE, DURABLE), and the opportunities for individual advancement (%PRO-DUCTION, MEAN SCHOOLING). Regional and urbanization variables are used to measure for differences in tastes.

Because the union penetration measure is limited to a zero—one continuum, ordinary least squares will not provide consistent estimates of the standard errors of coefficients. Linear estimates may also be highly sensitive to the values taken by the explanatory variables and fitted values may lie outside the range of the dependent variable. Use of the log-odds procedure provides consistent estimates of standard errors, restricts fitted values to the zero—one continuum, and eliminates the coefficient instability (Madalla 1984, 15—16). As with any regression procedure a log-odds equation can be used to generate predictions of the dependent variable and measure the relation between the explanatory and dependent variable.[5] Because the estimator is nonlinear, the coefficients are not directly comparable to OLS coefficients. The analog of an OLS coefficient is the derivative of the log-odds function with respect to an explanatory variable. This measures the change in the dependent variable for a one-unit change in the explanatory variable.[6]

The elementary unit of observation in the equation is the employee. The dependent variable was the log of the hourly wage in cents per hour. The coefficient of an explanatory variable measures the proportional change in the wage for a one-unit change in the explanatory variable. The personal characteristics included in the wage equations are measures of individuals traits. These are used to control for human capital, job market attachment, race and gender discrimination, and differences in the cost of living and labor market conditions among regions. The union penetration and concentration variables are measured at the industry level and were appended to the individual's data by PIC code. Variable definitions for the wage and penetration equation are provided in table 5.1.

The measure of concentration used in this study is the adjusted concentration ratio (ACR). This is the four-firm concentration ratio published in the 1977 Census of Manufacturers adjusted for geographically fragmented markets, product markets which are too narrowly or broadly defined by Census and imports. (Weiss and Pascoe 1986).

The data on individuals was obtained from the May 1978 *Current Population Survey*. Industry data was obtained from the 1977 and 1972 *Census of Manufacturers, Enterprise Statistics 1977, Annual Survey of Manufacturers 1968–1969* and *1970–1971*, and the *Annual Line of Business Report: 1974*. Some was constructed from the May 1978 CPS. Industry data was appended to individual records by matching population industry codes. The universe for the study was blue-collar manufacturing workers who were eligible for union membership. There were 2,005 observations in the sample used for estimation.

Results

Three nonsimultaneous systems were estimated for this study. The coefficients and standard errors for the union penetration equation are presented in table 5.2, and those for the wage equation are presented in table 5.3. For each system, the estimated value of UHAT derived from an equation in table 5.2 is used as an independent variable in table 5.3. There is no feedback from wages to unionism in these regressions.

The first system (columns 1 in the two tables) measures the indirect effect of concentration without controls for personal characteristics. ACR is the sole variable in the penetration equation. UHAT is the only variable in the wage equation. The effects of both are positive and significant, as required by the indirect effect hypothesis. The derivation of union penetration with respect to ACR is 0.36, indicating a 0.36 percent increase in penetration for a one-point increase in concentration.[7] In the wage equation a one-point increase in union penetration is associated with a 1.035 percent increase in the wage. The product of these two coefficients, the measure of the indirect effect, is 0.37 ($= 0.36 \times 1.035$). A one-point increase in concentration would cause a 0.37 percent increase in the wage.

Table 5.1
Variable definitions

ln WAGE	log of the hourly wage, in cents per hour
UNION MEMBERSHIP	the proportion of workers in an industry who belong to a union. The dependent variable in the penetration equation.
COLLECTIVE BARGAINING COVERAGE	the proportion of employees in an industry who are covered by collective bargaining agreements
ACR	a weighted average of adjusted concentration ratio, by population industry code based on employment weights. The range of this variable is 0.10 to 0.84.
UHAT	an estimate of the proportion of the industry employees belonging to a labor union. The estimate was derived from a log-odds equation and, after retransformation to a percentage form, is limited to a zero–one continuum.
CBCHAT	an estimate of the proportion of industry employees covered by a collective bargaining agreement. The estimate was obtained from a log-odds equation.

Control variables

Individual traits

WHITE	1 if individual is reported as white, 0 otherwise
EDUCATION2	1 if completed 5th through 7th grade, 0 otherwise
EDUCATION3	1 if completed 8th through 11th grade, 0 otherwise
EDUCATION4	1 if completed high school, 0 otherwise
EDUCATION5	1 if completed one or more years of college, 0 otherwise
EXPERIENCE	age — highest grade completed — 6
EXP^2	Experience squared
CRAFT	1 if classified as craftsman, 0 otherwise
OPERATIVE	1 if classified as an operative, 0 otherwise
SOUTH	1 if lives in the South, 0 otherwise. This and other regional variables are normalized on the West.
NORTHEAST	1 if lives in the Northeast, 0 otherwise
NORTH CENTRAL	1 if lives in the North Central region, 0 otherwise
DURABLE	1 if works in durable goods industry, 0 otherwise
CITY	1 if lives in SMSA with more than 500,000 inhabitants, 0 otherwise.
AFTERNOON SHIFT	1 if starts work between noon and 8 pm, 0 otherwise
GRAVEYARD SHIFT	1 if starts work between 8 pm and 4 am, 0 otherwise

Table 5.1 (continued)

Industry characteristics	
SPECIALIZATION	a measure of the specialization of firms in an industry. The proportion of enterprise output originating in the major enterprise classification of firms in the industry.
INJURY RATE	number of injuries reported to OSHA per 1,000 full-time equivalent employees in 1978.
DISPERSION	the dispersion of production. The number of federal regions in which output exceeds 10 percent of national production
SALES VARIANCE	the variance of monthly output from 1973 to 1976
INVESTMENT	the ratio of book value of investment from 1967 to 1976 divided by gross value of plant and equipment at the start of 1977.
IMPORTS/SHIPMENTS	the ratio of imports to total shipments, imports plus the value of domestic shipments, from 1973 to 1975
SMALL	1 if industry median plant employment less than 100, 0 otherwise
LARGE	1 if industry median plant employment exceeds 1,000 0 otherwise
%NC	percentage of workers in an industry living in northcentral United States
%WHITE	percentage of workers in industry who are white
%MALE	percentage of workers in industry who are male
SCHOOLING	average educational attainment of workers in an industry (in years)
%CITY	percentage of workers in an SMSA with a population of more than 500,000.
%PRODUCTION WORKERS	percentage of industry employees who are production workers

Since the mean ACR is 29, the elasticity of the wage with respect to cencentration is 0.13.

Model II differs from model I in two respects: ACR is included among the explanatory variables in the wage equation, and personal and geographic characteristics are included in the penetration and wage equations. Inclusion of ACR permits measurement of the direct effect. Inclusion of personal and geographic variables in the wage equations provides controls for human capital, discrimination, and differences in the cost of living between regions. In the penetration equation these variables control for differences in the value of unionization to workers.[8]

The results from model II support both the direct and indirect effects hypotheses. The coefficient of ACR in the wage equation is positive and significant as required by the direct effects hypothesis. A one-point increase in ACR would be associated with a 0.19 percent increase in the

Table 5.2
Union penetration equations (standard errors in parentheses, t ratios in brackets)

Variables	Model I	Models II and III
CONSTANT	−0.7979[a]	−17.669[a]
	(0.3184)	(3.252)
	[−2.51]	[−5.50]
ACR	1.7586[c]	1.9145[a]
	(0.764)	(0.6617)
	[2.30]	[2.89]
	0.36	0.40
INJURY RATE		0.02487
		(0.02195)
		[1.13]
NORTH CENTRAL		1.0191[d]
		(0.5484)
		[2.11]
%WHITE		2.152
		(1.815)
		[1.19]
%MALE		1.7178[a]
		(0.5578)
		[3.08]
MEAN SCHOOLING		0.7475[a]
		(0.2282)
		[3.28]
%CITY		1.2996[c]
		(0.5721)
		[2.27]
DURABLE		−0.5017[b]
		(0.1940)
		[−2.59]
%PRODUCTION WORKERS		0.06082[a]
		(0.01185)
		[5.13]

Note: $S = 0.6283$, $n = 66$. Dependent variable is percentage of union membership. Derivative of the log-odds function for ACR appears under the t ratios.
a. Significant in a 0.995 test (two-tailed 1 percent test).
b. Significant in a 0.99 test (one-tailed 1 percent test).
c. Significant in a 0.975 test (two-tailed 5 percent test).
d. Significant in a 0.95 test (one-tailed 5 percent test).

Table 5.3
Wage equations: models I through III (standard errors in parentheses, *t* ratios in brackets)

Variables	Model I	Model II	Model III
CONSTANT	5.97998	5.32952	5.61624
ACR		0.19388[a]	0.10313
		(0.05538)	(0.6654)
		[3.50]	[0.15]
UHAT	1.03463[a]	0.20388[a]	0.17622[a]
	(0.07838)	(0.0339)	(0.0408)
	[13.20]	[6.01]	[4.32]

Personal, location, and industry controls

WHITE		0.04916[c]	0.05185[c]
		(0.02464)	(0.02454)
		[2.00]	[2.11]
MALE		0.29746[a]	0.29115[a]
		(0.01905)	(0.01954)
		[15.61]	[14.90]
EDUCATION2		0.11795[d]	0.11474[d]
		(0.06253)	(0.06221)
		[1.86]	[1.84]
EDUCATION3		0.18087[a]	0.19711[a]
		(0.05633)	(0.05605)
		[3.21]	[3.52]
EDUCATION4		0.31562[a]	0.31168[a]
		(0.05680)	(0.05661)
		[5.56]	[5.51]
EDUCATION5		0.34530[a]	0.33622[a]
		(0.06028)	(0.06011)
		[5.73]	[5.59]
EXPERIENCE		0.02260[a]	0.02264[a]
		(0.00214)	(0.00214)
		[10.56]	[10.58]
EXPERIENCE^2		−0.00035[a]	−0.00035[a]
		(0.00004)	(0.00004)
		[−8.75]	[−8.75]
CRAFT		0.1377[a]	0.1470[a]
		(0.02913)	(0.02937)
		[4.73]	[5.01]
OPERATIVE		0.02042	0.02652
		(0.02586)	(0.02581)
		[0.79]	[1.03]
CITY		0.07096[a]	0.07355[a]
		(0.01771)	(0.01784)
		[4.01]	[4.12]

Table 5.3 (continued)

Variables	Model I	Model II	Model III
SOUTH		−0.17181[a] (0.02617) [−6.57]	−0.16210[a] (0.02642) [−6.14]
NORTHEAST		−0.18306[a] (0.02617) [−7.00]	−0.17282[a] (0.02723) [−6.35]
NORTH CENTRAL		−0.06514[b] (0.02567) [−2.44]	−0.05451[c] (0.02580) [−2.11]
DURABLE			−0.00952 (0.01906) [−0.50]
AFTERNOON SHIFT			0.06559[a] (0.02035] [3.22]
GRAVEYARD SHIFT			0.06442[d] (0.03440) [1.89]
SALES VARIANCE			0.000042 (0.00016) [0.26]
SPECIALIZATION			−0.00351[a] (0.00085) [−4.13]
INJURY TOTAL			−0.00019 (0.00160) [−0.12]
IMPORT			−0.12106 (0.13836) [−0.87]

Note: $n = 2,005$.
a. Significant in a 0.995 test (two-tailed 0.95 test).
b. Significant in a 0.99 test.
c. Significant in a 0.975 test (two-tailed 0.95 test).
d. Significant in a 0.95 test.

wage. The coefficients of ACR in the penetration equation and UHAT in the wage equation are also positive and significant. The product of the coefficients is 0.08, indicating a one-point increase in concentration would cause a 0.08 percent increase in the wage through the indirect effect. The total effect of concentration on the wage, the sum of the direct and indirect effects, is 0.27. The elasticity of the wage with respect to concentration declines to 0.09. These results indicate that the indirect effect is about half the magnitude of the direct effect and that the measure of the indirect effect in model I was biased upward by omission of a measure of the direct effect.

Model III adds controls for a number of further industry characteristics expected to yield compensating differentials to the model II wage equations. Results from model III indicate that while the indirect effect is not influenced by the inclusion of the industry variables, the direct effect becomes unimportant in their presence. The coefficient on ACR in the wage equation is positive but is not statistically significant.[9] Both coefficients associated with the indirect effect are positive and statistically significant. The measure of the indirect effect, 0.08 ($= 0.176 \times 0.0045$) is trivially smaller than the model II estimate. The total effect of concentration on the wage is 0.18.[10] The elasticity of the wage with respect to concentration declines to 0.07.

The results from these three models demonstrate the value of allowing for the indirect effect. Despite large changes in specification it remains an important component of concentrations's total effect on the wage. It is never less than half the magnitude of the direct effect. The model III results suggest the indirect effect is the primary mechanism through which concentration influences the wage. The varied conclusions of previous research on concentration's wage effect may be attributable in part to a failure to allow for the indirect effect.[11]

A Simultaneous Equations Approach

The alternative to the nonsimultaneous system used in models I through III is a system in which wages and unionization are modeled as simultaneous. Although the techniques required for estimating these systems with aggregate data are well established, the use of individual data poses particular econometric difficulties because the dependent variable of the membership equation is qualitative. The research reported in this section, taken from a longer study of firm resistance to unionization, was estimated with the two-stage probit procedure developed by Lee.[12]

Following Lee, the system used in this study has three equations The first equation determines the union status of the individual. The second and third equations are individual's union and nonunion wage equation, respectively:

$$I^* = a_0 + a_1(\ln W_{ui} - \ln W_{ni}) + a_2 ACR + \underline{a}_3'\underline{X} - v_i, \tag{1}$$

$$\ln W_{ui} = b_{u0} + b_{u1} ACR + b_{u2} U + \underline{b}_u'\underline{Z} + e_u, \tag{2}$$

$$\ln W_{ni} = b_{n0} + b_{u1} ACR + b_{n2} U + \underline{b}_n'\underline{Z} + e_{ni}, \tag{3}$$

where

  I^* = a latent variable indicating the net gain from union membership. If $I^* > 0$, union membership is observed. If $I^* \leqslant 0$, union membership is not observed.

  u, n = subscripts designating union and nonunion explanatory variables and error terms,

 $\ln W_u$ = the natural log of the union wage,

 $\ln W_n$ = the natural log of the nonunion wage,

 ACR = a measure of market concentration,

  U = union penetration, a measure of the proportion of employees who are union members in an industry,

UHAT = log-odds estimate of penetration, used in place of the observed value to eliminate simultaneity with the wage,

 $\underline{X}, \underline{Z}$ = vectors of additional independent variables in the wage and status equations, respectively,

e_u, e_n, v = error terms in the status and wage equations.

The first equation, the status equation, is derived from a choice theoretic model of union membership. The individual joins a union if his net benefit from membership is positive. The benefits and costs of union membership are determined by the difference in an individual's union and nonunion wage as well as by nonwage factors. Since individual membership outcomes are qualitative and dichotomous, the status equation is estimated with probit. Equation (1) is simultaneous with equations (2) and (3) because the wage difference term, $\ln W_u - \ln W_n$, is one of the variables determining union penetration.

Equations (2) and (3) are used to determine individual's union and non-union wage. Although an individual union status variable is not included in these equations, separation of the equations by status causes coefficient estimates to be conditioned on status. Because status is an endogenous variable, OLS estimates of wage coefficients will be biased by sample selection, a form of simultaneous equations bias. This bias may be eliminated by inclusion in the wage equation of a selection bias variable generated from the status equation. Estimated standard errors must also be corrected.

The use of separate wage equations is advantageous because it allows for differences in the wage formation process in the two sectors. Separation is also useful as it permits distinguishing the wage effect of individual union membership and the effect of the bargaining power of the union in the market.[13] Whereas the former benefits only union members, the latter may benefit both members and nonmembers. The effect of bargaining power is reflected in the coefficient on the union penetration variables, the effect of individual membership as the mean difference between individual's union and nonunion wage.

Tracing the direct and indirect effects of concentration in this type of system is complex. The direct effect is measured by the coefficients on concentration in the two wage equations, b_{u1} and b_{n1}. These coefficients must be positive to support the direct effect hypothesis. The indirect effect has two stages: concentration's effect on union status and status's effect on the wage. The first stage requires that coefficient a_2 in the status equation be positive. The second stage of the indirect effect may operate through two channels, individual union membership or union penetration. For there to be an indirect effect through penetration, the coefficients on the UHAT variable, b_{u2} and b_{n2} in the wage equations, must be positive. The indirect effect through individual union membership requires a positive differential between union and nonunion wages. The conditions on the first-stage and at least one of the second-stage channels must be met for there to be an indirect effect. Because the equations in this system are fully simultaneous, concentration also influences the wage through feedback. The requirement for a positive feedback effect is that the net direct and indirect effect be positive and that the wage difference coefficient in the status equation, a_1, be positive. The total effect of concentration on the wage is the sum of the direct, indirect, and feedback effects.

Simultaneous Equations Results

The results from this simultaneous equations system, model IV, are provided in table 5.4. The wage equations were separated on the collective

Table 5.4
Wage and status equations: model IV (standard errors in parentheses, t ratios in brackets)

Variables	Status equation	Wage equations	
		Union	Nonunion
CONSTANT	−1.3757[a]	5.4331	5.4358
	(0.6439)	(0.1632)	(0.2254)
	[−2.14]	[33.29]	[24.12]
ACR	1.6302[b]	−0.0924	0.3533[b]
	(0.3566)	(0.0710)	(0.1267)
	[1.20]	[−1.30]	[2.79]
CBCHAT		0.5376[b]	−0.1356
		(0.1187)	(0.1747)
		[4.53]	[−0.78]
WAGEDIFF	2.1064[b]		
	(0.52783)		
	[3.99]		

Personal, location, and industry controls

WHITE	−0.2969[b]	0.0611[a]	0.0862
	(0.0694)	(0.0296)	(0.5054)
	[−4.28]	[2.06]	[0.17]
MALE	0.1576[a]	0.2929[b]	0.2456[b]
	(0.0805)	(0.0245)	(0.0369)
	[1.96]	[11.96]	[6.66]
EDUCATION2	0.0989	0.1067	0.1207
	(0.2395)	(0.0701)	(0.0959)
	[0.24]	[1.52]	[1.26]
EDUCATION3	0.2993	0.1628[b]	0.1893[a]
	(0.2142)	(0.0626)	(0.0887)
	[1.40]	[2.60]	[2.13]
EDUCATION4	0.5872[b]	0.2637[b]	0.3259[b]
	(0.2180)	(0.0653)	(0.0945)
	[2.699]	[9.78]	[3.45]
EDUCATION5	0.3342	0.2877[b]	0.3586[b]
	(0.2311)	(0.0661)	(0.0948)
	[1.45]	[4.35]	[3.78]
EXPERIENCE	0.0099[b]	0.0183[b]	0.0236[b]
	(0.0024)	(0.0029)	(0.0043)
	[4.13]	[6.31]	[5.48]
EXPERIENCE^2		−0.00028[b]	−0.00038[b]
		(0.00005)	(0.0008)
		[−5.6]	[0.48]
CRAFT	0.0491	0.1627[b]	0.1704[b]
	(0.1104)	(0.0288)	(0.0517)
	[0.45]	[5.65]	[3.30]

Table 5.4 (continued)

Variables	Status equation	Wage equations	
		Union	Nonunion
OPERATIVE	−0.2555[a] (0.1071) [−2.39]	0.0699[b] (0.0263) [2.66]	−0.0123 (0.0457) [−0.27]
CITY	0.0403 (0.0699) [0.58]	0.0981[b] (0.0186) [5.27]	0.0331 (0.0309) [1.07]
SOUTH	−0.2120[a] (0.0996) [2.13]	−0.1760[b] (0.0325) [5.42]	−0.1259[a] (0.0494) [2.55]
NORTHEAST	−0.0289 (0.1085) [−0.27]	−0.1632[b] (0.0282) [−5.79]	−0.2181[b] (0.0473) [−4.61]
NORTHCENTRAL	0.2062[a] (0.0962) [2.14]	−0.0742[b] (0.0269) [−2.76]	−0.0601 (0.0469) [−1.28]
DURABLE	[2.14]	−0.0020 (0.0186) [−0.10]	0.0438 (0.0304) [1.44]
AFTERNOON SHIFT		0.0623[b] (0.0221) [2.82]	0.0623 (0.0383) [1.63]
GRAVEYARD SHIFT		0.0207 (0.0360) [0.58]	0.0852 (0.0751) [1.13]
SALES VARIANCE	0.0015[a] (0.0006) [2.5]	0.0000 (0.0002) [0.15]	0.0000 (0.0003) [1.33]
SPECIALIZATION	−0.0136[b] (0.0038) [−9.47]	−0.0018 (0.0011) [1.64]	−0.0026 (0.0021) [−1.24]
INJURY TOTAL	0.0258[b] (0.0258) [−1.0]	−0.0048[b] (0.0018) [−2.67]	0.0044 (0.0304) [0.15]
IMPORT/SHIPMENTS	0.1296 (0.5190) [0.25]	0.0234 (0.1610) [1.15]	−0.2213 (0.2213) [−1.0]
DISPERSION	0.0777[a] [0.0327] [2.38]		
INVESTMENT/ASSETS	0.7089[a] (0.3370) [2.10]		

Table 5.4 (continued)

Variables	Status equation	Wage equations	
		Union	Nonunion
SMALL	0.0520 (0.0783) [0.66]		
LARGE	1.1501 (0.1208) [9.52]		
SELECTION BIAS		0.0706 (0.0095) [7.43]	−0.0277 (1.1368) [−0.20]

Note: Loglikelihood = −1241.88. Mean wage difference = 17.39 percent.
a. Significant in a 0.950 test.
b. Significant in a 0.975 test.

bargaining status of individuals. For this type of model, separation on collective bargaining status is preferred to separation on union membership because it more accurately indicates receipt of the gains from unionization.[14] The covered wage equation, the analog of the union wage equation, predicts the wages of individuals covered by a collective bargaining agreement. The noncovered equation predicts the wage of an individual who is not covered by a collective bargaining agreement. Industry coverage (CBCHAT), an estimate of the proportion of employees in an industry covered by collective bargaining agreements, was used in place of estimated union penetration.[15] Model IV was estimated with the same data as models I through III. Variable definitions may be found in table 5.1. The model includes a number of variables to control for personal, occupational, geographic, and industrial characteristics. These variables perform the same function in the model IV wages equations as they did in previous equations. In the status equation these variables control for differences in the individual's benefits and costs of union coverage, tastes for coverage, and firm's costs of resisting coverage.

Results from model IV indicate that concentration affects the wages of covered and noncovered employees through different mechanisms. Although the coefficient on ACR (the measure of the direct effect) is small, negative, and not statistically significant in the covered wage equation, it is large, positive, and statistically significant in the noncovered equation. A one-point increase in concentration would be associated with 0.36 percent increase in the noncovered wage.

Table 5.5
Wage and status equations: model I (standard errors in parentheses, t ratios in brackets)

| Variables | Status equation | Wage equations | |
		Union	Nonunion
CONSTANT	−1.667[a]	5.5721[a]	5.4155[a]
	(0.5841)	(0.1841)	(0.1850)
	[−2.85]	[30.27]	[29.27]
ACR	0.0191[a]	−0.0723	0.36[a]
	(0.0034)	(0.068)	(0.11)
	[5.62]	[1.06]	[3.27]
DURABLE		0.0149	0.0379
		(0.0194)	(0.0289)
		[0.77]	[1.31]
AFTERNOON SHIFT		0.0667[a]	0.0613
		(0.0231)	(0.0373)
		[2.89]	[1.64]
GRAVEYARD SHIFT		0.0250[a]	0.0780
		(0.0368)	(0.0698)
		[0.67]	[1.12]
SALES VARIANCE	0.0014[b]	−0.0001	−0.0001
	(0.0006)	(0.0002)	(0.0003)
	[2.33]	[−0.50]	[−0.33]
SPECIALIZATION	−0.0141[a]	−0.0022[b]	−0.0027
	(0.0037)	(0.0010)	(0.0017)
	[−3.81]	[−2.20]	[−1.59]
INJURY RATE	0.0267[a]	−0.0050[b]	0.0050
	(0.0058)	(0.0018)	(0.0026)
	[4.60)	[2.78]	[1.92]
IMPORT/SHIPMENTS	−0.1069	−0.1014	−0.2031
	(0.5228)	(0.1709)	(0.2043)
	[0.20]	[−0.59]	[−0.99]
DISPERSION	0.0329[a]		
	[0.0323]		
	[1.02]		
INVESTMENT/ASSETS	0.9712[a]		
	(0.3215)		
	[3.02]		
UHAT		0.4955[a]	−0.2097
		(0.1243)	(0.1924)
		[3.986]	[−1.09]
WAGEDIFF	2.898		
	(0.4187)		
	[6.921]		

Table 5.5 (continued)

Variables	Status equation	Wage equations	
		Union	Nonunion
Personal, location, and industry controls			
WHITE	−0.2473[a]	0.0592	0.0867
	(0.0972)	(0.0298)	(0.0461)
	[−2.54]	[1.99]	[1.88]
MALE	0.0397	0.2837[a]	0.2272[a]
	(0.0812)	(0.0256)	(0.0356)
	[0.49]	[11.08]	[6.38]
MARRIED	0.3537[a]	0.0763[a]	0.1088[a]
	(0.0728)	(0.0253)	(0.0341)
	[4.86]	[3.02]	[3.19]
EDUCATION2	0.2404	0.1130	0.1578
	(0.2435)	(0.0705)	(0.0935)
	[0.99]	[1.60]	[1.69]
EDUCATION3	0.3711	0.1733[a]	0.2107[a]
	(0.2175)	(0.0626)	(0.0867)
	[1.71]	[2.77]	[1.23]
EDUCATION4	0.6439	0.2750[a]	0.3334[a]
	(0.2201)	(0.0652)	(0.0921)
	[2.93]	[4.22]	[3.62]
EDUCATION5	0.4258	0.2429[a]	0.3750[a]
	(0.2340)	(0.0665)	(0.0924)
	[1.82]	[3.65]	[4.06]
EXPERIENCE	0.0051[b]	0.0151[a]	0.0171[a]
	(0.0025)	(0.0032)	(0.0044)
	[2.04]	[4.72]	[3.89]
EXPERIENCE^2		−0.00022[a]	−0.00027[a]
		(0.00006)	(0.00008)
		[−3.67]	[−3.38]
CRAFT	0.0359	0.1411[a]	0.1578[a]
	(0.1125)	(0.0301)	(0.0481)
	[0.32]	[4.69]	[3.28]
OPERATIVE	−0.1301[a]	0.0516	−0.0181
	(0.1033)	(0.0270)	(0.0420)
	[−1.26]	[1.91]	[−0.43]
CITY	−0.0390	0.0965[a]	0.0263
	(0.0698)	(0.0194)	(0.0300)
	[−0.56]	[4.97]	[0.88]
FARM	−0.0478	0.0083	0.0213
	(0.0993)	(0.0613)	(0.0805)
	[−0.48]	[0.14]	[0.27]
SOUTH	−0.2450[a]	−0.1801[a]	−0.1334[a]
	(0.0993)	(0.0347)	(0.0481)
	[−2.47]	[−5.19]	[−2.77]

Table 5.4 (continued)

| Variables | Status equation | Wage equations | |
		Union	Nonunion
NORTHEAST	−0.1482	−0.1634[a]	−0.2306[a]
	(0.1090)	(0.0302)	(0.0453)
	[−1.36]	[−5.41]	[−5.09]
NORTH CENTRAL	0.1123	−0.0759[a]	−0.0697
	(0.0979)	(0.0281)	(0.0439)
	[1.15]	[−2.70]	[−1.59]
SMALL	0.0939		
	(0.0789)		
	[1.19]		
LARGE	−0.2946[b]		
	(0.1247)		
	[−2.36]		
SELECTION BIAS		0.0731	−0.0751
		(0.0984)	(0.1451)
		[0.74]	[−0.52]

Note: Loglikelihood = −1218; n = 2005. Mean wage difference = 16.05 percent.
a. Significant in a 0.975 test.
b. Significant in a 0.950 test.

In contrast, only covered members' wages are influenced by the indirect effect. The coefficent of ACR in the status equation is large and positive. The elasticity of coverage with respect to concentration is 0.44. The derivative of ACR at the mean of the independent variables, the analog of a linear coefficient, indicates a one-point rise in market concentration would cause mean individual coverage to rise by 0.64 percent. The second stage of the indirect effect operates through industry coverage or individual coverage. The results from the wage equation indicate there is an indirect effect through industry coverage for covered employees but not for the non-covered. The coefficient on CBCHAT is positive in the covered wage equation. A one-point increase in concentration would cause the covered wage to rise by 0.34 percent.[16] The coefficient in the noncovered wage equation is negative but is not statistically significant. There is also a positive indirect effect through individual coverage. A one-point increase in market concentration would cause an additional 0.65 percent of the sample to be covered by collective bargaining agreements. On average, their wage is 17.3 percent above the noncovered wage. Industry wages would rise by 0.11 percent.[17]

Concentration's total effect on the wage is the sum of the direct effect, the indirect effects, and feedback through the status equation. Using the estimates from model IV, a one-point increase in ACR would cause a 0.34 percent increase in the wage. As in the nonsimultaneous systems, indirect effects are the major component of the wage change. The direct effect accounts for 0.12 percent of this change, the indirect effect through industry coverage and associated feedback for 0.14 percent, and the indirect effect through individual coverage and associated feedback for 0.11 percent.[18] The elasticity of the wage with respect to concentration is 0.13, half again as large as the estimate obtained in the nonsimultaneous system.[19] The increase in the elasticity is due to the simultaneity, more accurate measurement of the relation between concentration and union penetration, and the addition of the indirect effect through membership.

Conclusion

This study provides empirical evidence that increases in industrial concentration are associated with substantial increases in the industry wage bill. Although part of the increase in wages is directly related to concentration, much of concentration's wage effect is intermediated through unionization. These results are not sensitive to assumptions about the relation between unionization and the wage or to the specification of the equations. The estimated total elasticity of the wage bill with respect to concentration ranges between 0.07 to 0.20 in the area of the means of the independent variables.

An implication of this result is that increases in market concentration may be associated with declining social effeciency in production for reasons other than the possession of monopoly power by the firm. Firms in concentrated industries are apparently subject to efficiency problems with respect to labor costs. Increases in labor costs will cause reductions in output and price increases beyond those caused by firms's utilization of monopoly power. A complete measure of the social inefficiency of concentrated markets must account for this efficiency loss as well as the more commonly measured costs associated with elevated profits or price cost margins.

Appendix: The Log-Odds Procedure

The Procedure

While the linear probability model takes the form

$$U_i = \underline{\beta_i X_i} + w_i, \tag{A.1}$$

the log-odds model has the form

$$U_i = \frac{1}{1 + e^{-\beta x + w}} \qquad (i \text{ subscripts have been dropped on the RHS}), \qquad \text{(A.2)}$$

where

U_i = the union coverage in industry i,

$\underline{X}_i$ = a vector of industry characteristics,

w_i = an error term.

The log-odds model imposes an S-shaped functional form on the relationship between the dependent and independent variables. This is used to constrain the dependent variable to the zero–one continuum. The coefficient and consistent estimates of the standard errors for the log-odds model may be estimated by OLS, using the form

$$\ln\left(\frac{U_i}{1 - U_i}\right) = \underline{\beta}'_i \underline{X}_i + w_i. \qquad \text{(A.3)}$$

Fitted Values

Predictions of the dependent variable may be calculated as

$$E(U_i) = E\frac{1}{1 + e^{-\beta x + w}}, \qquad \text{(A.4)}$$

where the estimate of β is used in place of the parameter in the calculations. Although the expectation of the error in the log-odds estimate is zero, the expectation of the exponential error is nonzero (although $E(w) = 0$, $-E(e^w) \neq 0$). Under the assumption that errors are homoscedastic and independent, the expectation of the exponentiated error is $e^{\sigma/2}$. The correct estimate of the dependent variable is

$$E(U_i) = \frac{1}{1 + e^{-bx + \sigma/2}}, \qquad \text{(A.4')}$$

where b is the estimate of β.

The Derivative

The coefficients obtained from a log-odds estimate are not directly comparable to linear coefficients because their value changes with changes in the values of the independent variables. An analog to a linear coefficient can be constructed by taking the derivative of the log-odds function with respect to the variable of interest. The derivative is

$$\frac{\delta U}{\delta X} = \frac{1}{1 + e^{-bx + \sigma/2}} \times \frac{e^{-bx + \sigma/2}}{1 + e^{-bx + \sigma/2}} \times b, \qquad \text{(A.5)}$$

where the derivative is typically evaluated at the means of the explanatory variables. Note that this expression may also be written as

$$\frac{\delta U}{\delta X} = u \times (1 - u) \times b_x, \tag{A.6}$$

where u is the value of the log-odds function evaluated at the means of the independent variables.

Notes

1. Because the literature on concentration's wage effects predate the controversy over the relation between market concentration and monopoly power, the terms concentration and monopoly are sometimes used interchangeably. While some traditional arguments depend on the firm's possession of monopoly power, others require only that there are relatively few firms in the market. The latter theories indicate that the existence of a relation between market concentration and the wage does not require that concentration act as a proxy for monopoly power, only that it is a sufficient measure of the fewness of firms in a market. There is no controversy on this point.

2. Arguments 1, 3, and 5 are from Weiss (1966). Segal (1964) develops arguments 3, 4, and 5.

3. Arguments 1 and 3 were taken from Weiss (1966). Arguments 2, 3, and 4 are developed by Segal (1964). Weiss has referred to argument 3 as economies of scale in organizing.

4. Since the wage equations were omitted from the article, it is not possible to comment on the direct effect or the second stage of the indirect effect.

5. An explanation of the log-odds procedure can be found in appendix A.

6. The union penetration measure was constructed from a 6,100 person sample of blue-collar manufacturing workers. In 16 of the 72 PIC industries there were fewer than 20 persons in the sample. Because of the potential for inaccuracy in the measurement of the dependent variable, these industries were not used in the estimation of the log-odds equation. The log-odds equation was used to predict values for these industries.

7. The calculation of the derivative of union penetration with respect to an independent variable in a log-odds equation is discussed in appendix A. The derivative with respect to ACR was calculated as $0.36 = 1.7586 \times (0.29 \times 0.71)$, where 0.29 is the mean value of the estimate of union penetration.

8. The coefficients on the control variables are mostly conventional in both the wage and penetration equations. Education and experience have a positive effect on the wage; the wage profile is concave in experience. White and male workers receive wage premiums, as do skilled workers and urban workers. Workers outside the West receive lower wages. Results are less clear-cut in the penetration equa-

tion. Race and injury rates do not have statistically significant effects on union penetration. Location in the industrial North Central region has a weak positive effect. Industries that have a high proportion of male employees, that have better-educated workers, and that provide limited opportunities for advancement because of a limited number of nonproduction positions show higher rates of penetration. Surprisingly, durable goods industries were less likely to have high rates of union penetration.

9. This statement should be interpreted cautiously as it is not possible to reject the null hypothesis in a test of the joint significance of the added variables. The decline of the significance of the coefficient of ACR may be caused by multicollinearity.

10. This measure includes the wage coefficient of concentration. This provides a consistent measure of the total effect. The sum of the coefficients of UHAT and ACR is significant in any conventional statistical test against the null hypothesis.

11. The measured effect of concentration on the wage could be increased by a third if a measure of simple concentration was substituted for the adjusted concentration measure used in this study. Most of this increase is due to the stronger relation between concentration and union penetration. While the statistical results are clear, the reasons for this difference are not.

12. A more complete discussion of Lee's two stage probit model may be found in Lee (1978, 1979). Details of the procedures used for this equation system may be found in Belman (1988).

13. As in the previous section, the measure of union penetration is generated from a log-odds equation. This equation is a reduced form equation and cannot be used to measure a structural relationship between concentration and union penetration. The estimate of the elasticity of status with respect to concentration is a structural elasticity and is used to measure both the relation between ACR and status and ACR and union penetration.

14. Except where there are provisions in the collective bargaining agreement compelling union membership, employees can refuse to join the union. By law these nonmembers must be provided with the same wages and benefits as members. While 51.1% of the sample employees were covered by a collective bargaining agreement, 48.7% were members of labor unions. A version of this system using union membership as the separating variable is reported by Belman (1988).

15. CBCHAT was estimated by the same procedures used to estimate UHAT.

16. This is calculated as the increase in CBCHAT caused by the increase in concentration multiplied by the wage coefficient of CBCHAT. Using the linearized coefficient from the status equation to estimate the relation between concentration and industry coverage, this is $0.5376 \times 0.6495 \times 0.1 = 0.034 = 3.4$ percent. The status equation coefficient is used because, unlike its counterpart in the industry coverage equation, it is a structural estimate.

17. The calculations in this paragraph do not allow for the feedback.

18. These summary measures were calculated by linearizing the status equation and computing restricted reduced form coefficients for ACR for each equation. These coefficients summarize both the immediate and feedback effects of independent variables. The direct effect of a one-point increase in concentration would cause a 0.09 percent decline in wages of covered employees. Noncovered wages would increase by 0.36 percent. The net direct effect, the sum of these two effects weighted by the proportion of workers in each sector, is 0.12 percent. The indirect effect of a one-point change in ACR through industry coverage is 0.34 percent for covered employees and -0.09 percent for noncovered employees. The weighted average is 0.14 percent. The indirect effect through individual coverage is the product of the change in concentration due to a one-point change in ACR (0.6332) and the wage advantage of covered employees (0.173). A discussion of the derivation of restricted reduced form coefficients and these calculations may be found in Belman (1988).

19. When union membership is used to separate the wage equations, the estimated elasticity is 0.20. See Belman (1988).

References

Ashenfelter, O., and G. C. Johnson. 1972. "Unionism, Relative Wages, and Labor Quality in U.S. Manufacturing Industries." *International Economic Review* 13 (October), 488–508.

Belman, D. 1988. "Concentration, Unionism, and Labor Earnings: A Sample Selection Approach." *Review of Economics and Statistics* (August), 391–397.

Dalton, J. A., and E. J. Ford. 1978. "Concentration and Labor Earnings in Manufacturing and Utilities." *Industrial and Labor Relations Review* (June), 45–60.

Duncan, G. M., and Leigh, D. E. 1980. "Wage Determination in the Union and Non-union Sectors: A Sample Selectivity Approach." *Industrial And Labor Relations Review* (October), 24–34.

Dunlop, J. T. 1948. "Productivity and Wage Structures." *Income, Employment, and Public Policy*. New York: W. W. Norton.

Galbraith, K. 1952. *American Capitalism*. Boston: Houghton Mifflin.

Goldberger, A. S. 1964. *Econometric Theory*. New York: Wiley and Sons.

Haworth, C. T., and D. W. Rasmussen. 1971. "Human Capital and Interindustry Wages in Manufacturing." *Review of Economics and Statistics* (November), 375–380.

Haworth, C. T., and C. J. Reuther. 1978. "Interindustry Concentration and Interindustry Wage Determination." *Review of Economics and Statistics* (February), 85–95.

Hendricks, W. 1975. "Labor Market Structure and Union Wage Levels." *Economic Inquiry* (September), 401–416.

Heywood, J. S. 1986. "Labor Quality and the Concentration-Earnings Hypothesis." *Review of Economics and Statistics* (May), 342.

Hirsch, B. T. and M. C. Berger. 1975. "Labor Market Structure and Industry Characteristics." *Southern Economic Journal* (September), 665–679.

Johnson, G. E., 1975. "The Economic Analysis of Trade Unions." *American Economic Review* (May), 23–28.

Kahn, L. M. 1979. "Unionism and Relative Wages: Direct and Indirect Effects." *Industrial and Labor Relations Review* (July), 520–532.

Kwoka, J. E. 1983. "Monopoly, Plant, and Union Effects on Worker Wages." *Industrial and Labor Relations Review* (January), 251–257.

Lee, L. 1978. "Unionism and Wage Rates: A Simultaneous Equations Model with Qualitative and Limited Dependent Variables." *International Economic Review* (June), 415–433.

Lee, L. 1979. "Identification and Estimation in Binary Choice Models with Limited Dependent Variables." *Econometrica* (July), 977–996.

Levinson H. M. 1967. "Unionism, Concentration, and Wage Change: Toward a Unified Theory." *Industrial and Labor Relations Review* (January), 198–205.

Lewis, H. G. 1963. *Unionism and Relative Wages in the United States.* Chicago: University of Chicago Press.

Lewis, H. G. 1983. "Union Relative Wage Effects: A Survey of Macro Estimates." *Journal of Labor Economics* (January), 1–27.

Madalla, G. S., 1984. *Limited Dependent and Qualitative Variables in Econometrics,* Cambridge: Cambridge University.

Masters, S. 1969. "An Interindustry Analysis of Wages and Plant Size." *Review of Economics and Statistic* (August), 341–345.

Mishel, L., and P. Voos. 1986. "The Effect of Unions on Industry Profits." *Journal of Labor Economics* (January), 105–133.

Mitchell, D. J. B. 1980. *Unions, Wages, and Inflation.* Washington, DC: Brooking Institute.

Rees, A. 1977. *The Economics of Trade Unions.* Chicago: University of Chicago Press.

Segal, M. 1964. "The Relation Between Union Wage Impact and Market Structure." *Quarterly Journal of Economics* (February), 96–114.

Weiss, L. 1966. "Concentration and Labor Earnings." *American Economic Rreview* (March) 96–117.

Weiss, L. W., and G. A. Pascoe. 1986. *Adjusted Concentration Ratios in Manufacturing, 1972 and 1977.* FTC (June).

6 Industry Competition and the Formation of the European Common Market

Hideki Yamawaki,
Leo Sleuwaegen, and
Leonard W. Weiss

With the signing of the Treaty of Rome in 1957, six Western European countries—France, West Germany, Italy, the Netherlands, Belgium, and Luxemburg—set out to create a common market known as the European Economic Community (EEC). The community members agreed to remove tariffs and quantitative restrictions on trade among themselves by staged reductions and completed the removal of internal tariffs by 1968. The member states also agreed to adopt a common external tariff on all goods flowing from the outside world.[1]

The formation of the Common Market provides researchers a great opportunity for studying its effects on economic variables. One research area that has been most intensively analyzed so far is its effects on international trade flows. Attempts to estimate trade creation and trade diversion abound and have found that in the Common Market trade creation exceeded trade diversion.[2] It has also been observed that the creation of the Common Market caused an increase in intraindustry trade among the Common Market countries.[3]

However, surprisingly little attention has been paid to the effects of the Common Market's formation on market structure and competitive performance in the member countries. The liberalization of trade among the EEC countries leads to a number of interesting hypotheses including specialization in production, the scale of production, recognition of mutual dependence across national boundaries, and the effects of trade flows on competition.[4]

This chapter focuses on one of these hypotheses, namely, the effect of the creation of the enlarged market on competition. After the formation of the EEC the scope of competition should be widened geographically due to the enlarged market. For some product markets, domestic sellers in a member country may start to engage in a oligopoly game and to recognize interdependence with foreign sellers in another member country because they now meet and compete with each other in the common market. Market performance of each community member would then be affected to some extent by the state of communitywide competition.

One conventional and theoretically relevant element of market competition is seller concentration. Seller concentration constructed for the domestic market may not be relevant any more for the EEC countries because it fails to capture the effect of the enlarged market and the interdependence among domestic and foreign sellers within the common market. A relevant structural variable to capture the state of competition will be seller concentration on a communitywide basis.

Our main purposes are to present the estimates of EEC-wide seller concentration at the three-digit level of the EEC Industrial Classification System, and then to test the hypothesis that EEC-wide seller concentration will be a significant element of market structure affecting member country's performance after the integration of markets, but not before. We begin by explaining the method used in estimating EEC-wide concentration and present some summary statistics. Then we describe the hypothesis to be tested, variables, specifications of the statistical model, and statistical results.

Estimation of EEC-wide Seller Concentration

Some measures of EEC-wide seller concentration for very broadly defined industries have been published by the Commission of the European Communities.[5] However, no attempts have been made so far in estimating EEC-wide concentration at a disaggregated industry level that even begins to approach realistic economic markets.[6] The task of estimating EEC-wide concentration in a systematic way for number of industries is not easy due primarily to the scarcity of data. To compute the largest four firms' sales share within the EEC market, information on sales of each product line in the EEC market for companies operating in the market is needed. Unfortunately, such data are currently not easily obtainable.

The Method of Estimation

We adopt an alternative approach that employs industry statistics of the member countries. It requires information on the scale of operation accounted for by the largest firms in each EEC country. Due to data limitations we were obliged to use the number of employees instead of sales as the unit of measurement.[7] The estimation method proceeds as follows:

1. First estimate, for each of the EEC countries,[8] the number of employees in an industry controlled by largest four firms ($E4_{ij}$, where i = industry and j = country). Since this information is not available directly from official statistics, we estimated it from data on the firm size distribution by employment size class for the EEC countries. The estimation method was originated by Bain (1966) and has been employed by Phlips (1971), George and Ward (1975), and Owen (1983).[9]

2. Rank the member countries' $E4$'s in the descending order for each industry. For example, if $E4_{in}$ ranked for industry i and nation n such that

$$E4_{iG} > E4_{iF} > E4_{iI} > E4_{iB} > E4_{iNL},$$

where G stands for Germany, F for France, I for Italy, B for Belgium, and NL for the Netherlands, then $E4$ for Germany ($E4_{iG}$) which shows the highest number is registered for industry i. The assumptions underlying MIN $E4$ are (a) that the four leading firms in an industry in each country are independent from all other EEC firms in that industry and (b) that each of the four largest producers in the nation where $E4_i$ is greatest has more employees than any other EEC firm in that industry.

3. Our MAX $E4$ assumes that the owners of the four largest employers in a given industry are the same for the four leading EEC countries in that industry. Then MAX $E4$ is just the sums of the four nations' $E4_i$'s. There is no good reason for leaving out the fifth smallest country, but we did. It cannot have done much damage.

4. To obtain minimum and maximum estimates of four-firm concentration in the original EEC market (MIN EEC $CR4$ and MAX EEC $CR4$, respectively), we divide MIN $E4$ and MAX $E4$ by total employment in the industry in the Common Market, thus

$$\text{MIN EEC } CR4 = \frac{\text{MIN } E4}{\text{Total employment in the Common Market}}$$

and

$$\text{MAX EEC } CR4 = \frac{\text{MAX } E4}{\text{Total employment in the Common Market}}.$$

5. Our estimate of EEC-wide concentration is finally obtained by averaging out the minimum estimate and the maximum estimate of concentration obtained in 4,

$$\text{EEC } CR4 = \tfrac{1}{2}(\text{MIN EEC } CR4 + \text{MAX EEC } CR4).$$

It is essentially arbitrary to assign the mean of the maximum and minimum estimates to EEC $CR4$. It might also introduce bias. Common ownership of leaders in all four countries is surely rare, but quite a lot of international mergers involving major firms did occur in the 1960s and 1970s. To the extent that this occurred, our estimates of EEC $CR4$ in 1978 are understated relative to the 1963 estimate. Turning to an alternative assumption, market dominance is rare in the United States (Weiss and Pascoe 1984), but it is likely to be more common in the smaller national markets of Europe. The automobile is one product where leading four firms may have had close to dominant shares in many of the national markets. Volkswagen, Peugeot-Citroen, Renault, and Fiat are among the four leaders of the EEC market excluding Denmark, Ireland, and the United Kingdom, and they account for very large shares within their national markets.[10] The true EEC $CR4$ for the automobile industry based on market share data is 68 percent for 1970 and 62 percent for 1977.[11] Although our estimate of MAX EEC $CR4$ for 1978, 59 percent, approximates the true EEC $CR4$, the arbitrary downward adjustment that occurs in our procedure deflates our estimate of EEC CR4 to 42 percent for 1978. We feel that this is an extreme case.

Estimates of EEC-wide Concentration

We estimated EEC-wide concentration for 1963 and 1978 using the method just described. The choice of these two years is dominated by data limitations. Since data on the firm size distribution by detailed employment size class are not available for the years before 1963, the year the first EEC Census was published, we were obliged to pick 1963 as the earliest observation point. Unpublished data for 1978 were made available to us by the Statistical Office of the European Communities.[12] The data for both years are available at the three-digit level of the EEC Industrial Classification.[13] However, we had to eliminate from the entire sample 56 industries for which figures are omitted from the size distribution tables for disclosure reasons. Thus our sample consists of 47 three-digit industries matched among the EEC countries.

Since our main concern is to test the hypotheses about the increasing importance of EEC-wide concentration after the formation of the EEC as an element of market structure in determining industry performance, we are interested primarily in the Common Market defined by the original six members. To make the estimate of EEC concentration in 1963 comparable to that in 1978 and to eliminate possible distortions associated with the enlargement of the Common Market that occurred after 1973, 1978 employ-

Table 6.1
Unweighted means of national concentration (NCR4), EEC concentration (EEC CR4), and changes in concentration, for 47 three-digit manufacturing industries

	West Germany	France	Italy	The Netherlands	Belgium	EEC5
NCR4(63)	0.189	0.233	0.220	0.353	0.366	—
NCR4(78)	0.231	0.305	0.283	0.397	0.418	—
NCR4(78) − NCR4(63)	0.041	0.082	0.063	0.044	0.052	—
EEC CR4(63)	—	—	—	—	—	0.163
EEC CR4(78)	—	—	—	—	—	0.185
EEC CR4(78) − EEC CR4(63)	—	—	—	—	—	0.022
EEC CR4(78) − NCR4(63)	−0.004	−0.039	−0.035	−0.168	−0.181	—

Note: Figures attached after each variable stand for observation years, 63 for 1963 and 78 for 1978. Concentration is measured in terms of employment. Luxembourg is omitted from the estimation. EEC CR4 is thus estimated based on data for West Germany, France, Italy, the Netherlands, and Belgium.

ment of Britain, Denmark, and Ireland is subtracted from the denominators of the minimum and maximum estimates of 1978 EEC-wide concentration.[14] Thus the denominators of both 1963 and 1978 EEC-wide concentration are defined as the sum of employment in West Germany, France, Italy, the Netherlands, and Belgium.[15]

In table 6.1 we present the unweighted means of EEC-wide concentration (EEC CR4), national concentration (NCR4), and changes in concentration. National concentration for the community members was also estimated from the firm-size distributions to make one country's measure comparable to another country's. Seller concentration here is thus measured in terms of employment. The estimates of EEC CR4 and NCR4 by industry are presented in appendix B. Table 6.1 yields the following conclusions:

1. The unweighted mean values of EEC CR4, 0.16 for 1963 and 0.19 for 1978, are smaller than the unweighted mean values of NCR4 in any EEC country. This is inevitable, given the method of estimation of EEC CR4. However, the result fits direct observation in other data where both regional and national data are available.[16]

2. The mean values of NCR4 in West Germany, 0.19 for 1963 and 0.23 for 1978, are the smallest among the five EEC countries, and the mean values of NCR4 in the Netherlands, 0.35 for 1963 and 0.40 for 1978, and those in Belgium, 0.37 for 1963 and 0.42 for 1978, are the highest. The mean

values of NCR4 in France and Italy are in the middle. The difference in concentration levels among the EEC countries confirms the previous findings on the negative relationship between concentration levels and market size.[17]

3. Accordingly, the absolute difference between national concentration and EEC concentration decreases with the size of national market. The unweighted average difference between EEC CR4 in 1978 and NCR4 in 1963 for West Germany, −0.004, is the smallest among the five EEC countries. The average difference reaches −0.17 for the Netherlands and −0.18 for Belgium. France and Italy are again in the middle, each with a value of −0.04. This conclusion remains unchanged even when the absolute difference is computed between EEC CR4(78) and NCR4(78) and between EEC CR4(63) and NCR4(63).

The four leaders in Germany employed more persons than the leaders in any other EEC countries in 32 industries for 1963 and in 30 industries for 1978, of the 47 industries for which data could be secured. For the most part this merely reflected the fact that their manufacturing industry is larger than that of any other EEC member. For the rest of the sample either the four leading firms in France (9 in 1963 and 12 in 1978) or in Italy (6 in 1963 and 5 in 1978) were the leading producers.

The Effects of EEC Concentration on Industry Performance

One of the interesting questions that one may ask about the formation of the EEC is its effects on competition among the European firms. As we have shown in the preceding section, the mean values of EEC-wide concentration differ from and are smaller than the mean values of national concentration of the member countries. This implies that if the formation of the EEC has not only eliminated tariffs and other trade barriers but may also have increased competition across national boundaries, national concentration will not correctly capture the true state of competition in the EEC countries. Consequently empirical findings on the relationship between national concentration and market performance in the EEC countries may miss this aspect of intracommunity competition. In what follows we shall examine the relative importance of concentration on an EEC-wide base in determining the member country's performance.

Hypotheses about EEC Concentration

Most investigators of the relationship between concentration and price or price-cost margins in the EEC countries have assumed that domestic sellers do not compete directly with foreign sellers[18] and that the relevant market is at the national level even after the formation of the EEC. Our approach, instead, allows for the possibility that European firms became more interdependent in the Common Market as trade barriers fell. In most industries the geographic extent of market has been greatly enlarged by the removal of internal tariffs, so domestic sellers who were previously protected from international competition now meet foreign sellers in both domestic markets and in other EEC member nation markets. Some industries may be so concentrated, even at the Common Market level that domestic sellers recognize oligopolistic interdependence with their foreign competitors in the Common Market as well as among themselves. However, such recognition of oligopolistic interdependence between domestic and foreign sellers may be developed gradually over time. At the start, mutual understandings may be less easy to achieve since the rules of the game may be less uniform and less easy to formulate when there are several national leaders involved at least sometimes with greater cost differences than existed in the national markets.[19]

Our basic hypothesis is that seller concentration at the national level will be a market structure variable that may have become important and that affects the price decision of the industry before and at the beginning of the tariff reduction process and that EEC-wide concentration will be a structure variable after the completion of the process. Thus we predict that over time national concentration will decline in importance and communitywide concentration will grow in importance. However, we doubt that the effects of national concentration will disappear entirely.

The conventional analysis of the concentration-price relationship was that the industry leaders are more likely to succeed in collusion (tacit or explicit) the higher the share of the top few firms in total sales. When the few have a large share, they are most likely to be able to control price.[20]

Statistical Models on Change in Price in Germany

We first test the hypothesis about the relative importance of EEC-wide concentration in determining the pricing decision by investigating the determinants of change in price for West Germany between the years before the tariff reduction process, 1955 to 1957, and the years after the completion of the process, 1969 to 1971.

In trying to identify the effect of change in concentration on change in price in West Germany, we use the following variables:

$\Delta P = [P(69-71) - P(55-57)]/P(55-57) =$ percentage change in price (P) between the 1955–1957 period and the 1969–1971 period. P is a unit value defined as the value of production divided by quantity produced and averaged over the three years for each period.

$\Delta W = [W(69-71) - W(55-57)]/W(55-57) =$ percentage change in wage per worker-hour (W) between the 1955–1957 period and the 1969–1971 period. W is defined as total wages divided by total hours worked and averaged over the three years for each period.

$\Delta Q = Q(69-71) - Q(55-57) =$ difference between the rate of growth of physical quantity produced for 1955–1957 and that for 1969–1971.

$\Delta X = X(70) - X(56) =$ difference in the ratio of total exports to total shipment between 1970 and 1956.

CAP DUM $=$ dummy variable equal to one if the industry is judged to produce capital goods.

As the concentration variables, we alternatively use

$\Delta NCR4 = NCR4(78) - NCR4(63) =$ difference between the four-firm national concentration $(NCR4)$ in 1978 and that in 1963.

EEC $CR4(78) - NCR4(63) =$ difference between the four-firm EEC concentration (EEC $CR4$) in 1978 and the four-firm national concentration in 1963.

The observation periods for these two concentration variables were dictated by the data availability and therefore do not correspond to the two periods in the analysis. However, we assume that the national concentration ratio in 1963, which lies during the tariff reduction process, reflects the market structure in the pre-EEC period.

We specify a four-equation model, with change in price, change in wages, change in real output, and change in concentration as the endogenous variables.[21] The model including $NCR4$ is

$$\Delta P = f_1(\Delta W, \Delta Q, \Delta NCR4, \Delta X, CAP\ DUM), \tag{1}$$

$$\Delta W = f_2(\Delta P, \Delta Q, \Delta NCR4, SKILL, RAW), \tag{2}$$

$$\Delta Q = f_3(\Delta P, \Delta NCR4, RD, CONS), \tag{3}$$

$$\Delta NCR4 = f_4(\Delta P, \Delta Q, \Delta X, CONS, MDS), \tag{4}$$

where the additional exogenous variables introduced in equations (1) through (4) are the proportion of skilled workers in total industry production employment (SKILL), the percentage of inputs from primary producing sectors in total purchased direct inputs (RAW), the ratio of R&D expenditures to total industry sales (RD), the proportion of value of industry outputs going to final consumption (CONS), and the radius (in miles) within which 80 percent of industry shipments were made in the U.S. counterpart (MDS).[22] Each equation in the model was estimated by the two-stage least squares (2SLS) method since the misspecification may be present within individual equations. To save space, we will report only the 2SLS results for the price equation in which our primary concern lies.

Table 6.2 shows the 2SLS result on the equation explaining change in price for West Germany. In equation 1 in table 6.2, change in national concentration ($\Delta NCR4$) has a marginally significant positive sign, confirming the hypothesis that change in price is determined in part by change in national concentration. On the other hand, in equation 2 the coefficient on change from national to EEC-wide concentration (EEC $CR4 - NCR4$) has

Table 6.2
Regressions explaining change in price in West Germany: 2SLS results, $N = 38$
(standard errors in parentheses, t ratios in brackets)

Variable	Equation 1	Equation 2	Equation 3
ΔW	0.188	0.016	0.159
	(0.755)	(0.696)	(0.761)
	[0.25]	[0.02]	[0.21]
ΔQ	0.856	0.835	0.876
	(0.220)	(0.268)	(0.294)
	[3.85]	[3.11]	[2.98]
$\Delta NCR4$	4.500		4.433
	(2.931)		(2.901)
	[1.54]		[1.53]
EEC $CR4 - NCR4$		0.285	−0.824
		(3.000)	(3.363)
		[0.10]	[−0.245]
ΔX	0.023	−0.005	0.005
	(0.053)	(0.044)	(0.058)
	[0.44]	[−0.10]	[0.09]
CAPDUM	0.798	0.448	0.760
	(0.395)	(0.332)	(0.416)
	[2.03]	[1.35]	[1.83]
Constant	−0.481	0.314	−0.345
	(2.047)	(1.858)	(2.066)
	[−0.24]	[0.17]	[−0.17]
SEE	0.553	0.498	0.543
DF	32	32	31

no significant effect at all, thus failing to support the hypothesis that the importance of EEC-wide concentration in determining price increases over time.

This result is also confirmed from equation 3 in table 6.2 where the two concentration variables are both included. In equation 3 the coefficient for $\Delta NCR4$ is significant and has a positive sign, whereas that for EEC $CR4 - NCR4$ is negative and not significant.

This result suggests that change in price between the 1955–1957 and 1969–1971 periods is determined by change in national concentration and is not affected by EEC-wide concentration. The observed insensitivity of price to EEC-wide concentration could be caused by several factors. First, our concentration measures are constructed for 1963 and 1978 and may not reflect correctly the market structure before the tariff reduction process and after the process. In the estimated equations in table 6.2 change in real output (ΔQ) is always highly significant and has a positive sign. The influence of the formation of the EEC and the enlarged market may thus be represented by the industry growth variable that dominates the effect of EEC-wide concentration. Second, the effect of EEC-wide concentration may be realized only gradually. Even after the elimination of tariffs and thus the formation of the EEC, oligopolistic interdependence between domestic and foriegn sellers may be less easy to achieve, and its recognition may develop very slowly. To the extent that this is true, it is plausible that our observation period which ends in 1969–1971 may be too short to observe the effect of EEC concentration. This is consistent with our result in table 6.2 where change in national concentration is significant, which suggests the greater relative importance of national concentration in affecting price over the 1955–1957 and 1969–1971 periods. Over these periods domestic sellers still achieved mutual understandings more easily with their domestic rivals than they did with foreign ones.

Unfortunately, it does not appear to be possible to do similar studies in other nations that made up the initial European Economic Community. We can do smething with price-cost margins, however.

Statistical Models on Change in Price-Cost Margins

Our dependent variable is now changes in the price-cost margin:[23]

$PCM(78)/PCM(63)$ = price-cost margins in 1978 divided by price-cost margins in 1963. Price-cost margins are defined as value added minus payroll divided by value of shipments.

In addition to the two measures of change in concentration introduced in the preceding section, we include the variables which represent the extent of foreign competition. Concentration measured at the national level fails to capture the competitive force of imports originating both with other members of the EEC and with the non-EEC countries. On the other hand, concentration at the EEC-wide level takes into account the effect of intracommunity import competition but not the force of import copetition originating from the non-EEC countries. Thus we use two measures of changes in import competition:

$M(78) - M(63)$ = difference in the ratio of total imports (imports from other EEC countries plus imports from non-EEC countries) to apparent domestic consumption (total shipments + imports − exports) between 1978 and 1963.

NON EEC $M(78) - M(63)$ = difference between the ratio of imports originating from non-EEC countries[24] to apparent domestic consumption in 1978 (NON EEC $M(78)$) and the ratio of total imports to apparent domestic consumption in 1963.

We use two measures of changes in export opportunities without a clear prediction of their signs:[25]

$X(78) - X(63)$ = difference in the ratio of total exports (exports to other EEC countries plus exports to non-EEC countries) to total shipments between 1978 and 1963.

NON EEC $X(78) - X(63)$ = difference between the ratio of non-EEC exports[26] to total shipments in 1978 (NON EEC $X(78)$) and the ratio of total exports to total shipments in 1963.

West Germany is the largest economy in the Common Market, and her largest firms in many industries exceed their continental rivals in terms of production size.[27] One hypothesis implied from this observation is that West German firms as a group may have been able to behave as price-leader in the Common Market. Firms in other EEC countries, especially those from small countries, may have followed the price set by the West German firms. The largest West German firms, which are among the leading firms in the Common Market, could set prices more independently given their market shares in the EEC.[28] If so, price-cost margins of industries in other EEC countries will be positively related to the price-cost margin of West German industries. On the other hand, price-cost margins of West German industries should be related more closely to EEC-wide concentration, which closely reflects market position of the largest West German firms in the Common Market. Thus changes in price-cost margin in West German industries $(PCM(78)_G/PCM(63)_G)$ are included in equations explaining other member countries' price-cost margins.[29] In addition the variable may control for other industry-specific disturbances common to the Common Market countries.

An industry's long-run changes in profitability may be affected by long-run industry structural change or industry evolution. Innovations by the industry affect industry evolution through their effects on the industry's long-run growth rate. Thus a dummy variable that indicates those industries that are technologically innovative is included to control for the interindustry difference in industry evolution and its effect on long-run profit potential:

R&D DUM = dummy variable equal to one if the proportion of scientists and engineers in total employment in the U.S. counterpart industry is greater than its mean value, 1972.

The intertemporal effect of windfalls due to unexpected growth is taking into account:

GROWTH(75−78)/GROWTH(59−65) = the average annual national growth rates in value of total output over 1975−1978 divided by the average annual growth rates in value of total output over 1959−1965.

Appendix A describes the data sources from which these variables were constructed.

We estimated the following two models for five Common Market countries, namely, West Germany, France, Italy, the Netherlands, and Belgium:[30]

Model I

$$\frac{PCM(78)}{PCM(63)} = a_0 + a_1[NCR4(78) - NCR4(63)]$$

$$+ a_2[M(78) - M(63)]$$

$$+ a_3[X(78) - X(63)]$$

$$+ a_4\left[\frac{GROWTH(75-78)}{GROWTH(59-65)}\right]$$

$$+ a_5 R\&D\ DUM + e_1, \tag{5}$$

Model II

$$\frac{PCM(78)}{PCM(63)} = b_0 + b_1 [EEC\ CR4(78) - NCR4(63)]$$

$$+ b_2 [NON\ EEC\ M(78) - M(63)]$$

$$+ b_3 [NON\ EEC\ X(78) - X(63)]$$

$$+ b_4 \left[\frac{GROWTH(75-78)}{GROWTH(59-65)} \right]$$

$$+ b_5 R\&D\ DUM + e_2,\tag{6}$$

where e_1 and e_2 are random disturbances. All the variables except EEC CR4 and R&D DUM are constructed for individual countries. For France, Italy, the Netherlands, and Belgium, relative changes in German price-cost margins $(PCM(78)_G/PCM(63)_G)$ are added to both equations (5) and (6).

Model I hypothesizes that each community country's changes in price-cost margin are determined primarily by the factors affecting its national market—changes in national concentration and changes in total import and export shares. Thus it assumes that the effect of the formation of the EEC worked only through imports and exports. Its effect on tacit oligopolistic collusion is ignored. Model II hypothesizes the full effect of the formation of the EEC. Changes from national to EEC concentration, changes from total import share to non-EEC import share, and changes from total export share to non-EEC export share are expected to become the main variables affecting changes in price-cost margins.

Tables 6.3 through 6.7 show the final results of estimating these two models for each Common Market country. Equations (1) and (2) include $NCR4(78) - NCR4(63)$, whereas equations (3) and (4) include EEC $CR4(78) - NCR4(63)$. All the equations are estimated by the OLS method.

Comparison of equations (1) and (3) in each country clearly shows the importance of the choice of concentration measures for larger Common Market countries. For West Germany, France, and Italy, EEC $CR4(78) - NCR4(63)$ always has a significant positive coefficient, whereas $NCR4(78) - NCR4(63)$ has no significant effect. On the other hand, for Belgium and the Netherlands, neither variable is significant. To test the two competing hypotheses, the model that includes both EEC $CR4(78) - NCR4(63)$ and $NCR4(78) - NCR4(63)$ as regressors was also run (not reported). For Germany, France, and Italy, the coefficient on $NCR4(78) - NCR4(63)$ was not different from zero with 95 percent confidence in the nesting model. The coefficient for EEC $CR4(78) - NCR4(63)$ remains unchanged and has a significant positive sign.

Table 6.3
Regression equations explaining changes in price-cost margins for West Germany
(standard errors in parentheses, t ratios in brackets)

Independent variables	Model I		Model II	
	(1)	(2)	(3)	(4)
$NCR4(78) - NCR(63)$	0.123 (0.173) [0.71]	−0.010 (0.161) [−0.06]		
EEC $CR4(78) - NCR4(63)$			0.433 (0.156) [2.77]^a	0.329 (0.159) [2.07]^b
$M(78) - M(63)$		−0.033 (0.113) [−0.29]		
$X(78) - X(63)$		0.292 (0.132) [2.22]^{bb}		
NON EEC $M(78) - M(63)$				0.077 (0.137) [0.56]
NON EEC $X(78) - X(63)$				0.250 (0.156) [1.61]
R&D DUM		−0.062 (0.024) [−2.57]^{bb}		−0.041 (0.025) [−1.44]
GROWTH(75−78)/GROWTH(59−65)		0.027 (0.013) [2.00]^b		0.020 (0.014) [1.44]
Constant	0.266 (0.014) [18.61]^{aa}	0.227 (0.029) [7.85]^{aa}	0.273 (0.012) [23.77]^{aa}	0.253 (0.023) [10.79]^{aa}
$\bar{R}^2$	−0.011	0.210	0.127	0.234
F	0.50 (1,45)	3.44^e (5,41)	7.69^d (1,45)	3.81^d (5,41)

Note: For the statistics in brackets, levels of significance in one-tail tests are $a = 1$ percent; $b = 5$ percent. Levels of significance in two-tail tests are $aa = 1$ percent, $bb = 5$ percent, $cc = 10$ percent. Levels of significance in F statistics are $d = 1$ percent, $e = 5$ percent, $f = 10$ percent.

Table 6.4
Regression equations explaining changes in price-cost margins for France (standard errors in parentheses, t ratios in brackets)

Independent variables	Model I		Model II	
	(1)	(2)	(3)	(4)
$NCR4(78) - NCR4(63)$	0.124 (1.033) [0.12]	0.155 (0.113) [1.37]		
EEC $CR4(78) - NCR4(63)$			0.353 (0.160) [2.21][b]	0.281 (0.159) [1.77][b]
$M(78) - M(63)$		−0.063 (0.242) [−0.26]		
$X(78) - X(63)$		−0.014 (0.23) [−0.06]		
NON EEC $M(78) - M(63)$				0.203 (0.154) [1.31]
NON EEC $X(78) - X(63)$				−0.187 (0.152) [−1.23]
R&D DUM		0.036 (0.040) [0.89]		0.064 (0.041) [1.55]
$PCM(78)_G/PCM(63)_G$		0.550 (0.190) [2.89][a]		0.471 (0.189) [2.56][a]
Constant	0.317 (0.018) [17.62][aa]	0.165 (0.060) [2.73][aa]	0.341 (0.016) [21.37][aa]	0.199 (0.057) [3.48][aa]
$\bar{R}^2$	0.003	0.101	0.078	0.159
F	1.14 (1,45)	2.04[f] (5,41)	4.89[d] (1,45)	2.74[e] (5,41)

Note: For the statistics in brackets, levels of significance in one-tail tests are $a = 1$ percent, $b = 5$ percent. Levels of significance in two-tail tests are $aa = 1$ percent, $bb = 5$ percent, $cc = 10$ percent. Levels of significance in F statistics are $d = 1$ percent, $e = 5$ percent, $f = 10$ percent.

Table 6.5
Regression equations explaining changes in price-cost margins for Italy (standard errors in parentheses, t ratios in brackets)

Independent variables	Model I		Model II	
	(1)	(2)	(3)	(4)
$NCR4(78) - NCR4(63)$	0.032 (0.128) [0.25]	-0.015 (0.125) [-0.12]		
EEC $CR4(78) - NCR4(63)$			0.236 (0.107) [2.20]^b	0.216 (0.111) [1.95]^b
$M(78) - M(63)$		0.005 (0.011) [0.46]		
$X(78) - X(63)$		-0.030 (0.035) [-0.86]		
NON EEC $M(78) - M(63)$				0.002 (0.011) [0.18]
NON EEC $X(78) - X(63)$				-0.044 (0.041) [-1.09]
R&D DUM		0.038 (0.027) [1.39]		0.043 (0.026) [1.64]
$PCM(78)_G/PCM(63)_G$		0.374 (0.154) [2.43]^b		0.315 (0.152) [2.07]^b
Constant	0.263 (0.014) [18.23]^{aa}	0.159 (0.047) [3.39]^{aa}	0.274 (0.012) [22.69]^{aa}	0.176 (0.046) [3.79]^{aa}
$\bar{R}^2$	-0.021	0.028	0.077	0.117
F	0.063 (1,45)	1.27 (5,41)	4.85^d (1,45)	2.22^f (5,41)

Note: For the statistics in brackets, levels of significance in one-tail tests are a = 1 percent, b = 5 percent. Levels of significance in two-tail tests are aa = 1 percent, bb = 5 percent, cc = 10 percent. Levels of significance in F statistics are d = 1 percent, e = 5 percent, f = 10 percent.

Table 6.6
Regression equations explaining changes in price-cost margins for Belgium (standard errors in parentheses, t ratios in brackets)

Independent variables	Model I		Model II	
	(1)	(2)	(3)	(4)
$NCR4(78) - NCR4(63)$	-0.182 (0.119) [-0.99]	-0.248 (0.178) [-1.39]		
EEC $CR4(78) - NCR4(63)$			0.143 (0.161) [0.89]	0.124 (0.175) [0.71]
$M(78) - M(63)$		0.232 (0.171) [1.36]		
$X(78) - X(63)$		-0.189 (0.135) [-1.40]		
NON EEC $M(78) - M(63)$				0.049 (0.136) [0.36]
NON EEC $X(78) - X(63)$				-0.040 (0.105) [-0.38]
R&D DUM		0.143 (0.063) [2.26]^{bb}		0.131 (0.071) [1.85]^{cc}
$PCM(78)_G/PCM(63)_G$		0.812 (0.337) [2.41]^b		0.769 (0.364) [2.11]^b
Constant	0.305 (0.029) [10.63]^{aa}	0.034 (0.103) [0.33]	0.321 (0.040) [8.11]^{aa}	0.074 (0.117) [0.63]
$\bar{R}^2$	-0.001	0.105	-0.004	0.049
F	0.97 (1,45)	2.08^f (5,41)	0.80 (1,45)	1.47 (5,41)

Note: For the statistics in brackets, levels of significance in one-tail tests are $a = 1$ percent, $b = 5$ percent. Levels of significance in two-tail tests are $aa = 1$ percent, $bb = 5$ percent, $cc = 10$ percent. Levels of significance in F statistics are $d = 1$ percent, $e = 5$ percent, $f = 10$ percent.

Table 6.7
Regression equations explaining changes in price-cost margins for the Netherlands (standard errors in parentheses, t ratios in brackets)

Independent variables	Model I		Model II	
	(1)	(2)	(3)	(4)
$NCR4(78) - NCR4(63)$	-0.032 (0.718) $[-0.23]$	-0.106 (0.116) $[-0.91]$		
EEC $CR4(78) - NCR4(63)$			-0.150 (0.097) $[-1.55]$	-0.058 (0.105) $[-0.55]$
$M(78) - M(63)$		-0.140 (0.085) $[-1.64]$		
$X(78) - X(63)$		-0.090 (0.051) $[-1.76]^{cc}$		
NON EEC $M(78) - M(63)$				-0.214 (0.110) $[-1.95]^b$
NON EEC $X(78) - X(63)$				-0.022 (0.076) $[-0.29]$
R&D DUM		-0.064 (0.037) $[-1.74]^{cc}$		-0.111 (0.056) $[-1.97]^{cc}$
$PCM(78)_G/PCM(63)_G$		0.427 (0.209) $[2.04]^b$		0.182 (0.222) $[0.82]$
Constant	0.208 (0.019) $[10.83]^{aa}$	0.160 (0.040) $[2.65]^{bb}$	0.185 (0.023) $[8.13]^{aa}$	0.150 (0.078) $[2.01]^{cc}$
$\overline{R}^2$	-0.034	0.351	0.046	0.198
F	0.05 (1,28)	4.14^d (5,24)	2.41 (1,28)	2.43^f (5,24)

Note: For the statistics in brackets, levels of significance in one-tail tests are $a = 1$ percent, $b = 5$ percent. Levels of significance in two-tail tests are $aa = 1$ percent, $bb = 5$ percent, $cc = 10$ percent. Levels of significance in F statistics are $d = 1$ percent, $e = 5$ percent, $f = 10$ percent.

The significant positive effect of EEC $CR4(78) - NCR4(63)$ for Germany, France, and Italy is robust as we add other explanatory variables in equation.[31] Thus EEC $CR4(78) - NCR4(63)$ consistently takes a significant positive coefficient in equation (4) in every country except Belgium and the Netherlands. On the other hand, $NCR4(78) - NCR4(63)$ remains nonsignificant in equation (2). Correspondingly, the overall explanatory power of equation (4) is always higher than that of equation (2) for Germany, France, and Italy. On the other hand, it is lower in Belgium and the Netherlands.[32] The significant positive effect of EEC $CR4(78) - NCR4(63)$ and the nonsignificant effect of $NCR4(78) - NCR4(63)$ thus indicate that at least for larger countries—West Germany, France, and Italy—the formation of the Common Market has affected their price-cost margins through its effect on effective concentration. This provides support for our hypothesis on the increasing importance of EEC-wide concentration in determining price-cost margins.

Comparison of equations (3) and (4) across the five Common Market countries leads to other interesting findings. EEC $CR4(78) - NCR4(63)$ has the largest coefficient for West Germany, 0.33, in equation (4), but it has a smaller coefficient for France and Italy, 0.28 and 0.22, respectively. That is, it has the largest impact on changes in the price-cost margin in West Germany, whereas it has a more moderate effect for France and Italy and no effect for Belgium and the Netherlands. This result probably reflects the relative importance of West German firms in EEC-wide concentration. In most industries in our sample, West German firms are among the leading four firms in the Common Market, and to a lesser degree French and Italian firms. To the extent that EEC-wide concentration represents more closely the relative position of the largest West German firms in the Common Market, it should affect West Germany's price-cost margin more strongly.

On the other hand, Belgian and Dutch firms tend to be smaller,[33] and they are less likely to be among the leading firms in the Common Market. Thus Belgian and Dutch firms may have behaved as a competitive fringe, taking price as given, while West German firms were the price-leader. Then price in Belgian and Dutch industries should be directly determined by pricing decisions of West German industries and should be less closely related to EEC-wide concentration. When change in German price-cost margin $(PCM(78)_G/PCM(63)_G)$ is included in equations for France, Italy, Beligum, and the Netherlands, it tends to have a significant positive coefficient in each of them. For France and Italy, the inclusion of $PCM(78)_G/PCM(63)_G$ does not obscure the effect of EEC $CR4(78) - NCR4(63)$, indicating that pricing decisions of French and Italian firms are still influenced by their oligopolistic interdependence with West German firms. However, for Belgium and the Netherlands, change in German price-cost margin is a main determinant of change in the price-cost margin (equation (2)), whereas change in concentration has no effect on it.[34] The coefficient on $PCM(78)_G/PCM(63)_G$ in equation (2) for Belgium, 0.81, is the largest among these four countries, indicating that pricing decisions by West German firms have a large impact on pricing of Belgian firms. This finding lends some support for the argument that Belgian and Dutch firms behave as price-takers in the Common Market.

Summary and Conclusions

The main purposes of this chapter were to introduce an estimate of seller concentration at the European Economic Community level and to examine its effect on change in price and price-cost margins in the EEC countries. EEC-wide concentration was estimated for 47 three-digit manufacturing industries and compared with national concentration of each of the EEC countries. The unweighted mean values of EEC concentration were found to be smaller than the unweighted mean values of national concentration in any of the EEC countries, and the difference between these two measures tends to decrease with the size of national market. On average, concentration increased in each country separately and in the EEC as a group, but it grew more slowly at the EEC level than at any national level except the Netherlands.

The statistical analysis of the determinants of changes in price for West Germany has found that over the 1955–1957 to 1969–1971 period, change in price is determined by change in national concentration rather than change from national to EEC-wide concentration. By contrast, the statistical analysis on the determinants of change in the price-cost margin, which was implemented by using the data for 1963 and 1978, shows that for West Germany the effect of EEC-wide concentration is becoming more important. This result suggests that the recognition of mutual dependence between domestic and foreign sellers was not easy to achieve during the early period of the EEC, but it became increasingly easier during the later period.

The statistical analysis of the determinants of changes in price-cost margin has also found, for France and Italy, that the model incorporating the full effect of the formation of the EEC has a superior explanatory power to the model assuming the effect of the enlarged market only through imports and exports. We found evidence on the influence of EEC-wide concentration on the price-cost margin for larger EEC countries—West Germany, France, and Italy.

These findings imply, first, that for some industries concentration measured at the national level overstates effective concentration in the EEC countries. Concentration measured at the Common Market level will provide more correct information about effective concentration. EEC-wide concentration is able to capture the state of industry competition across national boundaries. Second, they imply that the largest manufacturing corporations from West Germany, France and Italy may have recognized oligopolistic interdependence after the creation of the Common Market, though it developed quite slowly. Thus the analysis of industrial competition for the EEC countries will be further enriched when we take into account intracommunity influences, especially the influence of the recognition of oligopolistic interdependence across national boundaries.

Appendix A: Selection of Samples and Sources of Data

Selection of Sample

The classification of industries used in this study is La Nomenclature générale des activités économiques dans les Communautés Européennes (NACE). This classification has its origin in La Nomenclature des industries établies dans les Communautés Européennes (NICE). The first common market census published in 1969 refers to the year 1963 and uses the NICE industry classification system. However, industry statistics published in later years follow the NACE classification system as a reference system. Industries from other data sources (input-output tables of the EEC countries, trade statistics, and the U.S. statistics) were therefore matched to the NACE industries. The level of aggregation used in this study is the NACE three-dight level.

Industries used in this study were selected on the basis of information contained in the 1978 employment-size distribution tables of the five countries, which were kindly made available by the Statistical Office of the European Communities in Luxemburg. The 47 industries were thus selected for the analysis. Appendix C lists the 47 industries in this sample.

Sources of Data

Price-cost margins, national concentration, EEC concentration, total employment, and value of total production for 1963:

Office Statistique des Communautés Européennes, *Etudes et enquetes statistiques 2* (Luxemburg: Statistical Office of the European Communities [SOEC], 1969).

Price-cost margins, total employment, and value of total production, for 1978:

Statistical Office of the European Communities, *Structure and Activity of Industry 1978* (Luxemburg: SOEC, 1983).

The average annual growth ratio in value of production over 1976–1978 was constructed from *Structure and Activity of Industry*, various years. The growth ratio over 1959–1965 and the ratio of depreciation to value of total output were computed from the input-output tables of individual countries:

Statistical Office of the European Communities, *Input-Output Table* (Luxemburg: SOEC).

The 1978 national concentration for Belgium, France, Italy, and West Germany was estimated from the unpublished data on the employment-size classes of enterprises. This information was made available by the Statistical Office of the European Communities in Luxemburg. National concentration for the Netherlands was provided by Centraal Bureau voor de Statistiek in Voorburg. The number of employees accounted for by the largest four firms in the Netherlands was obtained by multiplying the four-firm concentration by total employment. The 1978 EEC concentration is estimated based on the same data base.

Imports and exports for individual countries for 1963 were obtained from:

Statistical Office of the European Communities, *Foreign Trade Statistics: Analytical Tables-Imports* (Luxemburg: S.O.E.C., 1964).

Statistical Office of the European Communities, *Foreign Trade Statistics: Analytical Tables-Exports* (Luxemburg: S.O.E.C., 1964).

The SITC four-digit classification used there was converted to the NACE three-digit classification. Imports and exports for 1978 were obtained from:

Statistical Office of the European Communities, *Statistique du commerce extérieur* (Luxembury: S.O.E.C.).

This information was read from the microfiches coded SCE 2911, NACE-CLIO.

The number of scientists and engineers as a proportion of total employment in the U.S. counterpart industry was obtained from:

National Science Foundation, *Research and Development in Industry, 1972* (Washington, D.C.: U.S. Government Printing Office, 1973).

The statistical analysis of change in price for West Germany over 1955–1957 to 1969–1971 used the following data sources:

Price (P), wage per worker hour (W), physical quantity produced (Q), and export share (X) are obtained from Statistisches Bundesamt, *Statistisches Jahrbuch für die Bundesrepublik Deutschland*. P is a unit value at the industry level (comparable to the four-digit U.S. SIC). Q is defined also at the same level of industry classification. However, W and X are available for a more aggregated level of industry classification.

The raw material intensity (RAW) and consumer demand (CONS) variables were constructed from the Statistisches Bundesamt, *Input-Output-Tabellen 1975*, Fachserie 18, Reihe 2. RAW is measured as the sum of input coefficients for primary commodities divided by input coefficient for all inputs. SKILL was obtained from Statistisches Bundesamt, *Gewerbliche Wirtschaft und Dienstleistungsbereich Arbeiterverdienste. Angestelltenverdienste*, Fachserie M, Reihe 17/1, Table 7.1. Only Class 1 production workers were considered as skilled labor. R&D intensity for West Germany (RD) was constructed on the basis of unpublished data for 1975 which were obtained from the Stiftenverband für die Deutsche Wissenschaft. The 80 percent shipping radius in the U.S. counterpart (MDS) was esttimated by Weiss (1972).

Appendix B: EEC Four-Firm Concentration Ratios

		EEC four-firm concentration ratio (EEC $CR4$)	
Number	NACE code	1963	1978
1	140	0.40	0.38
2	221	0.49	0.38
3	224	0.28	0.26
4	241	0.06	0.14
5	243	0.09	0.12
6	247	0.19	0.26
7	248	0.19	0.17
8	311	0.13	0.17
9	313	0.04	0.05
10	315	0.17	0.18
11	321	0.23	0.22
12	322	0.08	0.09
13	323	0.23	0.24
14	324	0.12	0.10
15	325	0.17	0.15
16	327	0.18	0.17
17	328	0.18	0.16
18	342	0.35	0.25
19	345	0.35	0.30
20	346	0.24	0.38
21	351	0.33	0.42
22	361	0.27	0.28
23	371	0.21	0.24
24	412	0.09	0.10
25	413	0.12	0.15
26	414	0.17	0.16
27	419	0.05	0.15
28	420	0.32	0.44
29	421	0.23	0.24
30	427	0.09	0.16
31	428	0.12	0.23

32	436	0.06	0.07
33	437	0.23	0.12
34	439	0.06	0.11
35	442	0.04	0.09
36	451	0.10	0.09
37	453	0.04	0.04
38	461	0.03	0.10
39	462	0.11	0.20
40	463	0.02	0.08
41	465	0.07	0.13
42	471	0.18	0.21
43	472	0.08	0.08
44	473	0.04	0.04
45	481	0.29	0.41
46	483	0.07	0.05
47	491	0.07	0.13

Note: The method of estimation is described in the text. The European Common Market is defined here as a combined market of West Germany, France, Italy, the Netherlands, and Belgium.

Table 6B.2
National four-firm concentration ratio in 1978, $NCR4(78)$

Number	NACE code	West Germany	France	Italy	The Netherlands	Belgium
1	140	0.51	0.66	0.34	0.77	0.69
2	221	0.54	0.58	0.55	1.00	0.64
3	224	0.29	0.46	0.37	0.47	0.65
4	241	0.28	0.21	0.17	0.14	0.20
5	243	0.14	0.23	0.19	0.12	0.30
6	247	0.28	0.47	0.25	0.66	0.77
7	248	0.32	0.26	0.13	0.53	0.62
8	311	0.22	0.31	0.10	0.38	0.38
9	313	0.07	0.05	0.11	0.14	0.18
10	315	0.28	0.17	0.54	0.20	0.35
11	321	0.23	0.36	0.36	0.28	0.77
12	322	0.10	0.16	0.14	0.19	0.37
13	323	0.27	0.62	0.32	0.43	0.79
14	324	0.13	0.16	0.10	0.21	0.42
15	325	0.19	0.17	0.17	0.18	0.47
16	327	0.20	0.26	0.16	0.43	0.33
17	328	0.18	0.32	0.21	0.21	0.31
18	342	0.31	0.24	0.38	0.49	0.70
19	345	0.51	0.37	0.30	0.83	0.87
20	346	0.47	0.53	0.65	0.83	0.75

Table 6B.2 (continued)

Number	NACE code	West Germany	France	Italy	The Netherlands	Belgium
21	351	0.44	0.74	0.86	0.95	0.76
22	361	0.44	0.40	0.60	0.32	0.74
23	371	0.27	0.45	0.27	0.37	0.54
24	412	0.14	0.12	0.18	0.29	0.10
25	413	0.18	0.15	0.48	0.29	0.33
26	414	0.20	0.29	0.20	0.32	0.40
27	419	0.20	0.39	0.47	0.10	0.19
28	420	0.46	0.68	0.66	0.85	0.74
29	421	0.27	0.39	0.56	0.29	0.38
30	427	0.10	0.54	0.55	0.87	0.39
31	428	0.13	0.60	0.30	0.45	0.50
32	436	0.11	0.13	0.06	0.32	0.16
33	437	0.19	0.18	0.09	0.63	0.24
34	439	0.19	0.13	0.11	0.48	0.21
35	442	0.10	0.14	0.12	0.16	0.22
36	451	0.25	0.13	0.04	0.18	0.29
37	453	0.04	0.04	0.10	0.17	0.07
38	461	0.11	0.07	0.17	0.30	0.11
39	462	0.19	0.45	0.12	0.58	0.25
40	463	0.11	0.07	0.15	0.13	0.21
41	465	0.14	0.23	0.14	0.13	0.40
42	471	0.30	0.32	0.33	0.66	0.54
43	472	0.12	0.09	0.11	0.28	0.17
44	473	0.05	0.06	0.11	0.09	0.11
45	481	0.37	0.71	0.65	0.52	0.62
46	483	0.05	0.09	0.12	0.17	0.13
47	491	0.18	0.17	0.21	0.25	0.30

Note: Concentration is measured in terms of employment. The estimate for industry 420 for the Netherlands is based on data for 1976.

Table 6B.3
National four-firm concentration ratio in 1963, NCR4(63)

Number	NACE code	West Germany	France	Italy	The Netherlands	Belgium
1	140	0.50	0.66	0.41	0.95	0.87
2	221	0.42	0.40	0.56	1.00	0.62
3	224	0.37	0.54	0.30	0.71	0.48
4	241	0.07	0.11	0.06	0.09	0.23
5	243	0.08	0.24	0.13	0.15	0.29
6	247	0.21	0.39	0.14	0.49	0.61
7	248	0.26	0.24	0.17	0.20	0.43
8	311	0.18	0.19	0.07	0.33	0.17

9	313	0.07	0.02	0.05	0.21	0.21
10	315	0.27	0.15	0.37	0.32	0.27
11	321	0.29	0.34	0.14	0.29	0.59
12	322	0.08	0.13	0.09	0.20	0.39
13	323	0.29	0.23	0.33	0.29	0.55
14	324	0.15	0.13	0.12	0.25	0.36
15	325	0.21	0.14	0.20	0.20	0.41
16	327	0.19	0.33	0.25	0.34	0.51
17	328	0.23	0.27	0.12	0.38	0.19
18	342	0.43	0.42	0.12	0.46	0.77
19	345	0.37	0.43	0.35	0.97	0.79
20	346	0.28	0.25	0.43	0.35	0.36
21	351	0.39	0.50	0.72	0.42	0.41
22	361	0.40	0.37	0.62	0.29	0.58
23	371	0.17	0.29	0.24	0.47	0.88
24	412	0.08	0.24	0.17	0.28	0.18
25	413	0.14	0.16	0.27	0.17	0.15
26	414	0.12	0.15	0.20	0.31	0.60
27	419	0.04	0.15	0.16	0.08	0.09
28	420	0.23	0.42	0.63	0.94	0.74
29	421	0.25	0.15	0.35	0.25	0.30
30	427	0.07	0.24	0.49	0.64	0.20
31	428	0.14	0.22	0.18	0.26	0.35
32	436	0.10	0.07	0.04	0.28	0.10
33	437	0.15	0.37	0.26	0.75	0.22
34	439	0.05	0.10	0.12	0.24	0.12
35	442	0.05	0.06	0.06	0.12	0.12
36	451	0.19	0.13	0.04	0.31	0.16
37	453	0.07	0.02	0.02	0.07	0.04
38	461	0.05	0.02	0.03	0.10	0.07
39	462	0.19	0.10	0.13	0.63	0.60
40	463	0.02	0.01	0.02	0.19	0.12
41	465	0.08	0.09	0.10	0.08	0.18
42	471	0.25	0.26	0.22	0.59	0.56
43	472	0.13	0.05	0.07	0.13	0.27
44	473	0.04	0.07	0.10	0.08	0.09
45	481	0.34	0.50	0.53	0.42	0.55
46	483	0.10	0.06	0.09	0.19	0.17
47	491	0.11	0.09	0.08	0.14	0.26

Note: The estimates for France, Italy, the Netherlands, and Belgium are adapted from Phlips (1971, table A.1, pp. 184–194). Concentration is measured in terms of employment.

Appendix C: Names and European Industry Classification Numbers for the Sample of Industries

Industry		NACE code	NICE code
1	Petroleum refining	140	320
2	Iron and steel	221	341
3	Nonferrous metals	224	344
4	Clay products	241	331
5	Concrete, cement, or plaster products	243	335
6	Glass	247	332
7	Ceramic products	248	333
8	Foundries	311	345
9	Secondary transformation of metals	313	352
10	Boiler, tanks, and metal containers	315	354
11	Agricultural machinery	321	361
12	Metalworking machinery	322	363
13	Textile machinery, sewing machines	323	364
14	Food products machinery	324	365
15	Mining and steelwork machinery	325	366
16	Other special industry machinery	327	368
17	Other nonelectric machinery	328	369
18	Motors, generators, and electric distributing equipment	342	372
19	Radio, TV, and electronic components and accessories	345	375
20	Household electric appliances	346	376
21	Motor vehicles and parts	351	383
22	Shipbuilding	361	381
23	Measuring, controlling, and engineering instruments	371	391
24	Meat products	412	201
25	Dairy products	413	202
26	Preserved fruits and vegetables	414	203
27	Bakery products	419	206
28	Sugar	420	207
29	Cocoa, chocolate, and sugar confectionary	421	208
30	Brewing and malting	427	213
31	Soft drinks	428	214
32	Knitting mills	436	237
33	Textile finishing	437	238

34	Miscellaneous textile products	439	239
35	Leather products	442	292
36	Footwear	451	241
37	Clothing	453	243
38	Sawmills	461	251
39	Semifinished wood products	462	252
40	Carpentary, floors	463	253
41	Other wood products	465	255
42	Pulp, paper, and paperboard mills	471	271
43	Paper and paperboard products	472	272
44	Printing	473	280
45	Rubber products	481	301
46	Plastic products	483	302
47	Jewelry, silverware, and lapidary work	491	395

Notes

We are grateful to David B. Audretsch, Richard E. Caves, Alexis P. Jacquemin, as well as to seminar participants at the Catholic University of Leuven and the International Institute of Management, Berlin, for helpful comments and suggestions. We thank W. Knuppel of the Statistical Office of the European Communities for providing access to the data base employed for this project.

1. For a description of the Common Market, see Swann (1984).

2. See, for example, Kreinin (1974). Mayes (1978) provides a survey on the literature.

3. For example, Balassa (1966) and Grubel (1967).

4. Auquier (1977) tests some of these hypotheses. See also Mueller and Owen (1985). Some suggestions for research design in testing hypotheses on the effects of the formation of the EEC are given in Caves (1976).

5. For example, Commission of the European Communities (1983) presents the estimates of EEC-wide concentration for only eight broadly defined industries such as food, chemicals, electrical engineering, mechanical engineering, metal industries, transport equipment, paper, and textiles.

6. Owen (1983) shows concentration within the EEC for some product lines.

7. Concentration measured in employment may understate true concentration because smaller firms are commonly more labor intensive than large firms.

8. Luxemburg is excluded from the estimation due to missing data. Thus Luxemburg is totally omitted in the analysis below.

9. For a detailed discussion, see Bain (1966, pp. 26–29).

10. Volkswagen accounted for 45 percent of total automobile production in West Germany for 1965 and 42 percent in 1977. In France, Renault's share was 35 percent in 1965 and 41 percent in 1977, while Peugeot-Citroen's share was 43 percent in 1977. Fiat accounted for 88 percent of Italian automobile production in 1965 and 83 percent in 1977. Owen (1983), table 4.2, p. 48, table 4.3, p. 49, and table 4.4, p. 52.

11. Based on Owen (1983, tables 4.2–4.4).

12. Firm-size distribution based on the only three employment-size classes has been published from the Statistical Office of the European Communities. However, the size classes as used there are not appropriate for our purpose.

13. The 1963 Census uses the NICE (La Nomenclature des Industries établies dans les Communautés Européenes) classification. The 1978 data follows the NACE (La Nomenclature générale des activitiés économiques dans les Communautés Européennes) classification. The concordance between these two systems is perfect.

14. It is true that British firms may be among the four leaders in EEC. But in most cases that does not change concentration much because the British firm is likely to be displacing a continental firm that is only a bit smaller in size.

15. Employment of Luxembourg is not included in the denominators for both 1963 and 1978. See footnote 8.

16. See, for example, the 1963 Census of Manufacturers, Vol. 2, for the United States.

17. See Pryor (1972) and Phlips (1971, ch. 6).

18. The one exception is a study by Auquier (1977).

19. See also Caves (1974) on the argument on international oligopoly.

20. For an overview of the theoretical relationships among theories of oligopoly, measures of concentration, and price-cost margins, see Waterson (1984). For an empirical application of the theoretical models of the concentration-price relationship, see Yamawaki (1984).

21. For the development of a four-equation system similar to this, see chapter 3.

22. MDS is supposed to capture the existence of regional markets within the industry. We assume that the industry characteristics that create the regional markets in the United States are also present in the EC market.

23. For a previous study on the determinants of change in price-cost margins, see Cowling and Waterson (1976).

24. Britain, Denmark, and Ireland are treated as non-EEC countries in order to make the construction of NON EEC $M(78) - M(63)$ symmetrical to that of EEC $CR4 - NCR4$.

25. See Caves (1985) for a survey.

26. Exports to Britain, Denmark, and Ireland are again counted as non-EEC exports for the same reason given in note 24.

27. On this account, see the preceding section of this chapter.

28. Kervyn (1979) observes that West German manufacturing industry acts as price-leader.

29. Yamawaki (1986) applies a similar approach to the analysis of pricing decisions of U.S. and Japanese firms.

30. Due to missing observations, the sample size for the Netherlands is 30.

31. GROWTH (75–78)/GROWTH (59–65) was dropped from the equation in every country except for Germany because we found that the variable had no significant effect and reduced $\bar{R}^2$, and thus the F statistics, when it was included in the equation. For instance, in model II specifications, $\bar{R}^2$ dropped from 0.16 to 0.14 for France, from 0.12 to 0.10 for Italy, from 0.05 to 0.03 for Belgium, and from 0.20 to 0.19 for the Netherlands. Omitting the variable caused no major change in the coefficients for other independent variables. The coefficient for EEC $CR4(78) - NCR4(63)$ was 0.275 for France, 0.215 for Italy, 0.122 for Belgium, and -0.073 for the Netherlands when the growth variable was included in equation (4). To control for gross returns to capital, we included, in an unreported set of regressions, the change in the depreciation–sales ratio as a proxy for the capital–sales ratio which is not available for the EEC countries. As the variable again turned out to be insignificant and its inclusion reduced $\bar{R}^2$ of the regression equation, it was eventually dropped from the equation.

32. $\bar{R}^2$ in equation (4) is always higher than $\bar{R}^2$ in equation (2) for West Germany, France, and Italy, but it is lower for Belgium and the Netherlands.

33. See Phlips (1971, ch. 6).

34. In the unreported equations, changes in the average of price-cost margins for West Germany, France, and Italy were included instead of changes in the German price-cost margin. The explanatory power of that variable was much smaller than that of changes in the German price-cost margin.

35. We tested our model further by assigning the national rather than EEC end-of-period concentration figures for commodities that sell on geographically limited markets. They were clay products (NACE 241), concrete and cement products (243), meat products (412), dairy products (413), bakery products (19), brewing (427), soft drinks (428), and printing (473). The choice was based on Weiss (1972, app.) and Schwartzman and Bodoff (1971, table II). Meat products and brewing were included because of disparate national tastes within Europe. The result of this experiment were almost the same as for the original study.

References

Auquier, Antoine A. 1977. *Industrial Organization in an Opening Economy: French Industry and the Formation of the European Common Market*. Ph.D. dissertation. Cambridge, MA: Harvard University.

Bain, Joe S. 1966. *International Difference in Industrial Structure: Eight Nations in the 1950's*. New Haven: Yale University Press.

Balassa, Bela. 1966. "Tariff Reduction and Trade in Manufactures among the Industrial Countries." *American Economic Review* 56 (June), 466–473.

Caves, Richard E. 1985. "International Trade and the Industrial Organization: Problems, Solved and Unsolved." *European Economic Review* 28 (August), 377–95.

Caves, Richard E. 1976. "The Determinants of Market Structure: Design for Research." In A. P. Jacquemin and H. W. de Jong (eds.), *Markets, Corporate Behavior and The States*. The Hague: Martinns Nijhoff.

Caves, Richard E. 1974. *International Trade, International Investment, and Imperfect Markets*. Special Papers in International Economics No. 10 Princeton: Princeton University.

Commission of the European Communities. 1983. *Twelfth Report on Competition Policy*. Luxemburg: Office for Official Publications of the European Communities.

Cowling, Keith, and Michael Waterson. 1976. "Price-Cost Margins and Market Structure." *Economica* 43 (August), 267–274.

George, Kenneth D., and T. S. Ward. 1975. *The Structure of Industry in the EEC: An International Comparison*. Cambridge University Press.

Grubel, Herbert G. 1967. "Intra-Industry Specialization and the Pattern of Trade." *Canadian Journal of Economics and Political Science* 33 (August), 374–388.

Kelton, Christina M. L., and Leonard W. Weiss. 1987. "Change in Price, Change in Cost, Change in Demand and Change in Concentration." This volume.

Kervyn de Lettenhove, A. 1979. "Taux de change, inflation et compétitivité externe." *Recherches Economiques de Louvain* 45, 55–94.

Kreinin, Mordechai E. 1974. *Trade Relations of the EEC: An Empirical Investigation*. New York: Praeger.

Mayes, David G. 1978. "The Effects of Economic Integration on Trade." *Journal of Common Market Studies* 17 (September), 1–25.

Mueller, Juergen, and Nicholas Owen. 1985. "The Effect of Trade on Plant Size." In J. Schwalbach (ed.), *Industry Structure and Performance*. Berlin: Edition Sigma.

Owen, Nicholas. 1983. *Economies of Scale, Competitiveness and Trade Patterns within the European Community*. Oxford: Oxford University Press.

Phlips, Louis. 1971. *Effects of Industrial Concentration: A Cross-Section Analysis for the Common Market*. Amsterdam: North-Holland.

Pryor, Frederic L. 1972. "An International Comparison of Concentration Ratios." *Review of Economics and Statistics* 54 (May), 130–140.

Schwartzman, David, and Joan Bodoff. 1971. "Concentration in Regional and Local Industries." *Southern Economic Journal* 37 (January), 343–348.

Swann, Dennis. 1984. *The Economics of the Common Market*. 5th ed. Harmondsworth, England: Penquin Books.

Waterson, Michael. 1984. *Economic Theory of the Industry*. Cambridge: Cambridge University Press.

Weiss, Leonard W. 1972. "The Geographic size of Markets in Manufacturing." *Review of Economics and Statistics* 54 (August), 245–257.

Weiss, Leonard W., and George Pascoe. 1984. The Extent and Permanence of Market Dominance." IIM/IP discussion paper 84-23 (July). Berlin: International Institute of Management.

Yamawaki, Hideki. 1986. "Exports, Foreign Market Structure, and Profitability in Japanese and U.S. Manufacturing." *Review of Economics and Statistics* 68 (November), 618–627.

Yamawaki, Hideki. 1984. "Market Structure, Capacity Expansion, and Pricing: A Model Applied to the Japanese Iron and Steel Industry." *International Journal of Industrial Organization* 2 (March), 29–62.

II   **Other Studies**

Concentration and the Price of Advertising Space and Time

The Stigler Study

The first concentration-price studies of which I am aware were done by George Stigler and incorporated in one of his most famous articles (1964). He reported on two studies he had made, one on milline rates on newspapers in 1939 and the other on charges for radio spot announcements in four midwestern states in 1961. His report is so short that it seems appropriate to simply reproduce it. After that I will report on two more recent studies, on milinch charges in newspapers in 1976 and the second on television spots in 1979.

Readers who have never run a regression on a desk calculater should know that Stigler's first study was really quite sophisticated for the late 1950s. A regression with one or two independent variables was reasonably easy, but if you got to three or more you had to turn to the "Doolittle method," one of the wildest misnomers in the English language. It look us half a day to regress some variable on three or four other variables, and then we had to do it again because there were so many opportunities for error, and then many of us had to do it a third time to see which of the first two results were right. I presume that the milline rate study was done in the era of desk calculators and the radio spot was run on a computer.

"Some Fragments of Evidence

"Before we seek empirical evidence on our theory, it is useful to report two investigations of the influence of numbers of sellers on price. These investigations have an intrinsic interest because, so far as I know, no systematic analysis of the effect of numbers has hitherto been made.

Table 7.1
Residuals from regression of advertising rates on circulation

Number of evening papers	n	Mean residual (logarithm)	Standard deviation of mean
One	23	0.0211	0.0210
With morning paper	10	−0.0174	0.0324
Without morning paper	13	0.0507	0.0233
Two	30	−0.0213	0.0135

Source: American Association of Advertising Agencies, *Market and Newspaper Statistics* 8a (1939).
Note: The regression equation is

$$\log R = 5.194 - 1.688 \log c + 0.139(\log c)^2,$$
$$\quad\quad\quad\quad (0.620) \quad\quad\quad (0.063)$$

where R is the $5M$ milline rate and c is circulation.

"The first investigation was of newspaper advertising rates, as a function of the number of evening newspapers in a city. Advertising rates on a milline basis are closely (and negatively) related to circulation, so a regression of rates on circulation was made for 53 cities in 1939. The residuals (in logarithmic form) from this regression equation are tabulated in table 7.1. It will be observed that rates are 5 percent above the average in one-newspaper towns and 5 percent below the average in two-newspaper towns, and the towns with one evening paper but also an independent morning paper fall nearly midway between these points. Unfortunately, there were too few cities with more than two evening newspapers to yield results for larger numbers of firms.

"The second investigation is of spot commercial rates on AM radio stations in the four states of Ohio, Indiana, Michigan, and Illinois. The basic equation introduces, along with number of rivals, a series of other factors. (power of station, population of the country in which the station is located, etc.). Unfortunately, the number of stations is rather closely correlated with population ($r^2 = 0.796$ in the logarithms). The general result, shown in table 7.2, is similar to that for newspapers: the elasticity of price with respect to number of rivals is quite small (-0.07). Here the range of stations in a county was from 1 to 13.

"Both studies suggest that the level of prices is not very responsive to the actual number of rivals. This is in keeping with the expectations based upon our model, for that model argues that the number of buyers, the

Table 7.2
Regression of AM spot commercial at end rates (26 times) and station characteristics, 1951 (n = 345)

Independent variables[a]	Regression coefficient	Standard error	t statistic
Logarithm of population of county, 1960	0.238	0.026	9.15
Logarithm of kilowatt power of station	0.206	0.015	13.73
Dummy variables of period of broadcasting:			
Sunrise to sunset	−0.114	0.025	−4.56
More than daytime, less than 18 hours	−0.086	0.027	−3.19
18–21 hours	−0.053	0.028	−1.89
Logarithm of number of stations in county	−0.074	0.046	−1.61
$R^2 = 0.743$			

Source: "Spot Radio Rates and Data," *Standard Rate and Data Service, Inc.* 43, 5 (May 1961).
a. Dependent variable: logarithm of average rate, May 1, 1961 (dollars).

proportion of new buyers, and the relative sizes of firms are as important as the number of rivals." (Stigler 1964, 56–57)

Studies related to both of Stigler's early efforts have been published since. The first, on newspaper ads, yield negative coefficients and must be included for that reason. It seems a natural extension of Stigler's first study, in any event.

Newspaper Advertizing Rates
James M. Ferguson

A more recent study (1983) estimates the effects of various media owner-ship and media competition variables on milinch advertizing rates—that is, the charge for a column inch per thousand circulation. The milinch adver-tizing rate is the relevant price, not the advertizing rate per column inch, because what advertisers buy is the opportunity to reach readers. This study worked with 815 general interest daily papers and their 445 Sunday papers with circulations of 10,000 or more continental United States and rates for ROP (run-of-paper) ads. Regressions were run on 1976 national and retail milinch advertizing rates separately in an attempt to identify the determinants of three different prices for national and retail ads for daily and Sunday editions: open or noncontract (spot) fees, fees for small annual contracts (714 column inches or 10,000 lines), and fees for large annaul contracts (7,143 column inches or 100,000 lines).

Table 7.3
Daily milinch advertising rate regressions dependent variable (standard errors in parentheses, t ratios in brackets)

Variable	National 10,000 line annual contract rates	Retail 10,000 line annual contract rates
Constant	−1.114 (0.139) [−8.02]	−1.175 (0.168) [−6.98]
Log city zone population	−0.156 (0.013) [−11.79]	−0.172 (0.016) [−10.77]
Log retail trade zone population	−0.091 (0.12) [−7.39]	−0.108 (0.015) [−7.24]
Log sum of these if 250,000 to 500,000	0.006 (0.004) [1.30]	0.004 (0.005) [0.75]
Log sum if in range 500,000 to 1,000,000	0.003 (0.007) [0.43]	0.008 (0.007) [1.09]
Log sum if in range 1,000,000 to 2,000,000	0.002 (0.01) [0.21]	0.006 (0.01) [0.60]
Log sum if 2,000,000 or more	0.024 (0.009) [2.65]	0.023 (0.011) [2.08]
Log mean income per city household	0.125 (0.051) [2.46]	0.083 (0.062) [1.34]
Log total retail sales in TV ADI	−0.005 (0.008) [−0.63]	0.007 (0.01) [0.73]
Log city area	0.030 (0.01) [2.89]	0.037 (0.013) [2.94]
Log number of radio and TV stations	−0.071 (0.018) [−4.02]	−0.110 (0.021) [−5.12]
Morning edition dummy	−0.027 (0.024) [−1.11]	−0.022 (0.029) [−0.76]
Morning-evening combo dummy	−0.111 (0.024) [−4.67]	−0.143 (0.029) [−4.97]

Table 7.3 (continued)

Variable	National 10,000 line annual contract rates	Retail 10,000 line annual contract rates
TV cross-ownership dummy	−0.068 (0.031) [−2.19]	−0.067 (0.038) [−1.77]
Radio cross-ownership dummy	−0.017 (0.022) [−0.77]	−0.030 (0.027) [−1.10]
Small chain dummy	0.040 (0.018) [2.28]	0.043 (0.022) [2.00]
Large chain dummy	0.089 (0.017) [5.21]	0.078 (0.021) [3.79]
Group membership dummy	−0.004 (0.014) [−0.29]	−0.041 (0.019) [−2.20]
Competing daily paper dummy	0.059 (0.036) [1.62]	0.018 (0.045) [0.40]
$\bar{R}^2$	0.670	0.667

The independent variables operate on newspaper milinch advertising rates by changing advertiser demand for space in daily newspapers and by changing readership—newspaper circulation. Advertiser demand and subscriber demand are interrelated: the demand for advertising space is a function of newspaper circulation, which depends on subscriber demand, and subscriber demand is a function of the information provided by retail advertising. The positive effect of retail advertising on circulation is important in the analysis of the newspaper price effects of the media competition and media ownership variables in the presence of substantial circulation economies of scale (more accurately, economies of longer production runs). Increases in circulation will lower marginal and average milinch advertising costs and advertising rates.

The word measures of concentration don't appear because very few cities had more than two general interest dailies in 1976. The closest variable is the competing paper dummy, and it *raised* milinch advertising rates. Its coefficient was not significant at the 5 percent level for any of the daily edition rates but was quite large and significant for Sunday papers facing

Table 7.4
Sunday milinch advertising rate correlations (standard errors in parentheses, *t* ratios in brackets)

Variable	National 10,000 line annual contract rates	Retail 10,000 line annual contract rates
Constant	−0.880 (0.223) [−3.95]	−0.617 (0.267) [−2.31]
Log city zone population	−0.177 (0.02) [−8.69]	−0.212 (0.024) [−8.71]
Log retail trading zone population	−0.099 (0.02) [−5.07]	−0.119 (0.023) [−5.08]
Log city retail trading zone population1	0.000 (0.01) [1.03]	−0.004 (0.007) [−0.54]
Log city retail trading zone population2	−0.007 (0.009) [−0.76]	−0.001 (0.007) [−0.15]
Log city retail trading zone population3	−0.008 (0.011) [−0.74]	−0.005 (0.013) [−0.39]
Log city retail trading zone population4	0.014 (0.013) [1.10]	0.017 (0.015) [1.10]
Log mean income per city household	0.050 (0.079) [0.63]	−0.079 (0.095) [−0.83]
Log total retail sales in TV ADI	−0.004 (0.013) [−0.32]	0.005 (0.014) [0.35]
Log city area in square miles	0.038 (0.015) [2.59]	0.042 (0.018) [2.38]
Log number of city radio and TV stations	−0.061 (0.027) [−2.24]	−0.096 (0.033) [−2.92]
TV cross-ownership dummy	−0.079 (0.037) [−2.15]	−0.109 (0.044) [−2.47]
Radio cross-ownership dummy	−0.028 (0.030) [−0.92]	−0.024 (0.037) [−0.65]

Table 7.4 (continued)

Variable	National 10,000 line annual contract rates	Retail 10,000 line annual contract rates
Small chain dummy	0.031 (0.027) [1.16]	0.016 (0.033) [0.49]
Large chain dummy	0.098 (0.025) [3.98]	0.082 (0.030) [2.77]
Group membership dummy	0.002 (0.022) [0.09]	−0.036 (0.028) [−1.28]
Competing Sunday dummy	0.122 (0.042) [2.90]	0.133 (0.05) [2.64]
$\bar{R}^2$	0.690	0.702
Sample size	455	455

other Sunday papers. This somewhat surprising result may be explained by the price increasing diseconomies of smaller circulation outweighing the price decreasing effect of greater price elasticity of advertiser demand. The presence of a competing paper provides more alternatives to advertisers and thereby may make advertiser demand for space in any paper more elastic, leading to lower advertising rates. At the same time the presence of a competing paper increases readers' options and, thereby, may reduce circulation of each paper. The circulation regressions show the significant reduction in circulation from a competing Sunday edition is twice that from a competing daily edition.

The number of local TV and radio stations has the expected competitive effect, however, and the reduction in rates as the number of broadcasters rises in highly significant. Here the price decreasing economies of greater circulation and greater price elasticity of advertiser demand work in the same direction. What explains the increase in newspaper circulation from a larger number of broadcasters? According to Ferguson, more broadcasters will tend to reduce audience per station, and diseconomies of smaller audience drive up broadcast advertising rates, shifting some retail advertising to newspapers. More retail advertising increases newspaper readership.

Joint ownership of two daily newspapers in a city results in significantly greater circulation and significantly lower combination advertising rates. This rate result is probably mainly due to the lower value of combination circulation to advertisers because of the overlap in readership.

Local newspaper-radio and newspaper-television station cross-ownership significantly increases circulation and always reduce newspaper advertising rates, but not significantly for radio. In 11 of the 12 daily and Sunday price regressions the coefficient of the newspaper-television cross-ownership dummy variable is significant at the 0.90 level or above. Why does cross-ownership reduce newspaper advertising charges? If newspapers and television stations are viewed as substitutes by most advertisers, joint profit maximization with cross-ownership is likely to result in higher advertising rates in a least one of the media. Possibly local cross-ownership achieves economies of size in news gathering, in securing advertising, and in coordination within the local market and thus lowers marginal and average costs. Also, if these lower costs lead to lower retail advertising rates and more editorial content, circulation will be higher, and greater economies of circulation can be achieved.

Yet one might expect economies of newspaper chain ownership to also produce lower advertising prices for chain papers. These economies would be reinforced by the greater daily circulation associated with large chain ownership. But chain newspapers charge significantly higher advertising rates. The tentative explanation is that chains often acquire family-owned papers. Many papers are still family owned. Profits may be much less important in the utility function of family owners, while nonpecuniary income (e.g., being well-liked in the community) may be much more important. The result would be that family owners is setting advertising rates to maximize utility do not charge prices as high as the ones that simply maximize profits. Chain owners and managers are more concerned about maximizing profits and may be superior at finding profit-maximizing advertising fees, so they set higher rates.

To complete this chapter we turn to the price of spot announcements on TV. This has been analyzed by Michael Wirth and Harry Bloch as part of a broader study of the future of the broadcast media (Wirth and Bloch 1985). They have prepared the following summary of the concentration-price part of their study.

Concentration and the Price of Local Television Advertising Time
Harry Bloch and Michael O. Wirth

Limitations of the supply of television advertising time arise from Federal Communications Commission limits on the number of over-the-air television stations licensed to broadcast. Other studies of advertising revenue of local television stations have treated the price of advertising spots as a hedonic function of audience characteristics. Fournier and Martin (1983) justify this by arguing that the "law of one price" applies to the sale of advertising time. They argue that advertisers shift their purchases to the station with the lowest price for reaching an audience of given characteristics.

We tested an oligopoly model against the hedonic model, using alternative regressions to explain the prices of 30-second spots during *MASH* in March 1984. These specifications were adopted to limit variation due to network affiliation, programming, and time of broadcast. We felt that the hedonic model pictured the product as viewer exposures of a given quality, whereas an oligopoly model would view the product as access to a particular audience. The hedonic model makes it reasonable to consider television stations in different viewing markets to be competing for the same advertising dollars so that the market is potentially very competitive. An oligopoly model is required if the product is access to a particular viewing audience, since broadcasters are always limited in number locally. Our purpose was to evaluate these two alternatives.

The variables used, their definitions, and their sources appear in table 7.5. Our sample consisted of the CBS affiliates in 105 cities.

The results of our basic formulation of the two models appear in table 7.6. We limit ourselves to the log-linear relationships here, though ordinary linear regressions were also run and yielded similar results. Weighted regressions were also calculated to deal with possible heteroskedasticity. Little change in coefficients occurred, and the t ratio of log Herfindahl index was increased moderately. Heteroskedastic-consistent estimates of t ratios were also calculated, but the significance of the coefficients generally stayed the same. The only change was to raise the t ratio of the VHF dummy enough to make it significantly positive by a one-tailed test (re-estimated $t = 1.93$).

The hedonic model follows that used by Fournier and Martin. The oligopoly model contains the changes that we feel were needed to characterize the local market with limited numbers of stations. Not only does it

Table 7.5
Variable definitions and data sources

Variable	Definition	Data source
R	List price of a 30-second spot for *MASH* or for highest price nonspecial event prime spot if *MASH* price was not directly available	Standard rate and data service Spot TV rates (March 1983)
H	Number of households in the designated market area (DMA) (in thousands)	A. C. Nielsen VIP'S (November 1982)
V	Average quarter hour audience for *MASH* (in thousands)	Nielsen
Herfindahl index	The sum of squared market shares for all local commercial broadcast stations of average daily viewers of local commercial stations. The share thus calculated differs from that provided directly in Nielsen which includes in the denominator viewers of noncommercial local stations, stations from other DMAs and cable programming.	Nielsen
S/H	Average total retail sales per DMA household (in thousands)	SRDS
VHF dummy	A dummy variable = 1 if station is a VHF station and = 0 if UHF. VHF has better reception.	SRDS
M	Average quarter hour metro area household audience for MASH (in thousands)	Nielsen
N	Number of television stations in DMA	Nielsen

contain a concentration variable, but price depends on the underlying number of households (an exogenous variable) and viewers per household, which is a response to concentration in part. The effect of concentration is very strong. We feel that this clearly supports the oligopoly model. Having derived our model from Stigler (1964), we tried his model where concentration was measured by log N. It had a negative effect as expected, but the relationship was weaker ($t = -1.77$). He had advocated the Herfindahl index in the same article.

In experimenting with the data after the basic model had been run, we found that the significance of the coefficients of log Herfindahl index and, alternatively, log N fell when we excluded from our sample the four stations with no competitors. For the 101 remaining cities the coefficients of our concentration indexes had the right signs, and the coefficient of the preferred Herfindahl index was still, clearly significant ($t = 2.05$ for log Herfindahl index), whereas the coefficient for the number of firms was clearly not significant ($t = -0.14$ for log N). We interpret this as saying

Table 7.6
Coefficients explaining price of 30-second spots on *MASH* in 1983 (standard errors in parentheses, *t* ratios in brackets)

Variable	Hedonic model	Oligopoly model
Constant	4.178	1.372
Log *V*	0.785 (0.058) [13.63]	
Log *S/H*	−0.235 (0.309) [0.76]	0.117 (0.285) [0.41]
VHF dummy	0.030 (0.120) [0.25]	0.185 (0.116) [1.59]
Log *M/V*	0.203 (0.155) [1.31]	0.159 (0.139) [1.14]
Log *H*		1.037 (0.080) [12.95]
Log *V/H*		0.089 (0.165) [0.54]
Log Herfindahl index		0.679 (0.197) (3.45]
$\bar{R}^2$	0.651	0.723

that prices were not at competitive levels when there were two or three stations in a city. We feel this reinforces the conclusion that television advertising markets are local. Viewers in Chicago and Denver are not pictured by advertisers as close substitutes for viewers in Cheyenne (which had a monopoly CBS station at the time).

Note

This chapter derives from research into the impact of new video transmission technolgies on the profitability of commercial over the air television broadcasting. The results of the research were presented to Columbia University's conference on "Rivalry among Video Transmission Media: Assessment and Implications" (see Wirth and Bloch 1985). Helpful comments from conference participants are gratefully acknowledged.

References

Ferguson, James M. 1983. "Daily Newspaper Advertising Rates, Local Media Cross Ownership, Newspaper Chains, and Media Competition." *Journal of Law and Economics* 26 (October), 635–654.

Fisher, F. M., J. J. McGowan, and D. S. Evans. 1980. "The Audience-Revenue Relationship for Local Television Stations." *Bell Journal of Economics* 11, 694–708.

Fournier, G. M., and D. L. Martin. 1983. "Does Government-Restricted Entry Produce Market Power?: New Evidence From the Market for Television Advertising." *Bell Journal of Economics* 14, 44–56.

Stigler, G. 1964. "A Theory of Oligopoly." *Journal of Political Economy* 72, 44–61.

Wirth, M. O., and H. Bloch. 1985. "The Broadcasters: The Future Role of Local Stations and the Three Networks." In E. M. Noam (ed.), *Video Media Competition: Regulation, Economics and Technology*. New York: Columbia University Press.

8   Deregulated Airlines

The airlines have become an almost ideal place to study concentration and price since deregulation. Price is necessarily public information because travel agents who write a large majority of tickets must know not only standard fares but all the "special deals" available at each point in time. Moreover, numbers of passengers carried by class are reported quarterly for each airline on each city-pair route and are computed quarterly on the basis of a 10 percent sample of all tickets sold.

In addition to readily available data, the airlines have provided plenty of incentive to study them. In the early 1980s there was an obvious need to evaluate regulatory reform. The changes had come in 1977 to 1978, fairly early in the regulatory reform movement, and had permitted drastic changes in pricing and entry almost at once. And then came the notion of contestable markets, of which airlines were supposed to be a clear case. Since perfect contestability was obviously inconsistent with a systematic positive effect of concentration on price, it was a natural invitation to regress price on concentration. It was an invitation to examine the effect of entry and of potential entry as well.

When the work on this book began, we knew of no systematic studies of the effects of concentration and entry on air fares. Two men who were then graduate students at Wisconsin developed studies for this book. The gap is much less serious now, but I feel that their papers still provide information not available elsewhere. The chapter therefore consists of three sections. The first describes the studies done by others in the 1980s. The second is a straightforward analysis that initially was like that of Keeler and Abrahams' done at about the same time. Its main contribution today is to include a wide range of alternative concentration measures. The last is a quite sophisticated analysis of potential entry. Altogether the three sections provide quite strong support for the conventional predictions about the effects of concentration, potential entry, and actual entry on price.

Other People's Studies

The first published concentration-price study with respect to airline fares that we know of was Keeler and Abrahams (1981). Keeler (1981) had reported the minimum unrestricted daytime fares for 88 of the 100 most important intercity routes as of September 1980 which he divided by a CAB formula fare that was supposed to reflect costs. He then compared these ratios for August 1975 to show how much more flexible and usually lower these fares had become after deregulation.

He and Abrahams went on to examine the 1980 fares more systematically (1981). They regressed minimum unrestricted daytime fares on a dummy if new entry had occurred on the route since 1978, the minimum amount of feed from other routes of firms flying the route in question, trip length, and the Herfindahl index. The coefficient for entry was of borderline significance; the feed and trip length variables had nonsignificant coefficients; but the Herfindahl index had a clearly significant positive effect. They had transformed the variable so that its new form could range from minus to plus infinity. This made it very difficult for outsiders to use the coefficient.

A few years later (Call and Keeler 1985) Keeler returned to the topic, using three different price variables for the same markets, but this time for 1977, 1978, 1979, 1980, and 1981. In addition, for 1980 they computed revenue yield per coach passenger-mile. The latter should reflect the special discounts available on many routes.

In 1977, before deregulation, the ratio of each of these fares to the old CAB formula was almost the same on all routes: about 1.01. After deregulation, these ratios diverged. The standard fares increases relative to the old CAB formula fares, and they rose significantly more on concentrated routes. The other two fare variables were the minimum unrestricted daytime fare by a trunk line on the route and the minimum unrestricted daytime fare by any airline, trunk or otherwise, including such lines as PeopleExpress and Pacific Southwest Airlines. The latter corresponded to the dependent variable in the previous study. This time they got the following coefficients for H: the coefficient for the minimum trunk line, the unrestricted daytime rate was 0.2052, (0.1826), [1.11], for overall minimum unrestricted daytime fares, it was 0.4992, (0.1822), [2.74], and for average yield per passenger-mile it was 0.1417, (0.0857), [1.65]. Other variables included entry by trunks, entry by others, percentage of seats on the route in wide body planes, and an estimate of price elasticity of demand by a method developed by Abrahams.

The next major work, by Graham, Kaplan, and Sibley (1983), was more elaborate. It was rerun by Bailey, Kaplan, and Graham (1985) to include a larger sample of routes. The dependent variable was average yield per passenger-mile on more than 5,000 routes. They controlled for distance, number of passengers on the route, per capita income, newly certified carriers on the route, and, sometimes, for interlining and circuity. In an OLS model the Herfindahl index has a powerful positive effect. In a two-stage least squares regression where number of passengers is endogenous, the log of the Herfindahl index still has a highly significant positive effect. However, when log H is made endogenous, its coefficient becomes negative ($t = -1.55$ to -1.96). After experimenting with data along these lines for the second quarter of 1981, they ran the two-stage model with number of passengers endogenous—surely appropriate for a demand equation—but with H exogenous. This yielded coefficients for H of 0.080, (0.009), [8.66], in the third quarter of 1980, 0.078, (0.010), [10.9], in the fourth quarter, 0.109, (0.010), [10.75], in the first quarter of 1981, and 0.086, (0.008), [10.75], in the second quarter of 1981 (Bailey, Graham, and Kaplan 1985, 162–163). They conclude that the airlines markets could not be characterized as fully contestable in that period.

Moore (1986) also set out to examine the effect of deregulation on air fares. He compared fares in 1983 with those in 1976 for a variety of issues. He reports that the Herfindahl index yielded a significant positive effect for 134 large city-pairs markets but that the coefficient for a dummy for more than four carriers yielded a better fit. This seems to be primarily a matter of long hauls. But according to Moore, on 96 non-long-haul markets the routes with one and two carriers had fare increases of 44 to 47 percent between 1977 and 1983, those with three and four had average increases of 31 to 33 percent, while the 13 city-pairs with five or more saw fare rise by only 3 percent. Discount fares were increasingly common as numbers of carriers rose. Moore also rejects contestability on airline markets because of the clear influence of numbers of carriers on price.

Morrison and Winston (1986) broaden the dependent variable to take into account changes in flight frequency and trip time as well as price. Their dependent variable is the "change in welfare" of individuals. They estimate compensating variation on the basis of a multimodal, intercity transportation demand function they have estimated. Then, using a method developed by Small and Rosen (1981), they estimate the combination of fares and flight frequencies that maximized the sum of travelers compensating variations on each of 812 routes. Their dependent variable was the welfare difference between this optimal combination and the actually prevailing fares and frequencies in 1983.

They regressed the difference on a series of type of route dummies (a large hub—large hub dummy, a large hub—medium hub dummy, etc.) and a series of variables for the numbers of actual and potential airlines in various categories flying on the route. A potential carrier is an airline presently flying to one of the termini of the route but not on the route itself. The estimated effects of current and potential carriers are quite systematic (Morrison and Winston 1986, 61):

Actual super majors	−0.7429 (0.1161) [−6.40]	Potential majors	−0.1385 (0.0599) [−2.31]
Actual other majors	−0.4577 (0.0851) [−4.34]	Potential newly certified carriers	−0.1006 (0.0374) [−2.70]
Actual newly certified carriers	−0.4898 (0.1129) [−4.34]	Potential other carriers	−0.0818 (0.0536) [−1.53]
Actual other carriers	0.0080 (0.0893) [0.09]		

They also controlled for airports that rationed slots and for the percentage of business travelers. Both had significant positive effects. Their "super majors" were United and American, the other majors were the usual list, including Republic, Pan Am, and USAir. Among newly certificated carriers were such airlines as PeopleExpress, World Airlines, and PSA. The other carriers must have been primarily the other old local service airlines.

The coefficients involved are quite large. It would only take one to three additional airlines on several of the most important types of routes to eliminate any loss of welfare in the affected routes. Like most of the others who had studied the issue, Morrison and Winston concluded that the airlines could not be characterized by contestable markets.

In sum, in less than a decade we have moved from a setting where almost all we knew about airline price competition derived from theory and a few intrastate airlines not regulated by the CAB to some remarkably sophisticated studies with very strong results. The conclusion of these studies is that concentration makes a lot of difference in setting price. The studies that have dealt with entry conditions have carried us much farther than might have been expected on the basis of studies in other fields available a decade ago. And despite the remarkably broad range of approaches used, these studies lead to the same conclusion, that competition in the form of reduced concentration and actual and/or potential entry has the conventional effect on price.

Our own contributions to the subject follow. Their main contribution is no longer to show that concentration raises price and that both actual and potential entry lower it. Our work supports these conclusions as do the other studies reviewed, but at this late date our emphasis will be on the choice among concentration measures and an alternative way to model entry conditions.

Competition in Deregulated Air Fares
Robert Town and Scott Milliman

The outbreak of price competition among airlines after deregulation provided us with an attractive basis for testing alternative functional forms of the concentration-price relationship. We used Theodore Keeler's ratios between the lowest unrestricted daytime airfare and the standard CAB cost-based industry fare level formula for 90 high-density routes in August 1980 (Keeler 1981). We regressed his fare ratios on many alternative measures of concentration and two alternative measures of entry. The left-hand section of table 3.1 shows regression coefficients relating Keeler's minimum unrestricted fare ratios to six alternative measure of concentration: H—the Herfindahl index; $CR1$, $CR2$, and $CR3$—the one-, two-, and three-firm concentration ratios; N—the number of firms; $1/N$—its inverse. We have also include three critical concentration-dummies with values of one if CRi equals or exceeds the level indicated in parentheses. There are two alternative measures of entry: E—the number of centrants between 1975 and 1980; and E/N—the number of entrants, divided by the 1980 number of firms. The values of $CCRi$ were chosen by trial and error to maximize the effect of $CCRn$. All the coefficients of concentration indexes have the expected signs, and all of them are statistically significant except for N and $1/N$ when entry is measured with E. The Herfindahl index yields the best fit based on R^2. Both entry indexes have significant negative effects regardless of concentration measures used. Of the two entry indexes, E/N has a higher t-ratio throughout. The best fit among all 18 regressions occurs where concentration is measured by H and entry by E/N.

The minimum unrestricted daytime fare may not be the best index of price, however. In some city-pair markets only a small number of passengers paid those fares. Their close association with E and E/N suggests that they were often fares offered by new entrants trying to build up their positions. Because of this we next calculated for each market weighted averages of unrestricted coach fares using the individual market shares of each airline in 1980 as weight.[1] We again divided the average dollar fare by the CAB standard fare.

Regressions relating these average ratios to concentration and entry are shown on the right in table 8.1. The fits are poorer compared to the minimum unrestricted daytime fares. The concentration variables' coefficients always have the expected signs, but they differ significantly form zero only for $CR2$, $CR3$, $CCR1$, $CCR2$, and $CCR3$, and marginally for N when entry is E/N. The entry variables have the expected negative coefficients in 14 of the 18 regressions, but they are never statistically significant. The best fit is for $CCR1$ of 39 and E/N, but these variables account for only 13.0 percent of the variability in average fare ratios.

The regressions were re-run with stage length as an additional independent variable, in part because much of the comment on fare competition emphasizes the longer routes. In addition, there may be a rough correlation between stage length and the price elasticity of demand in individual airline markets. The rationale is as follows: on very short routes, demand may be relatively elastic due to the presence of close substitutes, such as cars and buses. As distance increases, these alternative modes of transportation become less convenient relative to air travel, and accordingly demand may become less elastic. For very long routes, however, demand may once again become relatively elastic due to the increased number of tourist travelers who fly those routes because vacation flyers may be more sensitive to price then business travelers. If this rationale is correct, then stage length should be entered into the regressions in a quadratic form. We tried the log of stage length and a quadratic formulation—the latter yielded by far the better fit.

The introduction of the quadratic form of stage length left the results for minimum unrestricted fare virtually unchange. The coefficients for concentration and entry always had the expected signs and were significant for entry in all cases and for all measures of concentration except N and $1/N$.

Table 8.1
Coefficients relating air fare to concentration and entry, August 1980 (standard errors in parentheses, t ratios in brackets)

Minimum unrestricted daytime fare, August 1980				Weighted average unrestricted coach daytime fare, July 1980			
Constant	Concentration	Entry	R^2	Constant	Concentration	Entry	R^2
0.59	0.603H (0.181) [3.33]	−0.101E (0.027) [−3.77]	0.358	1.13	0.112H (0.135) [0.83]	−0.0224E (0.020) [−1.12]	0.040
0.56	0.680H (0.166) [4.09]	−0.449E/N (0.104) [−4.33]	0.386	1.08	0.178H (0.130) [1.38]	−0.0053E/N (0.076) [−0.07]	0.026
0.57	0.516CR$_1$ (0.163) [3.17]	−1.09E (0.261) [−4.18]	0.350	1.17	0.0183CR$_1$ (0.122) [0.15]	−0.029E (0.197) [−0.147]	0.033
0.55	0.573CR$_1$ (0.155) [3.69]	−4.68E/N (1.045) [−4.47]	0.366	1.12	0.077CR$_1$ (0.118) [0.65]	−0.025E/N (0.078) [−0.32]	0.008
0.43	0.511CR$_2$ (0.205) [2.49]	−0.108E (0.028) [−3.90]	0.322	0.91	0.036CR$_2$ (0.017) [2.08]	−0.010E (0.020) [0.51]	0.080
0.31	0.666CR$_2$ (0.181) [3.67]	−0.484E/N (0.103) [−4.68]	0.366	0.86	0.347CR$_2$ (0.134) [2.59]	+0.012E/N (0.080) [0.15]	0.078
0.16	0.770CR$_3$ (0.376) [2.05]	−0.114E (0.028) [−4.05]	0.307	0.56	0.650CR$_3$ (0.264) [2.46]	−0.0068E (0.019) [−0.35]	0.098
−0.15	1.107CR$_3$ (0.329) [3.34]	−0.500E/N (0.104) [4.80]	0.350	0.51	0.703CR$_3$ (0.239) [2.94]	+0.013E/N (0.076) [0.17]	0.097
0.95	−0.017N (0.018) [−0.92]	−0.129E (0.029) [−4.48]	0.279	1.24	−0.018N (0.013) [−1.38]	−0.017E (0.020) [−0.83]	0.054

Table 8.1 (continued)

Minimum unrestricted daytime fare, August 1980				Weighted average unrestricted coach daytime fare, July 1980			
Constant	Concentration	Entry	R^2	Constant	Concentration	Entry	R^2
1.05	$-0.042N$ (0.016) [-2.58]	$-0.536E/N$ (0.106) [-5.08]	0.317	1.25	$-0.023N$ (0.012) [-1.94]	$-0.014E/N$ (0.078) [-0.18]	0.046
0.81	$0.255\ 1/N$ (0.224) [1.14]	$-0.127E$ (0.028) [-4.53]	0.283	1.14	$0.123\ 1/N$ (0.160) [0.77]	$-0.023E$ (0.020) [-1.16]	0.039
0.73	$0.514\ 1/N$ (0.519) [2.58]	$-0.534E/N$ (0.105) [-5.07]	0.317	1.11	$0.196\ 1/N$ (0.146) [1.34]	$-0.022E/N$ (0.079) [-0.28]	0.025
0.81	$0.163CCR1(62)$ (0.047) [3.49]	$-0.106E$ (0.042) [-2.51]	0.308	0.85	$0.320CCR1(35)$ (0.183) [3.11]	$-0.007E$ (0.016) [-0.43]	0.124
0.77	$0.197CCR1(62)$ (0.048) [4.09]	$-0.290E/N$ (0.107) [2.71]	0.329	1.06	$0.123CCR1(39)$ (0.035) [3.49]	$+0.006E/N$ (0.075) [0.08]	0.130
0.73	$0.147CCR2(71)$ (0.069) [2.12]	$-0.107E$ (0.027) [-3.98]	0.246	0.84	$0.332CCR2(61)$ (0.099) [3.35]	$-0.0040E$ (0.071) [-0.056]	0.122
0.64	$0.215CCR2(71)$ (0.070) [3.06]	$-0.280E/N$ (0.111) [2.52]	0.167	1.10	$0.086CCR2(70)$ (0.050) [1.73]	$-0.0165E/N$ (0.018) [-0.91]	0.056
1.07	$0.123CCR3(90)$ (0.038) [3.22]	$-0.0002E$ (0.0185) [-0.01]	0.130	1.07	$0.123CCR3(90)$ (0.038) [3.22]	$-0.0002E$ (0.019) [-0.01]	0.130
1.06	$0.122CCR3(90)$ (0.036) [3.49]	$-0.006E/N$ (0.074) [0.38]	0.130	1.06	$0.122CCR3(90)$ (0.036) [3.49]	$+0.006E/N$ (0.074) [0.38]	0.130

The best fit for minimum unrestricted daytime coach fare was

$$0.586 + 0.5644H - 0.436E/N + 0.151SL - 0.087SL^2 \qquad R^2 = 0.458,$$
$$(0.107) \quad (0.1675) \qquad (0.079) \qquad (0.109) \qquad (0.040)$$
$$[5.45] \quad [3.37] \qquad [-4.40] \qquad [1.39] \qquad [-2.19]$$

where SL is stage length and is measured in thousands of miles. Fares rose out to a distance of 868 miles (553 to 859 miles with other concentration and entry indexes) and declined thereafter.

Stage length had a stronger effect on our average fare variable. The concentration coefficient still had the expected sign for all concentration indexes, but it only approached significance with CR_3. Entry had a negative effect in 10 out of 12 cases, but that effect was never statistically significant. The best fit for average unrestricted daytime coach fare was

$$0.705 + 0.325CR3 + 0.00297E/N + 0.431SL - 0.193SL^2 \quad R^2 = 0.595.$$
$$(0.159) \quad (0.167) \qquad (0.04950) \qquad (0.058) \qquad (0.021)$$
$$[4.43] \quad [1.95] \qquad [0.06] \qquad [7.48] \qquad [-9.02]$$

Stage length had a very strong effect here. Our average fare variable reached its maximum a 1,117 miles (1,112 to 1,122 miles with other concentration and entry variables). The sharp drop in the effect of $CR3$ from that estimated in table 8.4 suggests colinearity. In fact, the simple correlation between $CR3$ and SL is only -0.211. It is somewhat higher for other concentration measures reaching a maximum of -0.360 for the Herfindahl index.

Entry into Deregulated Airline Markets
Steven Berry

The now extensive literature on the price concentration relationship in airline city-pair markets provides evidence against the "contestable markets" hypothesis that potential competition alone is enough to enforce competitive outcomes. There is, however, still the possibility that *actual* entry in these markets will force prices down. If entry in airline city-pair markets is "easy," then rational potential entrants should choose to enter into concentrated markets. For example, in a free-entry Cournot model, the process of actual entry will force prices down.

In the traditional industrial organization framework, barriers to entry can impede the process of actual entry. These barriers might include cost advantages that stem from status as an incumbent. Also in a Cournot-type model the presence of economies of scale will prevent actual entry from driving price to marginal cost. Arguments for economies of scale as a barrier to entry are found in Bain (1956) and, interestingly, in Stigler (1987). There is also, of course, a very large literature on strategic entry-deterring behavior by incumbent firms.

In the airline industry, incumbency may offer several cost advantages. Incumbents have already paid the sunk costs of setting up a route. These sunk costs include the costs of publicizing its service, as well as the elevated costs and/or reduced revenue that may be expected in its early operations on the new route. Although these costs may be substantial, they are probably small compared to the sunk costs borne by a manufacturing firm that makes a large investment in firm-specific machinery.

The evidence for economies of scale in airline markets is mixed. Keeler (1978) reports that most econometric cost studies do not find evidence of economies of scale, although some engineering studies claim significant economies to plane size. Caves, Christensen, and Tretheway (1984) present an empirical cost function analysis that suggests that there are economies of scale for operation within a city-pair market, but not for the operation of a large route network. Their measure of an airlines network does not, however, take the "hub" structure of the network into account.

The fact that airlines are increasingly moving toward hubbed route networks provides evidence in favor of the engineering claim of economies of scale in aircraft size. A hubbed transportation network will increase costs by increasing the number of passenger-miles and by increasing the costs of transferring baggage and passenger. However, if there are economies of scale in aircraft size, these costs can be offset by the larger aircraft that a hubbed network can support.

The following section will provide a simple model of entry into airline markets that allows for the existence of economies of scale in city-pair markets and that will provide further evidence of the effect of market structure on entrants' profit expectations.

A Discrete Choice Model of Entry

Consider a model in which K potential entrants make an entry decision into a market that already contains N^1 incumbent firms. Each potential entrant will face fixed (and sunk) positive entry cost equal to F_k for the kth potential entrant. Postentry profits for an entering firm are $\pi(N^p, M) - F_k$, where $\pi(\ )$ is Cournot operating profits evaluated at N^p post entry firms and at a vector of market characteristics M.

Before we consider an equilibrium model of entry, we can consider some descriptive results based on this general framework. Note that if no other firm entered a given market, then entrant number 1 would enter if $\pi(N^1 + 1, M) > F_1$. This inequality condition is similar to the inequality conditions used in the traditional discrete choice framework. If we assume that there is no more than one entrant in each period and that F_1 is normally distributed, then we can estimate the parameters of the operating profits function π from a simple probit estimation. In the case with more than one potential entrant, we can think of F_1 as being the entry costs of the "most qualified" potential entrant.

Data for the analysis are from the Civil Aeronautics Board's Origin and Destination Survey of Air Passenger Traffic. This survey consists of a random sample of 10 percent of all domestic passenger tickets. The data set is from the Data Bank 4 summary of the O&D survey for the sumer quarter of 1980. The survey contains information on the number of passengers per quarter and passenger-miles per quarter broken down by firm within city pair for approximately 6,000 city pairs. Three quarters of retrospective information are provided. Information is for passengers carried "on-line." On-line passengers are those who do not switch airlines during their flight. Information is also available on the connecting portions of non-on-line flights, but there is no break down for nonstop passengers. We use a subsample of markets which consists of all routes connecting the 50 largest (by population) U.S. cities. This simplifies the task of collecting information on city characteristics.

The empirical work defines output quantity as number of on-line passengers. Following the work of Bailey et al. (1985), I define a firm as being "in" a market if it carries at least 10 passengers a day between the cities in the market pair.

The period of analysis is from the first quarter of 1979 to the third quarter of 1980. The year 1980 is appropriate because it is after the effective deregulation of the industry but before the air traffic controllers' strike which limited entry.

We would like to parameterize operating profits that control for market cost and demand conditions. Demand in a given city pair is assumed to depend on population and distance. Population is measured as the geometric mean of the population of the two cities and is in millions of persons. Distance is measured in thousands of miles. We expect that demand is larger as population increases and is smaller as distance increases. Marginal cost should increase with distance at a decreasing rate.

We also presume that entry will be affected by the number of "well-qualified" potential entrants in a market. The number of well-qualified entrants is defined to be the number of firms who already operate in at least one city of the city pair but who do not operate in this given city pair. A number of authors have suggested that these firms have the lowest cost of entry into airline markets. For example, these firms already have operating baggage-handling facilities and ticket counters in one of the two cities. Indeed, 98 percent of the entrants in our sample were well qualified (in our sense) prior to entry.

Some simple descriptive statistics on the data set are contained in table 8.2.

Results for the discrete choice entry model are provided in table 8.3. In the Cournot model with economies of scale, we expect entry to respond to cost and demand factors and to be more likely when the numbers of firms is small. We find evidence for both of these results in the estimated coefficients. Also, as suggested earlier, entry is more likely when the number of well-qualified entrants is large.

The results suggest that a decrease in the number of incumbents may be potentially offset by an increase in the probability of entry. However, the increase in the probability of entry is not large. Evaluated at the mean values of all other independent variables, a decrease in the number of firms from two to one will increase the probability of entry by 11 percent.

The results also provide some suggestion of the effects of economies of scale on the entry process. We find that at the mean values of the independent variables, the probability of entry given one incumbent is 0.20. However, in smaller markets the probability of entry is reduced. At an average city population of 500,000, the probability of entry is reduced to 0.165. This decline is not dramatic, but it does represent a 15 percent decline in the probability of entry.

An Equilibrium Model of Entry

The probit results in table 8.3 can be criticized because they are not based on any clear equilibrium notion that allows for a large number of potential entrants. We will therefore present a simple equilibrium model entry game that will suggest a somehat different approach to estimation.

Table 8.2
Summary statistics

	Number of observations: 917			
Variable	Mean	Maximum	Minimum	Standard deviation
Entry	0.2279	4.0000	0.0000	0.5004
Exits	0.1985	2.0000	0.0000	0.4382
N	2.0251	10.0000	1.0000	1.2240
$1/N$	0.6520	1.0000	0.1000	0.3046
Spread	0.0754	0.5542	0.0000	0.1081
Herfindahl	0.7274	1.0000	0.1889	0.2513
Well-qualified entrants	10.9444	19.0000	3.0000	3.3497
Population	2.1417	14.2025	0.7397	1.3770
Distance	1.0349	5.0950	0.0550	0.8467
Quantity	2.1705	60.3620	0.0910	4.5769

	Correlations				
Variable	Entry	Exits	N	$1/N$	Spread
Entry	1.0000	0.0275	0.1689	−0.1137	0.1344
Exits	0.0275	1.0000	0.3367	−0.3017	0.2555
N	0.1689	0.3367	1.0000	−0.8600	0.5567
$1/N$	−0.1137	−0.3017	−0.8600	1.0000	−0.6273
Spread	0.1344	0.2555	0.5567	−0.6273	1.0000
Herfindahl	−0.0800	−0.2558	−0.8029	0.9422	−0.3302
Well-qualified entrants	0.1671	0.1176	0.4000	−0.3956	0.2576
Population	0.2201	0.0683	0.6086	−0.4931	0.4236
Distance	0.0091	0.1051	−0.0170	0.0370	−0.0577

	Correlations				
Variable	Herfindahl	Well-qualified entrants	Population	Distance	Quantity
Quantity	0.2234	0.0314	0.6422	−0.4278	0.3697 #
Entry	−0.0800	0.1671	0.2201	0.0091	0.2234
Exits	−0.2558	0.1176	0.0683	0.1051	0.0314
N	−0.8029	0.4000	0.6086	−0.0170	0.6422
$1/N$	0.9422	−0.3956	−0.4931	0.0370	−0.4278
Spread	−0.3302	0.2576	0.4236	−0.0577	0.3697
Herfindahl	1.0000	−0.3687	−0.4154	0.0201	−0.3594
Well-qualified entrants	−0.3687	1.0000	0.4417	0.0898	0.2920
Population	−0.4154	0.4417	1.0000	0.0477	0.6521
Distance	0.0201	0.0898	0.0477	1.0000	−0.0937
Quantity	−0.3594	0.2920	0.6521	−0.0937	1.0000

Table 8.3
Probit results on entry

Dependent variable: entry
Observations: 1,170
Degrees of freedom: 1,164
-2^* Log likelihood: 1,112.147198

Variable	Parameter	t statistic	P value
Constant	-2.2430	-9.205	0.0000
Incumbent firms	-0.0806	-1.926	0.0540
Well-qualified entrants	0.0606	4.292	0.0000
Population	0.0995	2.302	0.0214
Distance	0.2027	1.515	0.1297
Distance squared	-0.0536	-1.594	0.1109

In our entry game the K potential entrants and the N^1 incumbent firms make simultaneous decisions on whether to be in or out of the market. Each firms has constant marginal cost, and as before, entrant k receives postentry profits of $\pi(N^p, M) - F_k$, where π is Cournot operating profits and F_k is a sunk entry costs. Incumbents are assumed to have no fixed costs; incumbent firms who choose to stay in receive $\pi(N^p, M)$. Firms who choose to stay "out" receive zero profits.

The Nash equilibrium to the entry game requires that each firm who chooses to stay in must make positive profits, conditional on the decisions of the other firms. In equilibrium, all incumbents remain "in" since Cournot operating profits are always positive given constant marginal costs. This no-exit result simplifies the estimation considerably.

The identities of the entering firms are not uniquely determined in equilibrium: all that is required is that $\pi(N^p) > F_k$ for potential entrants who enter and that $\pi(N^p) < F_k$ for potential entrants who do not enter.

Although the exact identity of the entering firms is not determined, the equilibrium is uniquely characterized by the following simple result:

Result 1: Entry occurs in the Nash equilibrium of the game described above if and only if $\pi(n^1 + 1) > F_1^*$, where N^1 is the number of incumbents and F_1^* is the lowest of the K entry costs.

In other words, entry occurs if and only if the "most-qualified" potential entrant would earn positive profits if it entered while no other potential entrant entered. Note that this does not ensure that the best-qualified potential entrant is the actual entrant. The proof of the result is a simple application of the definition of Nash equilibrium. A result similar to result 1 is that two or more firms will enter if and only if $\pi(n^1 + 2) > F_2^*$, where

F_2^* is the second lowest entry cost. This logic is pursued in the more complicated model found in Berry (1989).

Result 1 can be used as the basis for empirical estimation if we are willing to parameterize the operating profits term π as well as the process that generates the entry costs. A simple way to model entry costs for empirical work is to assume that each potential entrant draws its entry cost from an exponential distribution with mean M_k, with the draws assumed to be independent across firms. The exponential distribution has the advantage of being both theoretically and empirically tractable as well as ensuring that entry costs are nonnegative.

In particular, the exponential assumption allows for a simple derivation of the probability of entry in a given market. This probability can then be used in a traditional discrete choice framework to estimate the parameters of the operating profit term π as well as the parameters of the entry cost distribution.

Since the probability of entry is given by $\text{Prob}(F_1^* < \pi(n^1 + 1))$, we need to know the distribution of F_1^*. In other terms we want the distribution of the minimum order statistic of K^* single draws from K^* independent exponential distributions. Letting $v = \pi(n^1 + 1)$, the probability of entry is

$\text{Prob}(\min(F_1, F_2, \ldots, F_{K^*}) < v)$

$\quad = 1 - \text{Prob}(\min(F_1, F_2, \ldots, F_{K^*}) > v)$

$\quad = 1 - \text{Prob}(F_1 > v, F_2 > v, \ldots, F_{K^*} > v)$

$\quad = 1 - \text{Prob}(F_1 > v)\text{Prob}(F_2 > v)\ldots\text{Prob}(F_{K^*} > v)$

$\quad = 1 - \exp(-\text{sum}(v/\mu_k))$,

where μ_k is the mean of the kth entrant's cost distribution. Note that the last line of the equation uses the fact that for exponentially distributed variable x with mean M, the $\text{Prob}(x > v) = \exp(-v/M)$. In the simple case where $M_k = M$ for all k, the probability of entry reduces to

$$1 - \exp\left(-\frac{vK^*}{M}\right)$$

Following our earlier discussion, we assume that there are K_1 "well-qualified" entrants, who draw entry costs from a distribution with mean M_1, and $K_2 = K^* - K_1$ "less-qualified" entrants, who draw from a distribution with mean $M_2 > M_1$. The probability of entry then becomes

$$1 - \exp\left(-\left(\frac{K1}{M_1} + \frac{K2}{M_2}\right)v\right).$$

In empirical work that uses a discrete variable on the occurrence of entry in a market, the term $w = K1/M_1 + K2/M_2 = K1(1/M_1 - 1/M_2) + K^*/M_2$ will be identified only up to scale. Further the number of potential entrants, K^*, will typically be unobserved. I therefore scale K^*/M_2 to equal one and denote $(1/M_1 - 1/M_2)$ as α. The parameter α is increasing in the difference between the entry costs of "well" and "less" qualified entrants. This scaling gives $w = (1 + \alpha K_1)$, and a probability of entry of

$$1 - \exp(-(1 + \alpha K1)v).$$

We must still parameterize the operating profit v. We chose a to approximate the operating profits term by the simple expression $v = \exp(X\beta)$, where X is a vector of market characteristics and β is a vector of parameters to be estimated. This model is reduced form in the sense that it does not explicitly motivate the functional form of operating profits. The vector X should include the number of incumbent firms as well as variables discussed earlier that determine market costs and demand. This parameterization gives a probability of entry of

$$1 - \exp(-(1 + \alpha K_1)\exp(X\beta)).$$

Two estimation techniques are potentially appropriate. If we maintain an assumption that entry costs are uncorrelated between markets, the probability of entry can be used directly for maximum likelihood estimation. However, in airline markets the presence of network effects implies that entry costs may be correlated between markets. In this case we can define a dummy variable Y equal to one if entry occurs and equal to zero otherwise. Denoting the exogenous variables of the model as Z, we have that

$$E(y|Z) = \text{Prob(entry }|Z).$$

If we define a residual $u = y - \text{Prob(Entry }|Z)$, then $E(u|Z) = 0$. This last equality implies that $E(Z'u) = 0$, which suggests the use of a "method of moments" estimator (see Hansen 1982 and Hotz and Avery 1985). This method chooses a parameter vector that sets the sample analogue of $E(Z'u)$ as close to zero as possible. Hansen shows that this method is consistent even in the presence of a limited amount of cross-market correlation.

Results for the method of moments estimation are found in table 3.3. Once again, average city population and distance between the two cities are used to control for differences in cost and demand. Also the effect of

Table 8.4
Entry equation results

Observations: 917
Degrees of freedom: 910
Minimized value of objective function: 11.712408
Dependent variable: entry
Number of overidentifying restrictions: 5
Probability of entry at mean X: 0.1191

Variable	Coefficient	t statistic	P value	dPROB/dX
Constant	−4.01651	−5.0835	0.00000	−0.1680
$1/n$	0.73067	2.0052	0.04494	0.0306
Spread	1.11419	1.3592	0.17409	0.0466
Population	0.21727	3.8216	0.00013	0.0009
Distance	0.81309	2.8666	0.00415	0.0340
Distance squared	−0.26815	−3.1983	0.00138	−0.0112
Well-qualified potential entrants	0.15272	0.8666	0.38617	0.0064

incumbent firms is assumed to depend on the number of incumbents, measured by $1/N^1$ and by the "spread" in the distribution of firm market shares. The spread of market shares is measured by the sum of the squared deviations from the mean market share and is denoted NV. Note that the Herfindahl index, a traditional measure of market structure, is given by $H = 1/n^1 + NV$, so the present formulation includes the Herfindahl index as a special case (see Scherer 1980, 59).

We note from table 8.4 that the "market structure" variables have a significant impact on entry as do the cost and demand variables. This is consistent with a Cournot model of operating profits. The coefficient on the number of well-qualified entrants has the predicted sign, but we cannot reject the hypothesis that its coefficient is equal to zero.

When we evaluate the probability of entry at the mean of the x variables, we find that a reduction in the number of incumbent firms from two to one would increase the probability of entry by about 0.015, an increase of about 12.8 percent when the predicted probability of entry is evaluated at the means of the other independent variables. This increase has the expected sign, but its magnitude is not large: again, a dramatic increase in firm concentration will not lead to a dramatic increase in the probability of entry.

By now (January 1989) everybody knows that concentration raises airline fares. As a result of a series of mergers approved by the Department of Transportation in 1986 to 1988, many major hubs have found themselves dominated by one airline. Thereafter traffic into and out of those hubs, and in the airlines generally, became much more expensive in terms of both unrestricted fares and special deals. The newspapers reported the effect, and a half dozen economists seem to be working on the topic. The results show one of the most impressive upward adjustments in price with changes in concentration in our recent history.

Some of the acquired firms were losing money and faced bankruptcy, but that was not at all true of the big horizontal acquisition that started the airlines merger wave, the merger of Northwest and Republic airlines. Republic had been formed earlier in a pair of clearly pro-competitive mergers of North Central Airlines with Southern Airlines in 1979 and with Hughes Air West in 1980. All of them were local service airlines that served three quite different regions. Put together and renamed Republic Airlines, they became a potential transcontinental trunk. Republic Airlines created three hubs in Minneapolis, Detroit, and Memphis, something that would have taken years or decades before deregulation. It had to make heavy investment in low fares and/or half empty flights while building up its long-distance business, and many observers doubted that it would be able to handle the losses. It lost money each year from 1980 through 1983, but in 1984 it earned profits of $100 million and in 1985 it earned $177 million. By then it was selling almost as many domestic passenger-miles as their main competitor, Northwest. At that point Northwest, with net income of $73 million, set out to acquire Republic.[2] Under the Airlines Deregulation Act, which was passed in 1978, the decision to approve mergers lay with the Department of Transportation during the first ten years. The Antitrust Division argued against the merger and lost. The horizontal merger of two large prosperous, equal-sized trunks serving many identical routes was approved.

After that decision, many mergers were proposed and approved quickly before the DOT's power in the area ran out at the end of 1988. Many of these acquired firms really were losing money. Where that was true, some sort of merger was probably unavoidable, but it did not have to be with a trunk sharing the same hub. If Ozark had been acquired by Northwest or any other airline that did not serve St. Louis, or for which St. Louis was a minor part of its business, then travelers to and from St. Louis would have enjoyed more competition, not less. In general, deregulation had yielded a decade of competition in the airline industry, but the crazy merger policy of the DOT then took much of it away again.

Notes

1. Weights were taken from the 1980 *Origin and Destination Surveys of Passenger Traffic*, Air Transport Association, generously supplied to us by United Airlines. Coach pricing data were gathered from the *Official Airline Guide*, North American Edition, July 1, 1980.

2. The profit and volume figures come from *Moodies Transportation Manuals* for 1985 and 1986. Part of the reason why Republic's profits were so high compared with Northwest's is that Republic was able to reduce its taxes by writing off the losses it had incurred in 1980 to 1983.

References

Bailey, E., D. R. Graham, and D. P. Kaplan. 1985. *Deregulating the Airlines*. Cambridge, MA: MIT Press.

Bain, J. 1956. *Barriers to New Competition*. Cambridge, MA: Harvard University Press.

Berry, S. 1988. "Entry in the Airline industry." Ph.D. dissertation. Madison: University of Wisconsin.

Call, G. D., and T. E. Keeler. 1985. "Airline Deregulation, Fares, and Competitive Behavior: Some Empirical Evidence." In A. F. Daugherty (ed.), *Analytical Studies in Transport Economies*. Cambridge: Cambridge University Press.

Caves, D. W., L. R. Christensen, and M. W. Tretheway. 1984. "Economies of Density versus Economies of Scale: Why Trunk Local Service Airline Costs Differ." *The Rand Journal of Economics* 15 : 4 (Winter) 471−489.

Graham, D. R., Kaplan, D. P., and D. S. Sibley. 1983. "Efficiency and Competition in the Airline Industry." *Bell Journal of Economics* 14 : 1 (Spring), 118−138.

Hansen, L. P. 1982. "Large Sample Properties of Generalized Method of Moments Estimators." *Econometrics* 50(4) (July), 1029−54.

Hotz, V. J., and R. B. Avery. 1985 "Estimating Systems of Nonlinear Equations with Limited Dependent Variables." Discussion Paper 85-19. Economics Research Center, NORC, Chicago.

Keeler, T. 1980. "The Revolution in Airline Regulation." in L. W. Weiss and M. Klass (eds.), *Case Studies in Regulation*. Boston: Little, Brown.

Keeler, T., and M. Abrahams. 1981. "Market Service Quality in the Airline Industry under Deregulation." In W. Sichel and T. Geis (eds.), *Applications of Economics Principles to Public Utilities*. Ann Arbor: University of Michigan Press.

Moore, T. 1986. "U.S. Airline Deregulation, Its Effects on Passengers, Capital, and Labor." *Journal of Law and Economics* 29:1 (April).

Morrison, S., and C. Winston. 1986. *The Economic Effects of Airline Deregulation*. Washington, DC. Brookings Institute.

Scherer, F. M. 1980. *Industrial Market Structure and Economic Performance*. Boston: Houghton Mifflin.

Stigler, G. 1987 *The Theory of Price*. 4th ed. New York: Macmillan.

9   Retailing

Retailing might seem to be an especially difficult area in which to study concentration and price because of the many products involved. The first case, gas stations, involves the sale of one product, gasoline, so the multple product feature is circumvented.

The supermarket price study takes a different approach. The authors deal with the multiple product problems by pricing a fixed market basket specified even to the brand and package size. They make some attempt to control for production cost, and they get quite plausible results.

Concentration and Price in Gasoline Retailing
Howard P. Marvel

This section reports the results of a series of studies of the gasoline prices reported by the Bureau of Labor Statistics (BLS) for the 1960s and the 1970s for 22 of the BLS's 23 monthly reporting cities, excluding Honolulu. The BLS reports high and low prices for premium and for regular gasoline each month.

The first study (Marvel 1978) covered the years 1964 to 1971. The results were reported in two forms. The first, reproduced in table 9.1, was based on the average price in one of the four price categories over the entire period. Transport costs are from Oklahoma and date from 1961. Concentration is measured by the Herfindahl index based on 1970 market shares. In these overall average regressions concentration had the expected positive effect on price throughout, but the relationship was quite weak for the two high prices. Table 9.2 shows annual coefficients for three variables from each of the regular gasoline regressions. Concentration always had a positive effect on the low price, and it was significant in every year except

Table 9.1
Determinants of retail gasoline price levels in 22 cities, 1964–1971 (standard errors in parentheses, t ratios in brackets)

Dependent variable price series	Constant	Transport cost	(Transport cost)^2	Herfindahl index	Mean taxes	Population
Premium high	0.311	3.076	−143.800	0.229	0.585	0.135
	(0.022)	(1.472)	(19.889)	(0.128)	(0.344)	(0.058)
	[14.43]	[2.09]	[−1.80]	[1.79]	[1.70]	[2.32]
Premium low	0.200	6.372	−231.000	0.901	0.510	−0.056
	(0.292)	(2.004)	(112.683)	(0.192)	(0.429)	(0.076)
	[6.86]	[3.18]	[−2.05]	[4.70]	[1.19]	[−0.74]
Regular high	0.255	1.772	−83.670	0.203	0.925	0.137
	(0.023)	(1.554)	(84.516)	(0.137)	(0.381)	(0.059)
	[11.01]	[1.14]	[−0.99]	[1.48]	[2.43]	[2.31]
Regular low	0.186	5.960	−228.000	0.807	0.379	−0.114
	(0.025)	(1.723)	(96.610)	(0.167)	(0.383)	(0.064)
	[7.36]	[3.46]	[−2.36]	[4.84]	[0.99]	(−1.77)

Note: Method of estimation is weighted least squares. Dependent variable = mean retail gasoline (pump) price, 1964–1971. Mean transport cost = 0.825×10^{-2}.

1965. Its effect on the high price was rather random and never statistically significant in 1964 to 1968, but it had a significant positive effect on the high as well as the low prices in 1969 to 1971.

A second study working with the same data in Geithman, Marvel, and Weiss (1981) assigned a series of dummy variables for four-firm concentration ratios of less than 40, 40–44, 45–49, and 50–55, using overall averages like those in table 9.1. The results are shown in table 9.3. Using this overall set of average prices, virtually no concentration could be identified in the high prices, but the effect was very strong for the low prices.

It appeared that there was a critical concentration ratio using $CR4$ of about 50. It was about 40 using $CR3$ and about 35 using $CR2$. The $CR2$ data yielded a slightly better fit than the $CR4$ data did.

A third as yet unpublished study uses similar regressions from the 1970s to analyze the attempt of the federal government to control gasoline prices in the period October 1973 through December 1978. In these years the BLS reported only the mean price observed in a city in a month, so that became the dependent variable. The study's primary concern was to characterize the determinants of the price of gasoline as the controls period developed, so separate regressions were run for each month. Several variables were revised. Because of the end of import quotas, the transport costs were computed from the nearest major refining center rather than from

Table 9.2
Annual average price level regressions, regular grade gasoline: selected coefficients for
22 cities (standard errors in parentheses, t ratios in brackets)

Year	Price series	Transport cost	(Transport cost)^2	Herfindahl index
1964	High	2.222	−135.7	0.366
		(2.339)	(131.75)	(0.261)
		[0.95]	[−1.03]	[1.40]
	Low	3.490	−194.4	0.684
		(2.664)	(153.1)	(0.283)
		[1.31]	[−1.27]	[2.42]
1965	High	−0.456	38.48	−0.140
		(2.073)	(116.61)	(0.215)
		[−0.22]	[0.33]	[−0.65]
	Low	2.456	−52.84	0.321
		(2.579)	(146.78)	(0.147)
		[0.95]	[−0.36]	[1.30]
1966	High	0.250	15.25	−0.075
		(1.667)	(89.71)	(0.160)
		[0.15]	[0.17]	[−0.47]
	Low	4.344	−145.4	0.351
		(1.914)	(108.5)	(0.183)
		[2.27]	[−1.34]	[1.92]
1967	High	0.006	28.93	−0.083
		(1.50)	(82.66)	(0.136)
		[0.00]	[0.35]	[−0.61]
	Low	3.509	−107.8	0.494
		(2.005)	(112.3)	(0.194)
		[1.75]	[−0.96]	[2.55]
1968	High	1.197	−34.77	0.175
		(1.640)	(89.15)	(0.142)
		[0.73]	[−0.39]	[1.23]
	Low	5.188	−186.6	0.771
		(2.459)	(136.2)	(0.225)
		[2.11]	[−1.37]	[3.43]
1969	High	2.759	−146.5	0.274
		(1.524)	(83.2)	(0.130)
		[1.81]	[−1.76]	[2.11]
	Low	7.157	−253.3	0.867
		(2.324)	(127.9)	(0.213)
		[3.08]	[−1.98]	[4.08]
1970	High	4.615	−230.6	0.559
		(2.607)	(138.1)	(0.202)
		[1.77]	[−1.67]	[2.77]
	Low	14.45	−651.4	1.507
		(4.69)	(254.8)	(0.406)
		[3.08]	[−2.56]	[3.71]

Table 9.2 (continued)

Year	Price series	Transport cost	(Transport cost)²	Herfindahl index
1971	High	3.083	−171.8	0.474
		(1.976)	(105.4)	(0.155)
		[1.56]	[−1.63]	[3.05]
	Low	9.863	−350.1	1.336
		(3.437)	(189.2)	(0.295)
		[2.87]	[−1.85]	[4.53]

Table 9.3
Estimated effects of four-firm concentration ratios on average retail gasoline prices in 22 cities, 1964−1971 (standard errors in parentheses, t ratios in brackets)

	Regression coefficients: Concentration ratio class				
	Less than 40	40−44	45−49	50−55	R^2
Number of cities	4	3	8	7	
High premium price	—	0.0061	−0.0007	0.0021	0.61
		(0.0085)	(0.0078)	(0.0088)	
		[0.72]	[−0.90]	[0.24]	
Low premium price	—	0.0120	0.0167	0.0420	0.75
		(0.0125)	(0.0108)	(0.0135)	
		[0.96]	[1.55]	[3.11]	
High regular price	—	0.0024	−0.0033	0.0012	0.63
		(0.0083)	(0.0077)	(0.0092)	
		[0.29]	[−0.43]	[0.13]	
Low regular price	—	0.0130	0.0130	0.0374	0.75
		(0.0109)	(0.0094)	(0.0121)	
		[1.19]	[1.38]	[3.09]	
	Estimated prices based on these coefficients[a]				
High premium price	0.385	0.392	0.385	0.387	
Low premium price	0.316	0.328	0.332	0.358	
High regular price	0.347	0.350	0.344	0.349	
Low regular price	0.282	0.295	0.295	0.320	

a. Estimates based on mean values of tax, transport cost, and transport cost squared multiplied by their coefficients plus the concentration dummy coefficients at the top of this table plus the intercept term.

Table 9.4
Determinants of regular grade retail gasoline prices in 22 cities, October 1973–September 1975 (standard errors in parentheses, t ratios in brackets)

Month	Constant	Transport cost	(Transport cost)^2	Tax	Herfindahl index	Self-sufficiency ratio
1973						
October	0.33	0.04	−0.03	0.77	0.36	−0.005
	(0.02)	(0.01)	(0.01)	(0.15)	(0.15)	(0.002)
	[16.60]	[2.94]	[−3.02]	[5.15]	[2.35]	[2.54]
November	0.36	0.05	−0.03	0.71	0.39	−0.008
	(0.02)	(0.02)	(0.01)	(0.16)	(0.18)	(0.003)
	[16.38]	[2.74]	[−2.77]	[4.35]	[2.22]	[−2.39]
December	0.36	0.06	−0.03	0.71	0.37	−0.008
	(0.02)	(0.02)	(0.01)	(0.17)	(0.18)	(0.003)
	[14.97]	[3.11]	[−2.99]	[4.26]	[2.10]	[−2.53]
1974						
January	0.42	0.05	−0.03	0.68	0.12	−0.0006
	(0.03)	(0.02)	(0.01)	(0.22)	(0.24)	(0.0003)
	[15.01]	[2.44]	[−2.65]	[3.09]	[0.49]	[−1.81]
February	0.44	0.04	−0.02	0.72	0.26	−0.007
	(0.03)	(0.02)	(0.01)	(0.19)	(0.23)	(0.002)
	[17.19]	[2.06]	[−2.14]	[3.75]	[1.11]	[−2.49]
March	0.45	0.04	−0.02	0.82	0.22	−0.004
	(0.03)	(0.02)	(0.01)	(0.21)	(0.27)	(0.004)
	[14.96]	[1.77]	[−1.46]	[3.89]	[0.81]	[−1.05]
April	0.46	0.02	−0.01	0.84	−0.07	−0.001
	(0.02)	(0.01)	(0.01)	(0.14)	(0.19)	(0.001)
	[21.87]	[1.50]	[−0.74]	[5.96]	[−0.36]	[−0.47]
May	0.48	0.04	−0.02	0.61	0.41	−0.006
	(0.02)	(0.01)	(0.01)	(0.13)	(0.17)	(0.002)
	[25.08]	[2.99]	[−2.16]	[4.82]	[2.39]	[−2.63]
June	0.49	0.05	−0.02	0.66	0.24	−0.005
	(0.02)	(0.02)	(0.01)	(0.12)	(0.17)	(0.001)
	[26.49]	[3.29]	[−2.55]	[5.51]	[1.43]	[−2.29]
July	0.48	0.06	−0.03	0.74	0.24	−0.005
	(0.02)	(0.01)	(0.01)	(0.12)	(0.37)	(0.002)
	[25.74]	[4.19]	[−3.60]	[6.07]	[1.41]	[−2.23]
August	0.46	0.06	−0.03	0.62	0.42	−0.003
	(0.02)	(0.01)	(0.01)	(0.12)	(0.17)	(0.002)
	[24.91]	[4.22]	[−3.54]	[5.05]	[2.50]	[−1.59]
September	0.45	0.06	−0.03	0.65	0.42	−0.001
	(0.02)	(0.02)	(0.01)	(0.14)	(0.19)	(0.002)
	[21.71]	[3.85]	[−3.35]	[4.62]	[2.20]	[−0.54]

Table 9.4 (continued)

Month	Constant	Transport cost	(Transport cost)^2	Tax	Herfindahl index	Self-sufficiency ratio
October	0.43	0.06	−0.03	0.49	0.62	−0.002
	(0.02)	(0.02)	(0.01)	(0.15)	(0.19)	(0.002)
	[20.87]	[3.48]	[−3.10]	[3.36]	[3.18]	[−0.90]
November	0.42	0.07	−0.03	0.51	0.73	−0.003
	(0.02)	(0.02)	(0.01)	(0.16)	(0.21)	(0.003)
	[18.98]	[3.75]	[−3.58]	[3.24]	[3.54]	[−1.10]
December	0.41	0.06	−0.03	0.52	0.79	−0.002
	(0.02)	(0.02)	(0.01)	(0.16)	(0.21)	(0.002)
	[18.39]	[3.40]	[−3.16]	[3.28]	[3.75]	[−0.93]
1975						
January	0.43	0.06	−0.03	0.68	0.72	−0.003
	(0.02)	(0.02)	(0.01)	(0.17)	(0.25)	(0.003)
	[17.26]	[2.81]	[−2.83]	[4.05]	[2.86]	[−1.20]
February	0.42	0.05	−0.03	0.59	0.81	−0.002
	(0.03)	(0.02)	(0.01)	(0.17)	(0.26)	(0.002)
	[16.44]	[2.60]	[−2.55]	[3.40]	[3.08]	[−0.88]
March	0.43	0.06	−0.03	0.53	0.86	−0.003
	(0.03)	(0.02)	(0.01)	(0.18)	(0.28)	(0.003)
	[15.57]	[2.51]	[−2.44]	[2.87]	[3.09]	[−0.98]
April	0.44	0.06	−0.03	0.55	0.87	−0.004
	(0.03)	(0.02)	(0.01)	(0.19)	(0.29)	(0.003)
	[15.48]	[2.48]	[−2.43]	[2.89]	[3.01]	[−1.31]
May	0.45	0.06	−0.03	0.43	0.84	−0.003
	(0.03)	(0.02)	(0.01)	(0.18)	(0.28)	(0.003)
	[16.72]	[2.54]	[−2.46]	[2.39]	[3.05]	[−1.05]
June	0.48	0.05	−0.03	0.39	0.84	−0.004
	(0.03)	(0.02)	(0.01)	(0.17)	(0.26)	(0.003)
	[18.60]	[2.65]	[−2.41]	[2.33]	[3.22]	[−1.42]
July	0.51	0.04	−0.02	0.44	0.64	−0.003
	(0.02)	(0.02)	(0.01)	(0.16)	(0.25)	(0.003)
	[20.41]	[2.19]	[−1.82]	[2.79]	[2.52]	[−1.02]
August	0.51	0.05	−0.03	0.42	0.72	−0.004
	(0.03)	(0.02)	(0.01)	(0.16)	(0.25)	(0.003)
	[20.27]	[2.69]	[−2.32]	[2.65]	[2.83]	[−1.33]
September	0.51	0.05	−0.02	0.46	0.72	−0.003
	(0.03)	(0.02)	(0.01)	(0.16)	(0.26)	(0.003)
	[20.14]	[2.49]	[−2.21]	[2.81]	[2.80]	[−1.16]

Oklahoma. The average self-sufficiency ratio of the three largest gasoline marketers in the city was inserted as another independent variable because it might be expected to affect price under the control system that existed in the United States in that period. The results appear in table 9.4. The Herfindahl index had the predicted effect in the three months following the Yom Kippur War in 1973 and every month after July 1974, but its only significant effect in the first seven months of 1974 occurred in May of that year. This and other evidence[1] leads to the conclusion that price controls had relatively little effect during most of the period examined except for the first half of 1974 which was the one period of major shortages as well.

The Concentration-Price Relationship in Food Retailing
Bruce W. Marion

This section reports on two studies of the effects of market structure on prices in food retailing. Supermarkets are emphasized rather than all food retailing. We feel that prices should be defined in terms of type of store. It would be a major source of error to take some prices from convenience stores and others from supermarkets.

The JEC Study

The first study by Marion, Mueller, Cotterill, Geithman, and Schmelzer (1979) grew out of data collected by the Joint Economic Committee. It requested data on sales, profits, and prices from a number of large chains. The crucial request was for price comparisons made in October 1974. Three large chains provided extensive price information for 32 Standard Metropolitan Statistical Areas (SMSAs) in which one or more of the chains operated. Using these prices, we estimated the cost of a "market basket" containing 94 comparable grocery products. Only items that were identical as to brand, product, and size were included. Fresh fruits and vegetables, dairy products, and fresh meats were excluded from the "market basket" because of lack of data and difficulty in comparing quality. In total, we had 36 firm-in-market observations in 32 SMSAs. Twenty-three of the observations were from one chain, nine from a second chain, and four from a third. Two market basket values were computed, one based only on national brands and the second including private brands.

These market basket values were regressed on such variables as store size, SMSA size measured by grocery store sales, growth in grocery sales in the SMSA, average union wage rate in SMSA super markets, and "market rivalry" measured by the absolute change between 1972 and 1974 of the combined market shares of the four leading firms of 1974.

We tried a variety of concentration variables including $CR2$, $CR3$, $CR4$, H, and $\sqrt{H}$. These were mainly based on all grocery store sales, but $CR4$ based on just supermarket sales was also tried. Market share or relative market shares was included in most of our regressions. Relative market share is simply a firm's market share divided by $CR4$. We expected all of the concentration and market share variables to yield positive regression coefficients.

The results appear in table 9.5. The coefficients for concentration and market share are always positive and significant. Equations 1a through 1f evaluate the other variables. A comparison of 1a, 1b, and 1c shows that market rivalry makes a big difference. Prices are distinctly lower when market shares are very unstable, including relative market share, or later, market share. However, CR is still very significant. What we think of as the basic model appears in equation 1f. Several alternative concentration measures are tried in equations 1g, 1h, 1i, and 1k. $CR3$ offers the best fit, but the differences are not great. On lines 1j and 1m we substitute ordinary market share for relative market share. The substitution of market share reduced the coefficients on the concentration variables, although they remain clearly significant.

In regression 2c the dependent variable is the price of a market basket based on national brands only. The coefficients of interest barely change. The last equation contains two changes from 1c. Mean store size was dropped, and concentration was based on supermarket sales alone rather than sales of all grocery stores. Supermarket concentration figures were not available at the time of the JEC study. Dropping mean store size seems to weaken the effect of relative market share (see line 1e as well). The effect of substituting a supermarket concentration ratio for the grocery store concentration ratio is slight.

The overall effect of these experiments is to leave the original conclusion strongly in tact. In all of the models run, the effects of concentration, relative market share, and absolute market share are always positive and always highly significant.

These data were rerun by Geithman, Marvel, and Weiss (1981) to test for evidence of a critical level of concentration. Dummy variables were used for various ranges in concentration instead of the continuous variables for $CR2$ and $CR4$. The results are summarized in table 9.6. There is little

Table 9.5
Multiple regression equations explaining cost of a grocery basket of three chains in 36 SMSAs, 1974 (standard errors in parentheses, t ratios in brackets)

Equation number and dependent variable[a]	Intercept	Measure of concentration	Market concentration[b]	Relative firm market share (RFMS)	Firm market share (FMS)	Mean store size (SS)	Market growth (MG)	Market size (MS)	Market rivalry (MR)	Union wage rate (WG)	R/R^2	F Value
1a (NPC)	91.05	CR_4	17.097 (3.530) [4.842]ᶜ			-0.004 (0.002) [-2.299]ᵈ	-0.086 (0.021) [-4.103]ᶜ		-0.555 (0.096) [-5.805]ᶜ		0.59	13.36ᶜ
1b (NPC)	91.05	CR_4	11.957 (4.277) [2.796]ᶜ	10.284 (2.959) [3.475]ᶜ		-0.007 (0.002) [-3.141]ᶜ	-0.062 (0.026) [-2.405]ᵈ				0.38	6.30ᶜ
1c (NPC)	90.67	CR_4	15.645 (3.216) [4.864]ᶜ	6.582 (2.284) [2.882]ᶜ		-0.006 (0.002) [-3.148]ᶜ	-0.078 (0.019) [-4.067]ᶜ		-0.475 (0.091) [-5.247]ᶜ		0.66	14.87ᶜ
1d (NPC)	90.67	CR_4	15.259 (3.591) [4.249]ᶜ	6.449 (2.376) [2.714]ᶜ		-0.005 (0.003) [-1.931]	-0.078 (0.020) [-3.975]ᶜ	-0.158 (0.61) [-0.259]	-0.485 (0.099) [-4.875]ᶜ		0.65	12.02ᶜ
1e (NPC)	89.93	CR_4	11.121 (3.01) [3.694]ᶜ	5.025 (2.359) [2.130]ᵈ			-0.066 (0.019) [-3.400]ᶜ	-1.019 (0.437) [-2.333]ᵈ	-0.562 (0.095) [-5.917]ᶜ		0.62	12.53ᵃ
1f (NPC)	87.00	CR_4	16.074 (3.461) [4.644]ᶜ	6.259 (2.274) [2.752]ᶜ		-0.005 (0.003) [-1.781]ᵈ	-0.082 (0.020) [-4.110]ᶜ	-0.214 (0.601) [-0.356]	-0.518 (0.110) [-4.724]ᶜ	0.591 (1.033) [0.572]	0.69	11.89ᶜ
1g (NPC)	86.83	CR_3	16.278 (3.374) [4.825]ᶜ	5.563 (2.248) [2.475]ᶜ		-0.005 (0.003) [-1.900]ᵈ	-0.079 (0.019) [-4.092]ᶜ	-0.175 (0.589) [-0.297]	-0.510 (0.107) [-4.745]ᶜ	0.846 (1.017) [0.832]	0.70	12.44ᶜ
1h (NPC)	88.92	CR_2	16.494 (3.767) [4.378]ᶜ	5.46 (2.348) [2.325]ᶜ		-0.005 (0.003) [-1.641]	-0.073 (0.020) [-3.671]ᶜ	-0.324 (0.609) [-0.532]	-0.555 (0.113) [-4.896]ᶜ	0.689 (1.060) [0.650]	0.68	11.11ᶜ

Table 9.5 (continued)

Equation number and dependent variable[a]	Intercept	Measure of concentration	Market concentration[b]	Relative firm market share (RFMS)	Firm market share (FMS)	Mean store size (SS)	Market growth (MG)	Market size (MS)	Market rivalry (MR)	Union wage rate (WG)	R/R²	F Value
1i (NPC)	89.49	H	31.605 (9.51) [3.323]c	4.874 (2.632) [1.852]c		-0.002 (0.003) [-0.737]	-0.077 (0.023) [-3.365]c	-0.776 (0.645) [-1.204]	-0.507 (0.124) [-4.096]c	0.830 (1.167) [0.711]	0.61	8.47c
1j (NPC)	90.16	H	24.730 (10.748) [2.301]c		9.968 (5.112) [1.950]c	-0.003 (0.003) [-0.940]	-0.078 (0.023) [-3.449]c	-0.695 (0.648) [-1.072]	-0.503 (0.122) [-4.086]c	0.887 (1.159) [0.765]	0.61	8.62c
1k (NPC)	87.20	$\sqrt{H}$	21.053 (6.198) [3.396]c	4.886 (2.613) [1.870]c		-0.001 (0.002) [-0.492]	-0.078 (0.023) [-3.413]c	-0.798 (0.638) [-1.251]	-0.522 (0.123) [-4.240]c	0.554 (1.161) [0.477]	0.61	8.63c
1m (NPC)	92.54	CR_4	12.680 (3.612) [3.511]c	11.518 (4.266) [2.700]c		-0.006 (0.002) [-3.163]c	-0.082 (0.019) [-4.234]c		-0.484 (0.091) [-5.314]c		0.65	14.32c
2c (NC)	90.74	CR_4	14.624 (3.17) [4.607]c	6.604 (2.255) [2.929]c		-0.004 (0.002) [-2.048]d	-0.069 (0.109) [-3.655]c		-0.527 (0.089) [-5.898]c		0.68	15.83c
3c (NPC)	88.74	$SMCR_4$	13.321 (3.192) [4.173]d	4.458 (2.197) [2.029]d			-0.120 (0.032) [-3.703]c		-0.394 (0.093) [-4.236]c		0.62	14.07c

Source: Marion et al. (1979a, 1979b), plus additional runs.

Note: Numbers in brackets are t values. The statistical significance of the regression coefficients for the various measures of concentration, RFMS, FMS, SS, MR, and WG were tested by means of a one-tail t test; MG tested by means of a two-tailed t test.

a. The dependent variable (NPC) in equations 1a through 1m and 3c is the price of a grocery basket of national brand and private label products. The dependent variable (NC) in equation 2c is the cost of a grocery basket of only national brand products.

b. All grocery store sales are used as the product market in calculating market share and concentration figures except for equation 3c which is based upon supermarket sales in 1974.

c. Significant at 1 percent level.

d. Significant at 5 percent level.

Table 9.6
Coefficients of concentration dummies and their standard errors by level of two-firm and four-firm concentration ratio (standard errors in parentheses, t ratios in brackets)

Concentration	CR_2 regression coefficient	n	CR_4 regression coefficient	n
20–25	—	3		
25.1–30	2.127 (1.313) [1.62]	8		
30.1–35	1.960 (1.443) [1.36]	8		
35.1–40	3.414 (1.547) [2.21]	8	—	3
40.1–45	2.494 (1.419) [1.76]	4	3.221 (1.157) [2.05]	8
45.1–50	6.174 (1.751) [3.53]	2	4.112 (1.408) [2.92]	7
50.1–55			3.397 (1.387) [2.45]	7
55.1–60			4.512 (1.265) [3.57]	5
60.1–65	7.894 (2.133) [3.70]	2	5.837 (1.366) [4.27]	3
65.1 or more			9.235 (1.890) [4.89]	2
R^2	0.68		0.72	

Source: Geithman, Marvel, and Weiss 1981 plus additional runs by author.

evidence of a critical concentration ratio. A positive relationship between CR4 and prices is apparent even at low concentration levels. The coefficients on CR2 in the first two cells are significant at the 10 percent level; the coefficients in the remaining cells are significantly different from the base cell at the 1 or 5 percent levels. The explanatory power of these models is similar to the models using a continuous linear variable for concentration. These results confirm the earlier finding that CR4 is preferred to CR2 as a measure of concentration in this particular study.

Cotterill Study

During 1981 a court challenge to the Vermont blue law provided an opportunity to replicate the JEC study's market structure–price analysis (Cotterill 1986). The Vermont market basket of price-checked items contained the 94 grocery products analyzed in the JEC study, plus frozen foods, dairy products, and health and beauty aids. Prices were aggregated to produce a weighted price index value for 35 supermarkets in 18 markets. There was a 12 percent range in price across the 35 observations.

Vermont contains only one SMSA, Burlington, and it is far smaller than any of the metropolitan areas covered by the JEC study. Cotterill's remaining observations were for smaller cities and towns. He had price data for 35 supermarkets in 18 towns. Three of these towns contained only one supermarket, and only four had more than four supermarket companies (i.e., CR4 was 100 in 14 of the 18 markets). Two chains operated 26 of the 35 supermarkets.

Cotterill's basic format was similar to that used in the JEC study, but most of the control variables differed. Moreover in most of his regressions he calculated supermarket market share and concentration using the sum of supermarket sales rather than all grocery store sales in the denominator.

His results appear in table 9.7. CR1 fit better than CR2 and CR2 fit better than CR4 but the Herfindahl index did better than any of the CR_i's. Presumably this is because CR4 throws away information in markets with three or fewer firms. Of course the Herfindahl index avoids this problem. The effect of concentration on retail food prices declines markedly when the three towns with only one supermarket are excluded, but concentration still has a significant effect (see line 3 for the Herfindahl indexes and line 6 for CR1). The second equation offers the best fit. Independent supermarkets seem to charge higher prices. The control variables are plausible but all somewhat different from those used in the JEC study. Only the store size variables are significant.

Table 9.7
Multiple regression equations explaining the price level of Vermont supermarkets, August 1981

Sample and Number of OBS	Measure of market concentration	market concentration	Firm market share MS	Firm market share RMS	Independent supermarket	Square feet (1,000)	Square feet squared (millions)	Sales per square foot	Distance to warehouse	Population growth 1970–1980 (%)	1980 Per capita income (1,000)	Intercept	R² and F ratio
1. All firms, 35	Supermarket Herfindahl	8.912 (1.62) [5.49]ᵃ			2.24 (0.82) [2.72]ᵇ	0.007 (0.085) [0.82]		4.665 (2.22) [2.10]ᵇ	0.0019 (0.006) [0.33]	−0.017 (0.047) [0.36]	0.044 (0.25) [0.17]	99.84	0.63 (6.46)ᵃ
2. All firms, 35	Supermarket Herfindahl	7.779 (1.45) [5.37]ᵃ			2.07 (0.82) [2.51]ᵇ	−0.730 (0.30) [2.37]ᵇ	0.0268 (0.011) [2.35]ᵇ		0.0017 (0.006) [0.30]	−0.041 (0.047) [0.87]	0.175 (0.21) [0.82]	107.05	0.64 (6.82)ᵃ
3. All firms except monopolies, 32	Supermarket Herfindahl	6.476 (2.41) [2.68]ᵇ			2.11 (0.82) [2.57]ᵃ	−0.810 (0.31) [2.60]ᵇ	0.0294 (0.011) [2.56]ᵇ		0.0024 (0.006) [0.41]	−0.029 (0.049) [−0.59]	0.310 (0.24) [1.27]	107.09	0.55 (4.21)ᵃ
4. All firms, 35	Supermarket CR₄	0.167 (0.06) [2.70]ᵇ			1.20 (1.03) [1.16]	−0.381 (0.40) [0.95]	0.0127 (0.015) [0.86]		−0.0032 (0.007) [0.45]	0.006 (0.054) [0.11]	0.002 (0.03) [0.07]	93.28	0.41 (2.69)ᵇ
5. All firms, 35	Supermarket CR₁	0.081 (0.017) [4.81]ᵃ			1.87 (0.87) [2.16]ᵇ	−0.791 (0.33) [2.43]ᵇ	0.0294 (0.012) [2.42]ᵇ		−0.0026 (0.65) [0.00]	−0.040 (0.049) [0.81]	0.007 (0.028) [0.25]	107.36	0.60 (5.73)ᵃ
6. All firms except monopolies, 32	Supermarket CR₁	0.0561 (0.025) [2.25]ᵇ			1.97 (0.85) [2.33]ᵃ	−0.894 (0.320) [2.79]ᵃ	0.0325 (0.012) [2.75]ᵃ		0.0019 (0.006) [0.31]	−0.023 (0.05) [−0.46]	0.242 (0.249) [0.97]	107.69	0.52 (3.68)ᵃ
7. All firms, 35	Supermarket CR₄	0.089 (0.059) [1.49]	0.052 (0.017) [3.02]ᵃ		1.95 (0.942) [2.07]ᵇ	−0.678 (0.366) [1.85]ᶜ	0.0226 (0.013) [1.69]		0.0023 (0.007) [0.35]	−0.021 (0.54) [0.39]	0.176 (0.314) [0.56]	99.36	0.56 (4.21)ᵃ

Table 9.7 (continued)

Sample and Number of OBS	Measure of market concentration	market concentration	Firm market share		Independent supermarket	Square feet (1,000)	Square feet squared (millions)	Sales per square foot	Distance to warehouse	Population growth 1970–1980 (%)	1980 Per capita income (1,000)	Intercept	R^2 and F ratio
			MS	RMS									
8. All firms, 35	Supermarket CR_2	0.048 (0.022) [2.23]ᵇ		0.040 (0.018) [2.19]ᵇ	2.11 (0.968) [2.18]ᵇ	−0.756 (0.365) [2.07]ᵇ	0.0259 (0.013) [1.94]ᶜ		0.0020 (0.007) [0.29]	−0.044 (0.056) [0.79]	0.010 (0.032) [0.31]	105.42	0.53 (3.71)ᵃ
9. All firms, 35	Supermarket CR_1	0.080 (0.016) [4.55]ᵃ		0.005 (0.014) [0.35]	1.93 (0.898) [2.15]ᵇ	−0.803 (0.333) [2.41]ᵇ	0.0293 (0.012) [2.38]ᵇ		0.0006 (0.006) [0.10]	−0.040 (0.05) [0.80]	0.009 (0.028) [0.32]	106.97	0.60 (4.87)ᵃ

Source: Cotterill (1986).

a. Significant with two-tailed test at 1 percent.
b. Significant with two-tailed test at 5 percent.
c. Significant with two-tailed test at 10 percent.

The results of this study indicate that concentration is positively related to price even where concentration levels are very high as in the small cities and towns in Vermont.

In addition to the JEC and Cotterill studies, Lamm (1981) and Hall, Schmitz, and Cothern (1979) found that BLS food prices were positively and significantly related to SMSA concentration. Collectively, these studies indicate a clear linkage between concentration and prices in supermarket retailing.

References

Cotterill, Ronald. 1986. "Market Power in the Retail Food Industry: Evidence from Vermont." *Rev. Econ. and Stat.* 68 (August), 379–386.

Geithman, Frederick, Marvel, Howard, and Weiss, Leonard. 1981. "Concentration, Price, and Critical Concentration Ratios." *Rev. Econ. and Stat.* 63 (August), 346–353.

Hall, Lana, Schmitz, Andrew, and Cothern, James. 1979. "Beef Wholesale–Retail Marketing Margins and Concentration. *Econometrica* 46, 295–300.

Lamm, McFall. 1981. "Prices and Concentration in the Food Retailing Industry." *J. Ind. Econ.* 30, 67–78.

Marion, B. W., Mueller, W. F., Cotterill, R. W., Geithman, F. E., and Schmelzer, J. R. 1979a. *The Food Retailing Industry: Market Structure, Profits and Prices.* New York: Praeger.

Marion, B. W. Mueller, W. F. Cotterill, R. W. Geithman, F. E. and Schmelzer, J. R. 1979b. "The Price and Profit Performance of Leading Food Chains." *Amer. J. Agr. Econ.* 79 (August), 420–433.

Marvel, H. 1978. "Competition and Price Levels in the Retail Gasoline Market." *Rev. Econ. Stat.* 60 (May).

Concentration did not seem to be particularly relevant to rail freight rates during the long years when ICC rate regulation was effective, but it has fascinated many economists before and after that period.

The pathbreaking study of late-nineteenth-century freight rates by Paul MacAvoy revealed to us an extensive data set, including actual freight rates on a weekly basis and a running commentary on the actions of the colluding railroads as reported in the financial press of the day. A number of economists have worked with that data, but it continues to yield more insights. In the first study of this chapter Hugh Briggs briefly summarizes its content and tests a few more hypotheses.

You didn't hear a lot about concentration in discussing rail freight rates in the first four-fifths of this century. But in the 1980s the railroads were free to engage in a good deal of price competition again. After a century or so, economists were back trying to work out what determined freight rates on grain (and soybeans, this time) transported from the Midwest to ocean ports. James MacDonald has written a summary of his two articles on the subject which follows the section on nineteenth-century railroads.

The Effects of Concentration and Cartels on Nineteenth-Century Railroad Freight Rates
Hugh Briggs

Several railroads were able to establish control of through lines from Chicago to various cities on the East Coast in the late-nineteenth century. For exporters seeking transportation to Europe for the Midwest's grain, these railroads provided a homogeneous product—transportation to an ocean port—despite their different termini. The attempts by the railroads to collude on freight rates on these trunk line routes provides a rich sample of the problems cartels face. Modern analysis of the cartels is aided by both the importance of rail transportation during the period and the absence of antitrust legislation—contemporary accounts of the cartel's affairs are on the public record and researchers are afforded the opportunity of examining collusion in a situation in which the colluding parties were free from concern of prosecution.

In this short note, I contrast the findings of three analysts who come to different conclusions regarding the cartel's success: Paul MacAvoy (1965), Thomas Ulen (1978), and Robert Porter (1983). I then consider the effect of concentration on the Joint Executive Committee, an industry association whose raison d'être was to facilitate collusion among the firms.

Trunk Line Cartels and Instability

In his pioneering study of the trunk line railroads, Paul MacAvoy (1965) unearthed a variety of price and quantity data on railroads shipping grain from the midwest (mainly Chicago) to eastern ports in the decades after the Civil War. Although the price data, which was obtained from newspaper and trade journal reports, is somewhat suspect when supplied by colluding firms, he showed that the rail freight prices reported by the *Chicago Daily Commercial Bulletin* explain most of the variation on a weekly basis of the difference between grain prices in New York and Chicago.

MacAvoy showed that so long as there were only two rail systems, they were able of collude quite well. Technically, from 1871 to 1874 there were four eastern railroads: the Lake Shore and the Michigan Central, controlled by the New York Central, and the "Panhandle" (Pittsburgh, Cincinnati, and St. Louis) and the Fort Wayne, controlled by the Pennsylvania. There was a third route, by schooner or steamboat to Buffalo and from there by rail or the Erie canal to New York, but that route offered no competition when the Great Lakes were closed in the winter. The New York Central and the Pennsylvania systems engaged in little or no price cutting and charged much higher rates in the winter than in the summer. This blatant price discrimination is further evidence of collusion by the two firms.

This interlude ended with the entry of the Baltimore and Ohio in the winter of 1874. MacAvoy depicts the period from 1874 to 1887 as one of repeated attempts to collude that always failed until the ICC took over their administration. However, at least the high, discriminatory winter rates reappeared in many years. The average rates by year and season and the number of firms with through routes from Chicago to an eastern seaport are shown in table 10.1.

Table 10.1
Price by season and number of lines and firms from Chicago, 1871–1899

Year	Season[a]	Average rate[b]	Deflated rate[c]	Through lines to Chicago[d]	Number of firms
1871	Summer	0.476	0.366	LS, MC, PH, FW	2
	Winter	0.637	0.490	LS, MC, PH, FW	2
1872	Summer	0.540	0.397	LS, MC, PH, FW	2
	Winter	0.645	0.474	LS, MC, PH, FW	2
1873	Summer	0.500	0.376	LS, MC, PH, FW	2
	Winter	0.560	0.421	LS, MC, PH, FW	2
1874	Summer	0.445	0.353	LS, MC, PH, FW	2
	Winter	0.374	0.297	LS, MC, PH, FW, B&O	3
1875	Summer	0.328	0.278	LS, MC, PH, FW, B&O	3
	Winter	0.412	0.349	LS, MC, PH, FW, B&O	3
1876	Summer	0.192	0.175	LS, MC, PH, FW, B&O	3
	Winter	0.317	0.288	LS, MC, PH, FW, B&O	3
1877	Summer	0.332	0.313	LS, MC, PH, FW, B&Q	3
	Winter	0.312	0.294	LS, MC, PH, FW, B&O	3
1878	Summer	0.250	0.275	LS, MC, PH, FW, B&O	3
	Winter	0.265	0.291	LS, MC, PH, FW, B&O	3
1879	Summer	0.253	0.281	LS, MC, PH, FW, B&O	3
	Winter	0.379	0.421	LS, MC, PH, FW, B&O	3
1880	Summer	0.300	0.300	LS, MC, PH, FW, B&Q, GT	4
	Winter	0.336	0.336	LS, MC, PH, FW, B&O, GT	4
1881	Summer	0.171	0.166	LS, MC, PH, FW, B&Q, GT	4
	Winter	0.192	0.186	LS, MC, PH, FW, B&O, GT	4
1882	Summer	0.250	0.231	LS, MC, PH, FW, B&O, GT	4
	Winter	0.300	0.278	LS, MC, PH, FW, B&O, GT	4

Year	Season				
1883	Summer	0.253	0.250	LS, MC, PH, FW, B&O, GT, NP, E	5
	Winter	0.248	0.246	LS, MC, PH, FW, B&O, GT, NP, E	5
1884	Summer	0.212	0.228	LS, MC, PH, FW, B&O, GT, NP, E	5
	Winter	0.222	0.239	LS, MC, PH, FW, B&O, GT, NP, E	5
1885	Summer	0.171	0.201	LS, MC, PH, FW, B&O, GT, NP, E	5
	Winter	0.242	0.285	LS, MC, PH, FW, B&O, GT, NP, E	5
1886	Summer	0.248	0.302	LS, MC, PH, FW, B&O, GT, NP, E	5
	Winter	0.242	0.295	LS, MC, PH, FW, B&O, GT, NP, E	5
1887	Summer	0.250	0.294	LS, MC, PH, FW, B&O, GT, NP, E	5
	Winter	0.261	0.307	LS, MC, PH, FW, B&O, GT, NP, E	5
1888	Summer	0.229	0.266	LS, MC, PH, FW, B&O, GT, NP, E	5
	Winter	0.250	0.291	LS, MC, PH, FW, B&O, GT, NP, E	5
1889	Summer	0.229	0.283	LS, MC, PH, FW, B&O, GT, NP, E	5
	Winter	0.220	0.272	LS, MC, PH, FW, B&O, GT, NP, E	5
1890	Summer	0.213	0.260	LS, MC, PH, FW, B&O, GT, NP, E	5
	Winter	0.245	0.299	LS, MC, PH, FW, B&O, GT, NP, E	5
1891	Summer	0.244	0.298	LS, MC, PH, FW, B&O, GT, NP, E	5
	Winter	0.250	0.305	LS, MC, PH, FW, B&O, GT, NP, E	5
1892	Summer	0.234	0.308	LS, MC, PH, FW, B&O, GT, NP, E	5
	Winter	0.250	0.238	LS, MC, PH, FW, B&O, GT, NP, E	5
1893	Summer	0.244	0.313	LS, MC, PH, FW, B&O, GT, NP, E	5
	Winter	0.187	0.240	LS, MC, PH, FW, B&O, GT, NP, E	5
1894	Summer	0.200	0.286	LS, MC, PH, FW, B&O, GT, NP, E	5
	Winter	0.198	0.283	LS, MC, PH, FW, B&O, GT, NP, E	5
1895	Summer	0.187	0.263	LS, MC, PH, FW, B&O, GT, NP, E	5
	Winter	0.197	0.277	LS, MC, PH, FW, B&O, GT, NP, E	5

Table 10.1 (continued)

Year	Season[a]	Average rate[b]	Deflated rate[c]	Through lines to Chicago[d]	Number of firms
1896	Summer	0.188	0.276	LS, MC, PH, FW, B&O, GT, NP, E	5
	Winter	0.166	0.244	LS, MC, PH, FW, B&O, GT, NP, E	5
1897	Summer	0.141	0.207	LS, MC, PH, FW, B&O, GT, NP, E	5
	Winter	0.179	0.263	LS, MC, PH, FW, B&O, GT, NP, E	5
1898	Summer	0.155	0.218	LS, MC, PH, FW, B&Q, GT, NP, E	5
	Winter	0.184	0.259	LS, MC, PH, FW, B&O, GT, NP, E	5

a. The summer season is defined to include all weeks during which the railroads faced intermodal competition from steamships plying the Great Lakes. Thus the winter season for any particular year begins with the closing of the lakes in the fall and ends with the opening of the lakes in the following spring.

b. Average price refers to the average price of grain in dollars per hundredweight shipped from Chicago to New York, Philadelphia, or Boston as reported by MacAvoy as taken from the *Chicago Daily Commercial Bulletin.*

c. Average prices were deflated by using the wholesale price index for all commodities listed in Series E1-12 and 13-24, pp. 115–117 of *Historical Statistics of the United States, Colonial Times to 1957,* published by the Bureau of the Census, 1960. 1880 = 100.

d. Railroad lines are encoded as follows: LS is the Lake Shore and Michigan Southern Railroad, MC is the Michigan Central Railroad, PH is the "Panhandle," or Pittsburgh, Cincinnati, and St. Louis Railroad, FW is the "Fort Wayne," or Pittsburgh, Fort Wayne, and Chicago Railroad, B&O is the Baltimore and Ohio Railroad, GT is the Grand Trunk Railway, NP is the "Nickel Plate," or the New York, Chicago, and St. Louis Railroad, and E is the Eire Railroad.

MacAvoy noted that even the rates announced by the cartels fell drastically over time and were less than rates per ton mile on short-haul traffic which were set by monopolists in many cases. One of the reasons for the decline in rates was general deflation during the period. The fourth column of table 10.1 shows a deflated series of prices; the relative decline in prices is less striking in the deflated series.

The Joint Executive Committee and the ICC

In September 1879, after four years of sporadic rate wars and with a fourth line about to enter, the trunk line railroads created a Joint Executive Committee to oversee the cartel. This arrangement was a much more formal attempt to collude than the efforts that pre-dated it. Initially, the cartel's goal was to set rates and "pool" the market for allocation among the firms with through lines. A commissioner was hired to collect and distribute information on rates charged and quantities hauled by each firm in each week and a three-member board of arbitrators was established to determine market shares and resolve interfirm disputes. Although the cartel was unable to completely stabilize market shares, as had been its goal, Thomas Ulen (1978) maintains that it was fairly successful in getting its members to adhere to cartel rates. He examined contemporary trade journals and newspapers and found no reports of price cutting in three-fourths of the weeks from September 1879 to April 1886. He viewed these rates as collusive. Porter (1983) estimated a switching regression model in which the two regimes of the regression corresponded to weeks in which the cartel was either pricing collusively or fighting "price wars." The regime classification he estimated is very similar to Ulen's.

During this period three more firms entered the Chicago market, although one immediately merged. The Grand Trunk reached Chicago in the summer of 1880. In the summer it shipped grain from Canadian ports, and in the winter it connected with lines to Portland, Maine, and Boston. The Nickel Plate was completed in October 1883 and operated as an independent for only three days before being purchased by the New York Central; this purchase gave the New York Central three lines into New York City. The Erie, in a sense the first railroad on the route, finally reached Chicago by constructing the Chicago and Atlantic Railway in 1883. From a practical standpoint it was the standardization of the railroad gauges that ultimately gave the Erie access of Chicago because it had a wider than standard gauge track until 1880.

The years 1887 to 1896, when the ICC controlled rail rates, was a period of undisputed rail rate stability. This interlude of peaceful pricing ended with a series of Supreme Court decisions that effectively emasculated the ICC in 1897.[1] During the ten-year period when the ICC could control rates, the discriminatory winter rates largely disappeared. Summer and winter rates were similar, and winter rates were lower in four of the six years. In the last two years shown in table 10.1, the ICC had little power, and rates were set by rate bureaus (such as the Trans-Missouri Freight Association). During that period the high winter rates reappeared.

Table 10.2 contains two regressions that summarize the data in table 10.1. They can hardly be treated as separate tests since almost all of the variables were derived by looking at data like that in table 10.1. The dependent variable in both regressions is the "real price," which constitutes the reported freight rates for corn from Chicago to Atlantic ports deflated by a wholesale price index from the *Historical Statistics of the United States*. No constant term was estimated, so the five dummy variables cover the whole period. An observation is a season in a year, so we have 56 observations. Those for the period when the lakes was open (the length of which varied from year to year) bore a second dummy variable, Lakes × 18xx– 18yy. The only two cost variables that we could find that ran for the entire period were the real prices of anthracite coal and steel bars, both from *Historical Statistics* again. A linear trend was inserted in an attempt to allow for growth in population and technical progress. The only reliable concentration variables available for the entire period were N and $1/N$.

Winter rates were highest in the initial duopoly, as expected, but the period of effective ICC controls, 1887 to 1896, came in second. The ICC succeeded in eliminating interseasonal discrimination. Another way of saying the same thing is that summer rates of the ICC period were higher than those of any other period. The trend and our two cost variables had no effect. Freight rates tended to fall as number of firms rose and to increase with $1/N$, but only the latter was statistically significant.

The Joint Executive Committee Period

The most thoroughly studied period was 1879 to 1886 when the Joint Executive Committee was trying to make the cartel work. We have a good deal more information about that period than the others. A week is an observation in this case. We have wage data, better concentration data, and Ulen's judgment about whether the cartel was effectively controlling freight rates or not for a given week.

Table 10.2
An attempt to describe factors affecting real freight rates, 1871–1898 (standard errors in parentheses, t ratios in brackets)

Variable		
1871–1874 dummy	0.523	0.211
	(0.111)	(0.107)
	[4.71]	[1.97]
1874–1879 dummy	0.407	0.142
	(0.109)	(0.089)
	[3.73]	[1.60]
1879–1886 dummy	0.442	0.195
	(0.131)	(0.088)
	[3.37]	[2.38]
1887–1896 dummy	0.474	0.223
	(0.143)	(0.101)
	[3.31]	[2.21]
1897–1898 dummy	0.466	0.205
	(0.143)	(0.117)
	[3.26]	[1.75]
1871–1874 Lakes open dummy	−0.104	−0.101
	(0.038)	(0.035)
	[−2.74]	[−2.85]
1874–1879 Lakes open dummy	−0.040	−0.045
	(0.024)	(0.023)
	[−1.67]	[−1.96]
1879–1886 Lakes open dummy	−0.037	−0.035
	(0.022)	(0.020)
	[−1.68]	[−1.75]
1887–1896 Lakes open dummy	−0.00005	−0.0001
	(0.018)	(0.017)
	[−0.0003]	[−0.006]
1897–1898 Lakes open dummy	−0.048	−0.049
	(0.041)	(0.039)
	[−1.17]	[−1.26]
Real price of anthracite	−0.014	−0.011
	(0.017)	(0.014)
	[−0.82]	[−0.79]
Real price of steel	0.0007	−0.0001
	(0.001)	(0.0009)
	[0.70]	[−0.11]
Trend	−0.00005	−0.0001
	(0.0015)	(0.001)
	[−0.03]	[−0.10]
N (number of firms)	−0.029	
	(0.027)	
	[−1.07]	
$1/N$		0.630
		(0.231)
		[2.73]
$\bar{R}^2$	0.6853	0.7251

We developed a two-equations model estimated by two stage least squares. In the demand equation for each model, the dependent variable quantity of gain shipped in tons is regressed on a set of 12 dummy variables representing months, a time trend which takes on the values 1 to 75 for each month from January 1880 to April 1886, a dummy variable equal to 1 when the lakes were open and 0 otherwise, and the deflated average rates charged by the industry.

In the cost-price equations the deflated rate in dollars per ton is regressed on a dummy variable equal to one if the week was found to be collusive by Ulen, the deflated wages of fireman and conductors on the Nashville, Chattanooga, and St. Louis railroad in dollars per day, the deflated price of anthracite coal in dollars per ton, and the deflated price of steel rail, both in dollars per ton. During weeks in which the firms priced collusively, rates would be determined prior to the observation of demand and these cartel rates would determine the quantity demanded then. Therefore for collusive weeks, the supply equation does not include a quantity variable. On the other hand, for noncollusive weeks, we assume that the firms either produced according to some noncooperative single-period equilibrium or set rates competitively. In either case quantities should enter the firm's profit-maximizing calculus in noncollusive weeks. Thus an interactive term, one minus the collusion dummy constructed by Ulen times the quantity in each week, is included in all of the regressions.

We performed three sets of regressions on each of five different concentration measures: the Herfindahl index, the square root of the Herfindahl index, the number of firms, one divided by the number of firms, and the two-firm concentration ratio. In the first set of regressions we included the concentration measures for all weeks, regardless of whether the cartel was effective or not. In the second set of regressions the concentration measure was interacted with one minus the cartel dummy so that concentration was only allowed to affect rates during noncollusive weeks. In the last set of regressions the concentration measure was interacted with the cartel dummy so that concentration was only allowed to affect the rates during collusive weeks.

Table 10.3 shows the best-fitting regression results. Each run included a demand and a supply equation, but only the demand equation associated with the first supply equation is shown. The other demand equations were very similar. Twelve monthly dummies were also included in the demand equations, but they are left out to save space. The significant trend presumably reflects the growth in population and foreign trade in grain. Consistent with previous work (Porter 1983) demand for rail service fell when the

Table 10.3
Simultaneous equations models explaining tonnage shipped by rail and deflated freight rates, 1879–1886 (standard errors in parentheses, t ratios in brackets)

Variable	Demand	Freight rates dependent		
		Supply	Supply	Supply
Intercept		−0.621	−0.509	−0.541
		(0.180)	(0.187)	(0.184)
		[−3.45]	[−2.67]	[−2.94]
Trend	0.034	−0.002	−0.002	−0.002
	(0.015)	(0.0008)	(0.0007)	(0.0008)
	[2.27]	[−2.50]	[−2.86]	[−2.50]
Deflated freight rate	−13.58			
	(7.82)			
	[−1.74]			
Lakes open dummy	−8.98			
	(1.69)			
	[−5.08]			
Deflated steel price		0.0003	−0.0001	0.0003
		(0.0009)	(0.0009)	(0.0009)
		[0.33]	[−0.01]	[0.33]
Deflated coal price		0.130	0.112	0.118
		(0.062)	(0.061)	(0.062)
		[2.10]	[1.84]	[1.90]
Deflated firemen's wage		0.758	0.603	0.157
		(1.68)	(1.63)	(1.70)
		[0.45]	[0.37]	[0.09]
Deflated conductor's wage		−0.387	−0.253	−0.010
		(1.060)	(1.03)	(1.08)
		[−0.36]	[−0.25]	[−0.009]
Dummy for PA (period when the cartel was effective)		0.088	0.013	0.039
		(0.027)	(0.052)	(0.034)
		[3.26]	[0.25]	[1.15]
(1 − PA) × quantity shipped		0.001	−0.0006	0.0013
		(0.001)	(0.0017)	(0.017)
		[1.00]	[−0.04]	[0.76]
Herfindahl index		0.029		
		(0.046)		
		[0.63]		
Herfindahl index × (1 − PA)			−0.166	
			(0.103)	
			[−1.61]	
Herfindahl index × PA				0.151
				(0.073)
				[2.07]

Great Lakes were open. The price effect is negative but only marginally significant.

The three supply equations shown represent the best fits in each of three sets of five regressions run. In the first set concentration was introduced in every week; in the second set concentration was interacted with $(1 - PA)$ which implies it was only introduced when the cartel was not effective. In the last set concentration was introduced only when cartel rates were being observed.

The coefficients of most of the other variables have plausible signs but the effect of steel prices is nonsignificant and, in one case, negative. The negative effect of conductors' wage is also implausible. It is closely correlated with firemen's wage. When we experimented with other concentration measures the negative sign shifted to the firemen for three of the five concentration measures covered. Effective cartel pricing generally raised prices, and the level of demand when the cartel was not in force had a very weak tendency to increase market price.

Our main concern is with the effect of concentration. The effect of concentration over the entire period is nonsignificantly positive. During noncollusive weeks the Herfindahl index had a marginally significant negative coefficient. But in the cartel weeks concentration raised price by more than would occur by chance as often as one time in twenty. It seems unlikely that the negative effect of concentration in the noncollusive weeks can be interpreted as Nash equilibria. Price wars oriented toward enforcing the cartel seem likely for at least many of the noncartel weeks. But the significant positive effect of concentration in cartel weeks suggests that the cartel works through the ability of the cartel to enforce its price.

We tried five alternative concentration indexes. The Herfindahl always offered the best fit. In regressions like the last in table 10.3, the next best fit was for N: -0.024, (0.010), $[-2.40]$; the third was $\sqrt{H}$: 0.215, (0.097), $[2.22]$. The fourth was $1/N$: 0.349, (0.168), $[2.08]$; and the worst fit came with the two firm concentration ratio: 0.139, (0.079), $[1.76]$.

Clearly, even in collusive weeks the industry did not exploit its position as a pure monopolist would have. Evaluated at the mean deflated rates of 0.25 dollars per ton, the highest implied price elasticity of demand is -0.17 for the month of September. Therefore marginal revenues are negative, which is inconsistent with joint profit maximization.

It would appear that the cartel worked best when concentration was high. Collusive rates were higher, the higher was concentration; and the probability that any given week would be collusive was apparently higher, the fewer the firms involved. Thus even in the highly collusive world of the nineteenth-century railroads, concentration had its expected effect.

Concentration and Railroad Pricing
James M. MacDonald

The Staggers Rail Act of 1980 greatly increased the scope for individual rate setting by the railroads. The act removed many shipments from regulatory oversight and also eroded the influence of factors that encouraged interrail cooperation in setting rates, such as regional rate bureaus and the use of posted tariff rates. The act proposed to rely on competition to establish reasonable rates for services.[2] My research (MacDonald 1987) constructed measures of the extent of competition, among railroads and between railroads and barges, and estimated the impact of differences in competition on rail rates for the shipment of corn, wheat, and soybeans to ports for export.

There are at least four reasons for interest in the relation between rail rates and competition. First, as noted above, the success of rail deregulation relies on the existence of some competition among railroads. Levin's (1981) simulations confirm the sense of the act: "The most striking result obtained in simulating the outcome of complete deregulation is the importance of the degree of interrailroad competition ... a modest degree of interrailroad competition has profound effects relative to the pure monopoly case" (Levin, p. 396).

Second, because of the presumed existence of some pockets of monopoly in rail transportation, the Staggers Act retained Interstate Commerce Commission control over rates charged to captive shippers. The definition of a captive shipper is still a source of controversy but clearly should depend upon some estimate of the degree of monopoly power exercised by the shipper.

Third, mergers have consolidated the rail industry in recent years. The competitive effects of such mergers, and the relative desirability of "end-to-end" versus "horizontal" consolidations, clearly depend upon the extent of intermodal competition and the effectiveness of interrail competition as well as the impact of the merger on concentration.

Finally, the research relates to the more general debate in industrial organization over the relation between concentration and performance. The analysis will add to the small group of studies that are able to use observations on pricing, rather than profits, in order to avoid the serious conceptual problems that attend profit measures and analyses.

Measuring Competition in Rail Markets

Barges provide as important source of intermodal competition for the movement of grain, especially on the Columbia River in the Pacific Northwest and on the Mississippi River system (also including the Ohio, Illinois, Missouri, and Arkansas rivers) in the Midwest. Elevator operators may ship grain to barge loading locations by truck or by short-haul rail. Shipment costs to the river should be largely dependent on distance, so I measured the importance of water competition by calculating the distance from the origin of a rail shipment to the nearest location of water transport.

The importance of water competition varies geographically. Corn and soybean production areas are concentrated in Ohio, Michigan, Illinois, Iowa, Minnesota, Missouri, Nebraska, and South Dakota. At the sample means, water transport was 97 miles away from a corn shipper and 73 miles from a soybean shipper. Seventy-five percent of corn shippers were within 140 miles. By contrast, wheat production is concentrated in more arid areas of the Great Plains—Texas, Oklahoma, Kansas, Nebraska, Colorado, the Dakotas, and Montana—with some production in the Pacific Northwest. At the mean of the wheat sample, water competition was 300 miles away.

In order to measure competition among railroads, I calculated concentration measures based on all rail grain shipments originating in a region. I used crop-reporting districts (CRDs) as my regions. Most states have nine, and in the Midwest and Plains States they are large enough that movement from one to the other can impose nontrivial transport costs. Corn and soybean production areas are broadly contiguous, and my sample covers 678 corn shipments and 110 soybean shipments originating in 51 CRDs. At the median there are three railroads in a corn-soybean CRD, and three of the 51 are monopoly CRDs. Again, wheat production occurs in less populated, and less competitive, areas. Ten of the 52 wheat CRDs are monopoly districts, and the median number of railroads is 2.[3] The Northern Plains (Montana and the Dakotas) have the fewest railroads and are the farthest from water transport, whereas the Southern Plains production areas tend to have three and four railroads in a district.

A simple count of the number of railroads may be a poor measure of competition, if some railroads in a district are branch lines or shortline companies, while others operate major main lines. I therefore calculated

Herfindahl measures of railroad concentration (based on samples of all rail grain shipments originating in a CRD). My particular measure is the numbers equivalent Herfindahl, which is the reciprocal of the sum of squared market shares. The numbers equivalent Herfindahl ($1/H$) ranges from a low of one (in the monopoly districts) and increases as the number of railroads increases or as their shares become more equal. The mean Herfindahl in the corn-soybean sample is 2.3, with an interquartile range of 1.6 to 2.8; in wheat the mean is 1.9 with an interquartile range of 1.3 to 2.

I have not explicitly accounted for competition from trucks. Because entry into agricultural trucking is easy, if trucks are a strong enough competitive threat as to make grain transportation contestable, then we should see no effect of rail or barge competition on rail rates. That is, we can indirectly account for truck competition in the empirical analysis. But trucks are probably not an effective threat in most of these long-haul markets. Although some long-distance truck transport of grain exists (principally on backhauls), and although there is some stiff rail-truck competition on some important 100–300 mile routes (e.g., from Minnesota and the eastern Dakotas to the terminals at Duluth and Minneapolis) the truck share of long-distance export movements tends to be quite small.[4] Trucks do handle important flows to Great Lakes ports, but the analysis includes the distance to those ports in the measure of water competition.

The Data and Analysis

The analysis investigated the effects of competition on rail rates, measured as revenue per ton-mile. The principal data source was the 1983 ICC Rail Waybill File (Master Sample), a stratified sample of all rail waybills. Sampling probabilities in the waybill vary with shipment size and railroad waybill processing procedures, and range from 1 percent for some single car shipments to 50 percent for large unit trains. The water competition measure was calculated from a Rand McNally road atlas; all other data were taken directly or derived from the Waybill File. Observations consist of rail shipments of corn, wheat, or soybeans that originate in one of the ten leading producer states and terminate at an ocean port, a Great Lakes port, or points on the Mexican border. In the regression analysis each observation was weighted by the inverse of its sampling probability.

Table 10.4 contains the key results, from double logarithmic regressions run separately for each commodity. The regressions control for several

Table 10.4
Weighted least squares double-logarithm regression analysis of export rail rates for corn, soybeans, and wheat, 1983 (standard errors in parentheses, t ratios in brackets)

Independent variables	Regression coefficients		
	Corn	Soybeans	Wheat
Intercept	3.922	3.496	3.841
	(0.1183)	(0.2572)	(0.0717)
	[33.15]	[13.59]	[53.57]
Distance (miles)	−0.3645	−0.2782	−0.5091
	(0.0109)	(0.0205)	(0.0095)
	[−33.44]	[−13.57]	[−53.59]
Shipment size (tons)	−0.1189	−0.0549	−0.0433
	(0.0076)	(0.0088)	(0.0043)
	[−15.64]	[−6.24]	[−10.07]
Annual volume on route (tons)	−0.0148	−0.0826	−0.0551
	(0.0092)	(0.0167)	(0.0051)
	[−1.61]	[−4.95]	[−10.80]
Distance to water competition, (miles)	0.0864	0.0856	0.2576
	(0.0145)	(0.0324)	(0.0074)
	[5.96]	[2.64]	[34.81]
Shipment originates at riverport (0, 1)	0.5698	0.4130	0.7659
	(0.0554)	(0.1111)	(0.0443)
	[10.29]	[3.72]	[17.29]
Railroad competition, $1/H$	−0.2843	−0.1977	−0.1130
	(0.0228)	(0.0499)	(0.0145)
	[−12.47]	[−3.96]	[−7.79]
State regulated intrastate shipment (0, 1)			−0.1369
			(0.0114)
			[−12.01]
Second-quarter of year	0.0092	−0.0444	−0.0334
	(0.0223)	(0.0445)	(0.0127)
	[0.41]	[−1.0]	[−2.63]
Third-quarter of year	0.0578	0.0064	−0.0226
	(0.0210)	(0.0447)	(0.0111)
	[2.75]	[0.14]	[−2.04]
Fourth-quarter of year	0.0529	0.0999	−0.0443
	(0.0189)	(0.0325)	(0.0137)
	[2.80]	[3.07]	[−3.23]
R^2	0.811	0.858	0.774
N	678	110	1,535

Note: The dependent variable is revenue per ton-mile.

important shipment characteristics. Because some costs are fixed with re-spect to distance, costs (and rates per ton-mile) should decline with miles. Distance has a powerful negative impact on rates per ton-mile.[5] Because switching costs increase less than proportionately with shipment size, larger shipments should have lower incremental costs and rates per ton; rates should also be inversely related to annual volume on a particular route, because high volume routes are more likely to use unit trains and will achieve greater capacity utilization. Table 10.4 shows these shipment characteristics to be important determinants of rates. Rates may vary with the season, and to account for seasonal factors, I inserted quarterly dummy variables, which have some modest impacts. Some states continue to regu-late intrastate shipments. In Washington, Texas, and Minnesota I entered a dummy variable for these shipments. Rates are significantly lower, in a statistical and substantive sense, on intrastate moves.

Competition appears to have a strong impact on rail rates, even after we control for the other factors. The effect of water competition is highly significant and powerful. Using the coefficients of the wheat equation (where water competition varies quite widely), shippers who are 400 miles from the water pay rates 40 percent above those who are 100 miles from water, at median values of other variables. The corn and soybean sample has a much smaller, though still statistically significant, impact. Water competition is generally closer in those samples, and river conditions may vary across riverpoints. Such conditions that I could not statistically control affect tow sizes and therefore barge costs and rates.

Because some shipments originated at a river and the log of zero is undefined, I inserted a dummy variable for those originations (I then set the log of distance to water to zero for those river point observations). The result was surprising: rates from riverport originations were higher than inland points. The coefficient value was small and not important in wheat, but in the corn and soybean samples rates at river originations were much higher than almost all other originations.[6] Now very few shipments originate at river points (2 percent of wheat and 3 percent of corn and soybean observations) because barges have important cost advantages over railroads. Therefore a shipper will choose rail at a riverpoint only if some unexpected event, such as a time constraint, a freeze, or an inland sales opportunity, removes the constraint imposed by the barge line.

Competition from other railroads has important effects in the regres-sions. In each equation the coefficients are negative and highly significant—rail rates fall as the number of competitors increases. In the corn equation movement from monopoly to duopoly (or the Herfindahl equivalent) leads to an 18 percent decline in rates. Movement to triopoly leads to a further 11 percent decline.[7]

I explored the robustness of the competition results through the application of several alternative functional forms. First, it's likely that some interaction between rail and water competition will exist. That is, a rail monopolist will have little market power if there is a nearby barge line. I therefore added an interaction term to the regressions of table 10.4, multiplying rail competition by water competition. The results were statistically significant for corn and wheat, but not for soybeans (MacDonald 1987). The impact of rail competition was weaker, by modest amounts, where water competition was nearby.

In order to determine if rates were sensitive to different degrees of oligopoly, I reran the regressions of table 10.4 after deleting all observations from monopoly (single-railroad) CRDs. There were no monopoly CRD's in the soybean sample, and only three for corn (these three had no export soybean shipments). However, ten monopoly CRDs accounted for 23.3 percent of the tonnage shipped in the wheat sample. The regressions were remarkably similar to the old. Coefficient values and significance levels showed hardly any change at all. In particular the coefficients on rail competition in the corn and wheat samples each increased imperceptibly, to -0.283 in corn and -0.111 in wheat (or changes of 0.001 and 0.002). The degree of oligopoly appears to matter, as does the transition to monopoly.

Conclusion

Levin (1981) reported that some degree of interrail competition is required in order to keep rates from rising under deregulation. It appears, from this analysis, that most grain is shipped under conditions of some reasonable degrees of competition among railroads and from waterborne carriers. Railroads have a considerable degree of market power in some areas in the wheat growing regions of the Northern Plains States, and in some parts of western Nebraska and Kansas and eastern Colorado. In these areas competing railroads are few and water competition is far away. Continued maximum rate regulation may be desirable in these regions.

Grain rates are sensitive to changes in the degree of oligopoly in the analysis. The results suggest that potential reductions in competition should be taken seriously in analyses of rail mergers, and that serious efforts be made to measure and compare presumed efficiency gains.

Notes

1. ICC v. Cincinnati, New Orleans, and Texas Pacific Railway, 167 US 479 (1897) and ICC v. Alabama Midland Railway, 168 US 144 (1897).

2. See Title 1, Rail Transportation Policy, of the Conference Report of the Staggers Rail Act of 1980.

3. The distribution of CRDs by number of railroads is as follows:

Number of Railroads

	1	2	3	4	5	6	7	Total
Corn/soybeans	3	11	19	11	2	3	2	51
Wheat	10	19	10	7	6	0	0	52

4. Trucks handle the dominant share of short haul traffic to Great Lakes ports, such as movements into Toledo from northern Ohio and Indiana (Hill, Leath, and Fuller 1981). However, on a longer movement such as to Gulf ports from Kansas (600–700 miles), trucks had a 3.2 percent market share. The truck-barge combination had another 3.4 percent, and rails had 93.4 percent (Leath, Hill, and Fuller 1981).

5. Distance is the major determinant of rates, and a plot of distance versus rates showed a log-linear relationship. For that reason I used the double-logarithmic specification. I also specified the regressions in untransformed variables with quadratic terms entered. That specification yielded results that were quite similar to the double-log form, but tests on residuals showed a modest, statistically significant, pattern of heteroscedasticity. No such pattern appeared in the double-log specifications.

6. The result appeared to be robust to a series of other specifications (MacDonald 1987). The result also remains when I use data from 1981 through 1985. All other coefficients keep the same signs, significance levels, and magnitudes in the longer time span (MacDonald 1989).

7. Some CRDs in the Plains States have monopoly railroads and distant water competition. Using wheat sample coefficients, a shipper facing a monopolist 600 miles from water competition (the extreme of low competition) will pay rates 70 percent higher than a shipper facing a duopoly 200 miles from the water, for a first-quarter, 5,000-ton, 800-mile shipment on a route with 60,000 tons volume.

References

Hill, Lowell D., Mack N. Leath, and Stephen W. Fuller. 1981. *Corn Movement in the United States: Interregional Flow Patterns and Transportation Requirements in 1977*. North Central Regional Research Bulletin 275 (January). Agricultural Experiment Station. Champaign: University of Illinois.

Leath, Mack N., Lowell D. Hill, and Stephen W. Fuller. 1981. *Wheat Movements in the United States. Interregional Flow Patterns and Transportation Requirements in 1977.* North Central Regional Research Bulletin No. 274 (January). Agricultural Experiment Station. Champaign: University of Illinois.

Levin, Richard C. 1981. "Railroad Regulation, Deregulation, and Workable Competition." *American Economic Review, Papers and Proceedings* 71, 394–398.

MacAvoy, Paul W. 1965. *The Economic Effects of Regulation.* Cambridge, MA: MIT Press.

MacDonald, James M. 1989. "Competition and Rail Rates for the Shipment of Corn, Soybeans, and Wheat." *Rand Journal of Economics* Vol. 18, 151–163.

MacDonald, James M. 1987. "Railroad Deregulation, Innovation, and Competition: Effect of the Staggers Act on Grain Transportation." *Journal of Law and Economics* 32, 63–96.

Porter, Robert H. 1983. "A Study of Cartel Stability: The Joint Executive Committee, 1880–86." *Bell Journal of Economics* 14, 301–314.

Ulen, Thomas S. 1978. "Cartels and Regulation." Ph.D. dissertation. Palo Alto: Stanford University.

U.S. Bureau of Census. 1960. *Historical Statistics of the United States, Colonial Times to 1957.* Washington, DC.

U.S. House of Representatives. *Staggers Rail Act of 1980. Report of the Committee on Conference* 96th Congress. 2nd Session. House Report No. 96-1430.

11   Buyer Concentration and Cattle Prices

Thus far all of the cases developed or summarized in the book have dealt with seller concentration. Theory tells us that concentration among buyers will tend to depress prices. There seems to have been little empirical work on this topic to date except for several studies of the effects of deposit interest rates in banking which will be covered in chapter 12. There is one study of buyer concentration and price that should surely be in the book, however. Bruce Marion agreed to write the following brief summary of his work on the effect of regional concentration among slaughter houses on beef cattle prices.

Live Cattle Prices and Packer–Buyer Concentration
Bruce W. Marion and Frederick Geithman

Although U.S. beef packers sell in a national market, they buy in much more limited markets. Most fed cattle are purchased within 100 miles of the slaughtering plant.

Accurate data on beef packer concentration are available from the USDA Packers and Stockyards Administration. At the national level, concentration of fed steer and heifer slaughter was relatively low through the 1970s but then increased sharply. The four-firm concentration ratio was 27 in 1972, 32 in 1977, and then doubled to 64 by 1987 (Marion 1988). Increased concentration is due to several factors, including the shift from carcass to boxed beef shipments. By 1985 boxed beef accounted for 77 percent of the steers and heifers slaughtered. MES seems to be in the neighborhood of 250,000 head per year, or roughly 1 percent of national slaughter per year for specialized slaughtering plants. But most of the new combination slaughtering-processing plants have slaughtering capacity of 500,000 to 1 million head per year. (Cothern et al. 1978; USDA 1982)

More than two-thirds of the fed cattle are produced in Iowa, Nebraska, Kansas, Colorado, and Texas. Large commercial feedlots have grown in importance, but there are still over 100,000 feedlots in the country. This study uses as markets 13 of 14 defined in a study done for the House Committee on Small Business (1979). Region 14 (Nevada, Utah, and most of Wyoming) was omitted for lack of price data. The states south and east of the Ohio River—Mississippi River boundary are not included in the markets studied because of few fed cattle. Prices used were annual averages for choice steers weighing 900 to 1100 pounds for each of 32 locations for which USDA Market News reported prices. Where more than one USDA reporting points were in a region, they were combined in weighted averages.

Concentration of steer and heifer slaughter was calculated for each of the 13 regions based on data provided by the Packers and Stockyards Administration. Several indexes of concentration were calculated for each year covered by the study (1971–1980). Price was expected to fall as concentration rises because of increasing monopsony power.

Several other explanatory variables were included as well. Those used in the regressions are reported here. Packer labor costs in each region were proxied by the percentage of slaughter done in plants on the "master contract" of United Food and Commercial Workers. High labor costs (high percent on master contract) were expected to depress cattle prices, so a negative coefficient was expected. A second variable was a dummy with a value of one if prices were for livestock terminal sales instead of feedlot—packer direct sales. This was also expected to yield lower prices, and therefore a negative coefficient. A third control variable was the distance from New York for regions to the east of a line from Denver to Amarillo, and from Los Angeles for regions to the west of that. This implies that the price of beef in Los Angeles should be lower than that in New York by the transport cost of beef over a distance of 663 miles, because Los Angeles is that much closer to the "beefshed." A fourth variable was the percentage of beef coming from feedlots with more than 1,000 cattle capacity (USDA 1983). A positive coefficient was expected because packer transaction costs are lower per head with large feedlots and because large feedlot operators tend to be better informed about price. The fifth is a dummy with a value of one if the region contained one or more plants with a capacity of at least 250,000 head. Since more efficient plants should be able to pay higher prices for cattle, a positive sign was expected.

Several other control variables were introduced in some regressions not reported in this summary. (See Quail et al. 1986 for complete study.) They were the Census state level average hourly earnings for production employees in hog and beef slaughtering plants, which was available only for 1971 to 1978 (nonsignificant and varying in sign); a market share instability variable (with a nonsignificant positive effect); and the ratio of cattle marketings to slaughter in a region (which had a nonsignificant effect of varying sign).

The price of fed cattle is affected by many variables besides the regional variables of this model. To deal with year-to-year fluctuations in national beef prices, a dummy was introduced for each year in the sample. Since all years had dummies, no constant term appears in the regressions.

The regression results (table 11.1) indicate that the Herfindahl index has a negative and significant effect in all equations. The effect of CR4 is negative and significant in the two equations in which it is the measure of concentration although in one case it is significant at only the 10 percent level. CR3 (not shown) performed slightly better than CR4 but not as well as the Herfindahl index.

Labor cost is generally negative in effect but never significant. Distance has a negative effect as hypothesized and is usually significant. Feedlot size is positively related to cattle prices and consistently significant. The coefficient of the large plant dummy has a negative sign in the equation in which it is included, which is contrary to the hypothesized relationship.

The coefficient of the terminal dummy is always negative but only marginally significant. This variable is highly collinear with distance and feedlot size. The four regions with terminal prices are closest to the East Coast and have small feedlots. The terminal markets are dropped from the sample in equations 5 and 7. Concentration has a much stronger effect in the nonterminal market regions, perhaps suggesting that monopsony power is easier to exercise when transactions are direct rather than through terminal markets where several buyers are present. In the nonterminal equations, the distance variable drops slightly in significance, while the feedlot size becomes stronger.

In addition to the pooled time series and cross-section analysis, simple regressions on the Herfindahl index and multiple regressions including the Herfindahl index, distance, and feedlot size variables were run for each year separately. Since there were only 13 regions, the regressions had only 11 and 9 degrees of freedom. The coefficients of the Herfindahl index were always negative. In the simple regressions they were significant in 1971 through 1974 but not thereafter. They were significant in all the multiple

Table 11.1
Regression results explaining the price of live steers in 13 regional markets, 1971–1980 (standard errors in parentheses, t ratios in brackets)

	Equation number						
Variable	1	2	3	4	5[a]	6	7[a]
Herfindahl index	−287.92	−269.9	−218.7	−208.6	−319.59		
	(73.64)	(123.24)	(123.56)	(123.43)	(112.53)		
	[−3.91][b]	[−2.19][c]	[−1.77][c]	[−1.69][c]	[−2.84][b]		
CR4						−105.74	−226.98
						(71.45)	(72.29)
						[−1.48][d]	[−3.14][b]
Labor cost			−9.65	−15.76	28.73	−18.76	21.74
			(43.86)	(43.78)	(49.53)	(44.67)	(48.31)
			[−0.22]	[−0.36]	[0.58]	[−0.42]	[0.45]
Terminal dummy			−62.13	−81.80		−74.11	
			(50.93)	(55.65)		(55.72)	
			[−1.22]	[−1.47][d]		[−1.33][d]	
Distance from Los Angeles or New York City		−0.11	−0.14	−0.12	−0.13	−0.14	−0.10
		(0.067)	(0.069)	(0.072)	(0.073)	(0.082)	(0.078)
		[−1.63][d]	[−2.04][c]	[−1.66][c]	[−1.79][c]	[−1.70][c]	[−1.29][d]
Feedlot size		2.81	2.44	2.10	3.55	2.36	3.38
		(0.594)	(0.693)	(0.792)	(0.937)	(0.761)	(0.918)
		[4.73][b]	[3.52][b]	[2.65][b]	[3.79][b]	[3.10][b]	[3.68][b]
Large plant dummy				−22.16			
				(26.38)			
				[−0.84]			
Number of observations after correction for auto regression	126	110	110	110	74	110	74

a. Observations for four terminal market regions are excluded.
b. Significant with one-tailed test at 1 percent.
c. Significant with one-tailed test at 5 percent.
d. Significant with one-tailed test at 10 percent.

regressions except the last (1980). Prices fluctuated substantially during the ten years with troughs occurring in 1971−72 and 1976−77. In view of the persistance of the relationship despite the few degrees of freedom and the extreme changes in prices generally during the period, it seems quite clear that the effect of concentration was something more than statistical accident.

The natural hypothesis that buyer concentration depressed fed cattle prices is strongly supported by both the pooled and annual regressions. Monopsony power seems clear in this case.

The effect was not large, however. A ten-point rise in the four-firm concentration ratio reduced steer prices by 10 to 23 cents per hundred-weight in the different equations. Going from the least concentrated market to the most—from CR4 of 25 to 95—reduces cattle prices by $.70 to $1.60 per cwt. The mean price during the period was $46.61, so the greatest possible effect of concentration was only 1.5 to 3.4 percent of the total price.

Most of the production cost of meat products occurs on the farm, not in the slaughter house. The value added of the meat packer is only 16 percent of their shipments. Their gross margins are only 8.5 percent, and their average net margins are usually less than 1 percent! Although the effect of concentration on beef prices is small, it is relatively important when compared with the value-added, gross margins and, especially, net margins of meat packers.

References

Committee on Small Business, U.S. House of Representatives. 1979. *Small Business Problems in the Marketing of Meat and Other Commodities: Changing Structure of the Beef Packing Industry*. Pt. 4. Washington, DC: U.S. Government Printing Office.

Cothern, J. H., R. M. Peard, and J. L. Weeks. 1978. *Economics of Scale in Beef Processing, and Portion Control Operations: Northern California, 1976*. University of California Leaflet 21027.

Marion, Bruce. 1988. "Changes in the Structure of the Meat Packing Industries: Implications for Farmers and Consumers." In *Mergers and Concentration: The Food Industries*. Hearings before Subcommittee on Monopolies and Commercial Law of the Committee on the Judiciary, House of Representatives, May 11, 1988.

Quail, G., B. W. Marion, F. E. Geithman, and J. Marquardt. 1986. "The Impact of Packer Buyer Concentration on Live Cattle Prices." University of Wisconsin-Madison: NC-117 Working Paper Number 89 (May).

U.S. Department of Agriculture. 1982. "Boxed Beef: Production, Pricing and Distribution, 1979." *Packers and Stockyards Resume.* Packers and Stockyards Administration (November).

U.S. Department of Agriculture. 1983. *Livestock and Meat Statistics.* Statistical Bulletin Number 715 (and previous years). Economic Research Service.

12   Banking

As in many areas, banking offers something special. Here prices (interest rates) have been a matter of concern for a long time, and price data has been widely available for years. The first concentration-price study in banking (Edwards 1964) appeared only six months after Stigler's first concentration-price studies anywhere. As of 1987 the banking markets people has published at least 34 concentration-price studies, as well as various other studies of concentration and profitability or portfolio structure.

The banking studies are very mixed in quality and call for review rather than simple reproduction. In any event it would be outragenous to present anything like 34 summaries solicited from the authors. Most of this chapter is therefore a review of and an attempt to synthesize the concentration-price studies in banking, but you will also find at the chapter's end a brief report of a project that I requested Allan Berger and Timothy Hannon to do using data they had put together for one of the many bank studies. It contains regression results using many alternative functional forms of concentration.

A Review of Concentration-Price Studies in Banking
Leonard W. Weiss

Much of the research in this area was done by economists employed by the federal banking agencies, especially the Federal Reserve Banks and the Board of Governors. In a number of cases the data was created by questionnaires or tabulations of the Federal Reserve System. This seems wholly appropriate for an agency which was newly assigned responsibility for mergers whose effects neither it nor anyone outside had much empirical basis for judging. The Bank Holding Company Act of 1956 as amended in

1966 and in 1970, The Bank Merger Act of 1960, the Philadelphia National Bank decision in 1963, and the Bank Merger Act of 1966 assigned to the bank regulatory agencies responsibility for reviewing virtually every bank merger in the country. The Federal Reserve System was responsible for all mergers that took the holding company from. This has meant that the System had an increasing obligation since at least the large mergers were more and more holding company acquisitions. It was altogether appropriate for an agency, given such a new job, to develop staff suitable for its new activities, to encourage that staff to make studies relevant to it, and to collect the data needed to make the results of that work useful. We know a lot more about the effects of bank mergers today as a result.

In the first dozen studies the concentration-price relationships were the main focus, but after that the studies were often concerned about such subjects as the effect of holding company membership or the willingness of management to take risks. These were certainly matters for which the Federal Reserve Board and the Federal Reserve Banks had responsibility. The effect of concentration on price was a proper part of the models, but not the primary purpose of many of the projects.

Banking Markets

One reason why such studies are attractive in banking is that many of the markets on which bankers trade are local in character and therefore present us with many observations. There is need for care, however. Some bank prices are unquestionable determined in local markets. This is true of check charges, time deposit interest rates, and interest rates on personal loans.

Another group of bank prices are unquestionable determined on national markets. No one has yet tried to relate interest yields on securities held by banks to local concentration for the good reason that most of these are bonds issued by the federal, state, and local governments, and their prices are determined on national markets.

The most interesting case, however, is surely the interest rate charged on commercial loans. Here is a price that is of concern to many people and one that is often determined locally. Most small firms obtain most of their credit locally. However, a large part of the funds lent are also at interest rates that are determined nationally. Most large firms can with a little time borrow from hundreds of banks and many have the further option of issuing securities on the open market. Individual banks have little opportunity to exploit such borrowers.

The Effect of Business Fluctuations

The effect of business fluctuations on business loan interest rates was "well understood" when the concentration-interest rate studies began. It was commonly believed then that during periods of easy money, rates on money market-oriented loans fell while those on local, small business loans did not. In tight money periods money market rates rose, and the rates on small local loans were close to money market rates. Part of the reason was state usury laws which might apply to commercial loans, but even where this was not so, it appeared that some sort of "proper interest rate" near the top of the normal range set an effective ceiling on what banks felt they could charge small borrowers. It tended to reflect rates that had prevailed in peak periods of the past.

In this setting the fact that they weren't paying much more than GM during boom periods was of little value to many small borrowers, because the banks quite naturally rationed credit to them on the basis of such things as the stability of their business and the length of their relationship with the bank. New, small borrowers were particularly limited, but even those with long relationships to their banks were apt to be held to the old line of credit in tight money periods. This was probably a more important limitation on most small borrowers than high interest rates would have been.

In the nineteenth century the ability of the small town banker to control the prospects of individual local businesses was often a matter of highly emotional politics. Today that power is undoubtedly lessened because of greatly reduced transport and communication costs. Nevertheless, the banker is still one of the most powerful persons in a small town. I think this is the real issue about monopoly in banking, but it is not the main issue of this book.

The Fed studied it in the 1950s. The amounts of credit available to small borrowers during times of stringency then seemed to contract or to expand much more slowly than credit to large borrowers. Since then, of course, we have been through a period in the 1970s and 1980s that makes the interest rates of these early "tight money" periods seem low. One effect of the very high and widely fluctuating interest rates of the decade that began in 1973 was to shatter the ceilings on small business loan interest rates or at least to shift them to far higher levels. As a result many banks quoted interest rates such as "one point above the prime" for some small borrowers and "two points above the prime" for others. This could have reduced the tendency for nonprice rationing of credit, at least during the period of declining interest rates after 1982. It seems less likely that interest rates on small business loans were limited by an informal ceiling than in the 1950s and 1960s. Unfortunately, the Fed has made no more studies of the availability of bank credit by size of loan or borrower, so we do not know for sure.

Interest Rates on Small Business Loans

The rest of this chapter will be devoted to particular studies. Two tables appear in the text, which should make it more manageable. Table 12.1 defines the terms used in table 12.2.

The first study by Franklin Edwards (1964) set a high standard. He limited his work to fairly small loans and was able to report results for 1955, an easy money year, and 1957, then thought of as a tight money year.

A metropolitan area was an observation. There was a significant positive effect of concentration on loan interest rates within the smaller asset size classes, but the relationship was nonsignificantly positive in 1955 for borrowers whose assets fell in the range $250,000 to $1,000,000. In 1989 dollars this might correspond to assets of $1,000,000 to $4,000,000 after adjusting for inflation. The relationship was strongest to firms with assets under $50,000 in 1955 (perhaps those under $200,000 in 1989). In the subsequent "tight money" period of 1957, the concentration–interest rate relationship largely disappeared.

Flechsig (1965) did an extensive rework of Edwards and seemed to show that Edwards' results did not hold with a mild change in the model or with data for another year (1960). Using the data Edwards had used, he made several changes. First, he computed SMSA concentration ratios using FDIC figures for 1955 except that he had to depend on 1960 figures adjusted for mergers to get 1955 estimates in some states. This surely was a change for the better. Second, he excluded the loan maturity variable. It is hard to see how this helped, but it is also hard to see how it could have distorted the results much.

Then he inserted a series of dummies to represent regional differences. These undoubtedly did distort the results. How did Denver and Memphis get into the Midwest? When he gets to his 19 SMSA sample for 1960, his regions change. He combines the two midwestern regions that he used in reworking Edwards, and he now shifts Kansas City and St. Louis out of the Midwest and into the South!

The basis for choosing regions is never completely clear, but he regularly suggests that credit conditions differ interregionally—that it is right,

Table 12.1
Abbreviations used in table 12.2

CD	Certificate of deposit
CRi	The i firm concentration ratio. The share of the top i firms in total shipments, sales, deposits in the market, industry, etc. For example, $CR3$ is the share of the top three firms in some economic measure of size.
CU	Credit union
FDIC	Federal Deposit Insurance Corporation
FHLBB	Federal Home Loan Bank Board
FR	Federal Reserve. FRB = Federal Reserve Board; FRS = Federal Reserve System.
H	Herfindahl index. The sum of the squared market shares of all the firms selling on a market. $-1/H$ is derived from this measure. The ratio, $1/H$, is equal to the number of equal-sized firms that would produce such a Herfindahl index. When this is used as a measure of concentration, it is often assigned a negative value so that it will rise as concentration rises.
IL/TL	Interest, discounts, and service charges divided by total book value of loans outstanding, or, more simply, interest on loans divided by total loans, all derived from the report of condition of a commercial bank
ITD/TD	Interest paid on time and savings deposits divided by time and savings deposits outstanding, all derived from the bank's statement of condition
MSBk	Mutual savings bank
N	Number of firms, often used as a measure of concentration either directly or in inverse form: $1/N$
NPE	Number of potential entrants
Qi	The ith quarter of the year. For example, Q^2 refers to the second quarter of April through June.
r_{xy}	The simple correlation ratio relating x to y
SC/DD	Service charges on deposits divided by demand deposits outstanding, derived from the bank's statement of condition
SLA	Savings and loan association
SMSA	Standard metropolitan statistical area. The Bureau of the Census has recently changed the term to simply MSA or metropolitan statistical area, but the bulk of our studes reviewed here were done in the days of the SMSA.

Table 12.2

Author(s) (date)	Main concern	Data: Year(s) Unit of observation Source	Concentration variable(s)	Other independent variable(s)	Price variable(s)	Regression coefficients 1955	1957	Approximate percentage change in price with a ten-point rise in CR3	
Edwards (1964)	Effect of concentration on level and change in commercial loan interest rates by size of borrower	Oct. 1955, Oct. 1957 49 SMSAs FRB business loan surveys	CR3 for 1955, CR3 for 1957, both based on statewide data	Average loan size SMSA employment growth % loans maturing in one year rules SMSA size dummies	Effective interest rates on loans to firms with assets of: $1 thousand to $50 thousand	$0.0179CR3$ (0.0050) $t = 3.56$	$0.0074CR3$ (0.0057) $t = 1.30$	3.0%	1.2%
					$50 thousand to $250 thousand	$0.0070CR3$ (0.0021) $t = 3.33$	$0.0031CR3$ (0.0022) $t = 1.41$	1.2%	0.6%
					$250 thousand to $1 million	$0.0066CR3$ (0.0017) $t = 1.40$	$-0.0010CR3$ (0.0018) $t = 0.67$	1.3%	-0.2%
Flechsig (1965)	Same as Edwards but special emphasis on region	Oct. 1955 49 SMSAs FRB business loan surveys	CR3 based on SMSA data except 9 statewide branching states where 1960 CR3's adjusted for mergers	Average loan size Five regional dummies	Effective interest rates on loans to firms with assets of: $1 thousand to $50 thousand	1955 only $-0.001CR3$ (0.006) $t = -0.17$		-0.2%	
					$50 thousand to $250 thousand	$-0.001CR3$ (0.003) $t = 0.33$		-0.2%	

Study	Data	Concentration measure	Other variables	Dependent variable	Coefficient 1955	Coefficient 1957	1955	1957
Flechsig (continued)	June 1960 19 large SMSAs FRB survey of interest rates on short term business loans	SMSA CR3	Average loan size Four regional dummies	Average interest rates on loans of sizes:	1955 only			
				$1 thousand to $10 thousand	$0.0001CR3$ (0.002) $t = 0.50$		0.2%	
				$10 thousand to $100 thousand	$0.001CR3$ (0.002) $t = 0.50$		0.2%	
				$100 thousand to $250 thousand	$-0.002CR3$ (0.002) $t = -1.00$		−0.4%	
				More than 250 thousand	$-0.000CR3$ (0.003) $t = -0.00$		0.0%	
Murphy (1967)	Same as Edwards	CR3 at SMSA rather than state level	Similar to Edwards Growth in non-agricultural employment Average bank size	Effective interest rate on loans to firms of asset size:	1955	1957	1955	1957
				$1 thousand to $50 thousand	$0.0102CR3$ (0.0065) $t = 1.56$	$0.0134CR3$ (0.006) $t = 2.02$	2.0%	2.2%
				$50 thousand to $250 thousand	$0.0064CR3$ (0.0026) $t = 2.50$	$0.0018CR3$ (0.0295) $t = 0.61$	1.1%	0.3%
				$250 thousand to $1 million	$0.0033CR3$ (0.0016) $t = 2.01$	$-0.0022CR3$ (0.0017) $t = -1.30$	0.6%	−0.4%

Table 12.2 (continued)

Author(s) (date)	Main concern	Data: Year(s) Unit of observation Source	Concentration variable(s)	Other independent variable(s)	Price variable(s)	Regression coefficients				Approximate percentage change in price with a ten-point rise in CR3			
						Q4 1960	Q3 1962	Q2 1964	Q1 1966	1960	1962	1964	1966
						Coefficients of CR3							
Phillips (1967)	Effect of concentration on price	Q4 1960 Q3 1962 Q2 1964 Q1 1968 73–75 banks in 19 SMSAs FRS quarterly survey of short-term business loans	SMSA CR3 based on deposits	Bank size Region	Interest rate on short term business loans by loan size:								
					$10 thousand	0.0087 (0.0031) t = 2.81	0.0075 (0.0044) t = 1.87	0.0097 (0.0038) t = 2.55	0.0069 (0.0033) t = 2.09	1.5%	1.3%	1.6%	1.1%
					$10 thousand to $100 thousand	0.0090 (0.0029) t = 3.10	0.0107 (0.0031) t = 3.45	0.0097 (0.0029) t = 3.34	0.0076 (0.0029) t = 2.62	1.5%	1.8%	1.6%	1.3%
					$100 thousand to $200 thousand	0.0036 (0.0031) t = 1.16	0.0062 (0.0044) t = 1.41	0.0107 (0.0032) t = 3.34	0.0105 (0.0030) t = 1.50	0.7%	1.4%	2.4%	1.9%
					$200 thousand and more	0.0093 (0.0028) t = 3.32	0.0050 (0.0040) t = 1.48	0.0086 (0.0038) t = 2.26	0.0054 (0.0027) t = 2.00	1.9%	1.3%	1.9%	1.0%
Jacobs (1971)	Effect of tight money on small business	1966 7,614 borrowers Questionnaire sent to 600 banks	CR3	Population growth Branching rules Mean deposit Bank size Loan characteristics	Loan interest	0.5275CR3 (0.0526) t = 10.03				0.9%			

Table 12.2 (continued)

Author(s) (date)	Main concern	Data: Year(s) Unit of observation Source	Concentration variable(s)	Other independent variable(s)	Price variable(s)	Regression coefficients Nominal interest rates	Adjusted for compensting balances	Approximate percentage change in price with a ten-point rise in CR3 Nominal	Adjusted
Scott (1977)	Effect of CR on loan interest rates. Correction for compensating balances	July 1972 through June 1974; 80 banks in 29 SMSAs in Northeast; Monthly surveys of FR Bank of Boston	CR3; Herfindahl index (H); H − 1/N	Bank size; SMSA total employment per bank office; Number of branches; SMSA average wage rate	Nominal interest rate on small loans ($10 thousand to $25 thousand) business loans; Interest rates adjusted for compensating balances	1.0CR3 (0.45) t = 2.4; 1.9H (0.79) t = 2.4; 2.4(H − 1/N) (0.92) t = 2.6	1.3CR3 (0.57) t = 2.3; 2.4H (0.92) t = 2.6; 2.9(H − 1/N) (1.12) t = 2.6	1.1%; 0.7%	1.4%; 0.9%
Aspinwall (1970)	Effect of concentration on mortgage interest rates	1965; 31 SMSAs; FDIC survey	CR3 based on savings deposits at commercial banks, SLAs and MS banks; Number of such mortgage lenders	Increase in number of households; Loan to price ratio; Median family income; Average bank size	Contractual interest rate on conventional, single family home mortgages of commercial banks	0.0053CR3 (0.0020) t = 2.71; −0.070 log N (0.0252) t = −3.88		0.9%; 2.2%	

Table 12.2 (continued)

Author(s) (date)	Main concern	Data: Year(s) Unit of observation Source	Concentration variable(s)	Other independent variable(s)	Price variable(s)	Regression coefficients	Approximate percentage change in price with a ten-point rise in CR3
Marlow (1982)	Effect of inter-state branch banking on conventional home mortgage interest rates	1975 111 SMSAs FHLBB survey of SLAs, commercial banks and MS banks	CR3 CR5 N Firms N Offices All based on all major mortgage lenders	Market size Market growth Foreclosure rate Ratio of loan/property value Average term of mortgage	Average effective interest rate on conventional, single-family home mortgages of all major mortgage lenders	0.003CR3 (0.0013) $t = 2.38$ 0.003CR5 (0.0012) $t = 2.44$ −0.0009N firms (0.0004) $t = -2.17$ −0.0002N offices (0.00025) $t = -0.79$	0.3% 0.3% 1.0% 0.2%
Schweiger and McGee (1961)	How Chicago banks perform compared with other SMSAs	1954 Bank size class in an SMSA	CR3 1966 (We inserted. They did not test.)	Bank size class Unit banking dummy	Interest on $500 personal loans Interest on automobile loans	0.072CR3 (0.019) $t = 3.79$ 0.020CR3 (0.013) $t = 1.54$	6.9% 2.1%

Table 12.2 (continued)

Author(s) (date)	Main concern	Data: year(s) Unit of observation Source	Concentration variable(s)	Other independent variable(s)	Price variable(s)	Regression coefficients				Approximate percentage change in price with a ten-point rise in CR3
Taylor (1968)	Effect of loan mix on IL/TL	1962 1,315 commercial banks in 6th district (Atlanta) Statements of condition	Number of banks in town (1, 2, 3, or more)	Total deposits percent of loans that were: Business loans Farm loans Nonfarm residential mortgages Personal installment loans Financial and all other loans	IL/TL		Number of banks			
							1	2	3 or more	
						Mean IL/TL	7.592	7.331	7.150	
						Less mean deviation	−0.045	0.055	0.016	
						Equals estimated mean controlling for loan portfolio	7.547	7.386	7.166	
							Number of banks			
							1–2	2–3	1–3	1–2 2–3 1–3
						Differences between estimated means	0.161	0.220	0.381	2.2% 3.0% 5.2%
Edwards (1965)	Effects of concentration on performance variables derived from reports of condition	1962 36 SMSAs in 18 states. Does not include New York Averages based on reports of condition	SMSA CR2	Average bank size IL/TL Population Deposits per capita Consumer loans/ ITD/TD total loans		0.0095CR2 (0.0052) $t = 1.83$				1.2%
						−0.0049CR2 (0.0029) $t = 1.69$				−1.2%

Table 12.2 (continued)

Author(s) (date)	Main concern	Concentration variable(s)	Other independent variable(s)	Price variable(s)	Data: year(s) / Unit of observation / Source	Regression coefficients — Coefficient of CR3				Approximate percentage change in price with a ten-point rise in CR3		
						Year	IL/TL	ITD/TD	SC/DD			
Rhoades (1981)	Effects of concentration on bank charges over time	SMSA CR3	Branching dummies, Annual growth, Assets of SLAs, MS banks, and CUs divided by commercial bank time deposits, Total loans/total assets, Taxable payroll in banking/total banking employment, Bank holding company presence dummy	IL/TL, ITD/TD, SC/DD	1966, 1968, 1970, 1972, 1973, 1974, 1975; 167 SMSAs (averages for banks in those SMSAs); Statements of condition	1966	0.001 (0.00003) $t = 3.64$	−0.00000 (0.00000) $t = -0.016$	0.00004 (0.00002) $t = 1.90$	1.5%	−0.0%	6.0%
						1968	0.0001 (0.00003) $t = 2.92$	−0.00000 (0.00000) $t = -0.11$	0.00003 (0.00002) $t = 1.91$	1.4%	0.3%	6.0%
						1970	0.001 (0.00004) $t = 2.18$	−0.00007 (0.00003) $t = -2.11$	0.00003 (0.00002) $t = 1.24$	1.1%	0.03%	12.0%
						1972	0.0001 (0.000025) $t = 4.00$	−0.00008 (0.00003) $t = -2.58$	0.00006 (0.00002) $t = 3.04$	1.9%	0.02%	12.0%
						1973	0.00004 (0.00002) $t = 1.79$	−0.00005 (0.00004) $t = -1.15$	0.00006 (0.00002) $t = 3.40$	0.4%	0.03%	12.0%
						1974	0.00001 (0.00004) $t = 0.26$	−0.0001 (0.00005) $t = -1.99$	0.00006 (0.00002) $t = 3.14$	0.1%	0.3%	12.0%
						1975	0.00004 (0.00003) $t = 1.56$	−0.0001 (0.00005) $t = -2.10$	0.00006 (0.00005) $t = 1.31$	0.5%	0.3%	12.0%

Table 12.2 (continued)

Author(s) (date)	Main concern	Data: Year(s) Unit of observation Source	Concentration variable(s)	Other independent variable(s)	Price variable(s)	Regression coefficients	Approximate percentage change in price with a ten-point rise in CR3
Rhoades and Rutz (1982)	Effect of multi-bank holding companies on other banks in same SMSA	1970–1979 1,511 single market banks not holding companies in 154 SMSAs	CR3 based on deposits over 1970–1979	Total share of multibank holding companies Branching rules Portfolio ratios Market size and growth	IL/TL (ten-year average 1970–1979)	0.005823CR3 (0.00123) t = 4.75	0.7%
Whitehead (1978)	Competitive effect of multimarket holding companies	1974 47 Florida banking markets Statements of condition	CR3 H	Market growth 11 alternative multimarket links "Market rivalry" (instability of market shares)	IL/TL	−0.0100 (0.234) t = −2.34	−0.8%

Table 12.2 (continued)

Author(s) (date)	Main concern	Data: Year(s) / Unit of observation / Source	Concentration variable(s)	Other independent variable(s)	Price variable(s)	Regression coefficients — Coefficients from alternative regressions		Approximate percentage change in price with a ten-point rise in $CR3$
Kaufmann (1966)	Effect of concentration on interest rates, profits, and balance sheet ratios	1959, 1960 / All 99 Iowa counties / Statements of condition	Number of banks $CR1$ based on deposits	SLA assets/bank deposits; Distance from financial center; Level and change in incomes; Level and growth in population; Nonagricultural employment/total employment	1959	1959		$\Delta N = -1\Delta CR1 + 4$
					IL/TL	$-0.0517N$ (0.0157) $t = 2.95$	$0.0111CR1$ (0.0028) $t = 3.96$	1.8% 0.8%
					ITD/TD	$0.0544N$ (0.127) $t = 5.04$	$-0.139CR1$ (0.0027) $t = 5.15$	-5.0% -2.5%
					1960	1960		
					IL/TL	$-0.0473N$ (0.0168) $t = 2.82$	$0.0124CR1$ (0.0027) $t = 4.59$	1.6% 0.8%
					ITD/TD	$0.0652N$ (0.0194) $t = 3.36$	$-0.157CR1$ (0.0030) $t = 5.83$	-5.3% -2.8%

Table 12.2 (continued)

Author(s) (date)	Main concern	Data: Year(s) / Unit of observation / Source	Concentration variable(s)	Other independent variable(s)	Price variable(s)	Regression coefficients				Approximate percentage change in price with a ten-point rise in CR3
Fraser and Rose (1972a)	Difference in performance between isolated 1 bank and 2- to 3-bank towns	1965, 1968 — 71, 1-bank towns and 83.2- or 3-bank towns — Statements of condition	Number of banks (1 and 2 or 3)	Sample limited to 1-, 2-, 3-bank towns not in SMSA. No entry in past 6 years. Controlled for presence of SLA. Distance from financial center. Population level and growth. Deposit growth		**1965**	**1966**			Effect of increase N of banks
					IL/TL	$-0.386N$ (0.339) $t = -1.14$	$-0.279N$ (0.254) $t = -1.01$			N / 1965 / 1966 — 1-2 / -5.1% / -3.7% — 2-3 / -5.6% / -3.5% — 1-3 / -10.3% / -7.4%
					ITD/TD	$0.044N$ (0.440) $t = 0.10$	$0.330N$ (0.500) $t = 0.66$			1-2 / 1.4% / 10.4% — 2-3 / 1.3% / 9.7% — 1-3 / 2.8% / 20.8%
					SC/DD	$-0.027N$ (0.055) $t = -0.488$	$0.005N$ (0.500) $t = 0.088$			1-2 / -9.0% / 1.7% — 2-3 / -8.7% / 1.6% — 1-3 / -18.0% / 3.3%
Fraser and Rose (1972b)	Effect of entry on many variables, not just price	1960, 1961 (pre-entry) — 1965, 1966 (postentry) — 34 banks in towns where entry occurred and 58 towns where no entry — Statements of condition	1-, 2-, and 3-bank towns pre-entry. Became 2-, 3-, or 4-bank towns after entry. Median town went from 2 to 3 banks.	Sample chosen to match size of town (non-SMSA). 2 or 3 banks, all unit banks		**Differences between means or banks in entry and nonentry towns by year**				1965–66 mean less 1961–62 divided by four-year nonentry mean
						Pre-entry		**Post-entry**		
						1960	**1961**	**1965**	**1966**	
					IL/TL	-0.05 (0.28) $t = 0.18$	0.12 (0.30) $t = 0.40$	-0.28 (0.22) $t = -1.28$	-0.21 (0.20) $t = -1.03$	2.6%
					ITD/TD	-0.04 (0.15) $t = -0.26$	-0.44 (0.17) $t = -2.53$	0.07 (0.14) $t = 0.50$	-0.11 (0.17) $t = -0.63$	7.5%
					SC/DD	0.09 (0.07) $t = -1.38$	0.08 (0.06) $t = 1.28$	-0.01 (0.17) $t = -0.06$	-0.02 (0.08) $t = -0.26$	24.0%

Table 12.2 (continued)

Authors(s) (date)	Main concern	Data: Year(s) Unit of observation Source	Concentration variable(s)	Other independent variable(s)	Price variable(s)	Regression coefficients			Approximate percentage change in price with a ten-point rise in CR3
Fraser and Rose (1974)	The importance of several types of variables in determining bank performance putting all industry structure variables into one group	1969, 1970 All 245 Texas counties that have banks Statements of condition	A weighted group of three market structure variables: N of banks, $CR1$, dummy for SLA. Weighted to maximize their explanatory power with respect to a weighted combination of performance growth, and density.	Five other groups weighted to maximize the groups' explanatory power. The groups are costs (labor costs only): composition of deposits; types of loans; population size, growth, and density; local economic conditions.	The weighted performance grouping contained IL/TL, ITD/TD, SC/DD, but also contained T/L assets and a profit variable	Weights not reported but canonical correlations Group All Costs Loan types Deposit types Demographic factors Market structure Economic conditions	1969 0.7016 0.5042 0.4984 0.4804 0.4585 0.3786 0.3164	1970 0.7368 0.4590 0.4590 0.5212 0.4250 0.3989 0.3051	Not calcuable with results given

Table 12.2 (continued)

Author(s) (date)	Main concern	Data: Year(s) Unit of observation Source	Concentration variable(s)	Other independent variable(s)	Price variable(s)	Regression coefficients		Approximate percentage change in price with a ten-point rise in CR3
						Using share stability index	Best-fitting dynamic index and its t ratio	
Fraser and Rose (1976)	Effects of dynamic concentration indexes in banking markets	Performance data for 1973 Concentration change, 1961–1973	1973 Herfindahl index ($H73$) Three alternative dynamic market structure indexes: $H73-H61$	SLA dummy Labor cost Four types of loan percentages Population growth rate	IL/TL	0.0079 (0.0048) $t = 1.62$	$H73-H61$ $t = 1.62$	0.03%
		90 Texas counties, including some with very large banks	"Dynamic concentration index (depends on $X2$, $Y2$, and XY, where X and Y are $si - \bar{s}$ in 1961 or 1973)	Retail sales per capita	ITD/TD	−0.0004 (0.0029) $t = 0.14$	Share stability index $t = 1.62$	−0.01%
		Statements of condition	Share stability index $= r_{s_{61}s_{73}}$	Average bank size	SC/DD	−0.0012 (0.00053) $t = -0.75$	Dynamic concentration index $t = -1.65$	−0.1%
					Spread $= (IL/TL)$ $+ (ITD/TD)$	0.0082 (0.0052) $t = 1.57$	$H73-H61$ $t = 0.89$	0.03%
Heggested and Mingo (1966)	To determine what variables were most effective variables in attracting deposits	1970	H $-1/H$		Interest rate on auto loans	$0.00060(-1/H)$ (0.00014) $t = 4.15$		1.2%
		A bank						
		Federal Reserve Survey of Mergers			Interest rate on one year CD passbook interest rates	$-0.001548(-1/H)$ (−0.001025) $t = -1.51$		−5.0%

Table 12.2 (continued)

Author(s) (date)	Main concern	Data: Year(s) Unit of observation Source	Concentration variable(s)	Other independent variable(s)	Price variable(s)	Approximate percentage Regression coefficients	change in price with a ten-point rise in $CR3$
Hannon (1979)	To test the limit pricing hypothesis	1970 One of 53 banking markets in Pennsylvania Time deposit interest rates	N Number of potential entrants (NPE)		Time deposit interest rates	$0.062N$ (0.014) $t = 4.43$ $0.22NPE$ (0.07) $t = 3.14$ $0.0062N \times NPE$ (0.0024) $t = 2.58$	3.1%
Berger and Hannan (1987)	Effect of $CR3$ on money market deposit account	1983–85 A bank in a quarter Federal Reserve Board Survey	$CR3$ Herfindahl index (see special report in the chapter)	Money market fund rate One-year growth Bank branches Bank wage rate Per capita income Branching rules	Interest rates on money market account deposits	$-0.63CR3$ (0.15) $t = 4.08$ $-0.011N$ (0.0030) $t = -3.63$	0.9%

and the sort of study Edwards did tried to explain those differences in terms of concentration, among other things. When data can only vary with intercity differences, regional dummies should not be introduced without some obvious need, and then only on the basis of a criterion that is independent of the dependent variable. With a little care, it would probably be possible to show that latitude does not affect temperature in the United States, once six or eight regional dummies have been introduced!

If there is any reason to use a regional dummy, it would be to distinguish those cities where money market transactions are so large that they may affect interest rates on small loans. The obvious case is New York. The Fed excluded New York banks from the 1955 survey, so neither Edwards nor Flechsig included it. Flechsig did include New York in his 1960 regressions so that one of his 19 observations combined by far the largest center for large loans and security issues with one of the lowest concentration ratios in the country. Even in this case, however, I would prefer to introduce a continuous variable—such as size of city. Edwards did control for city size, through with dummy variables. Flechsig put New York in a box with Baltimore, Boston, and Philadelphia, where the money market is a far smaller part of the whole.

In general, I feel that Edwards made most of the right decisions. Interest rates were averages within borrower size classes. The years 1955 and 1957 were examined separately. New York was not included. He should have used SMSA concentration, and I wish he had controlled for average bank size in order to capture some of the effect of money market participation and any economies of scale. I don't feel that any of these faults were very serious.

Flechsig's regional dummies, on the other hand, leave both of his studies fatally flawed, in my opinion. The reason he was given so much space here is that he was Edward's main critic, and Edwards was the key study in the first decade of concentration-price studies in banking or anywhere else.

Murphy (1967) tried to correct the imperfections in Edwards' work in a more constructive way. He used SMSA rather than state concentration estimates, and he excluded the statewide branch banking states from his main regressions because he thought many SMSA figures were unrepresentative of conditions for the statewide branch systems. He controlled for average bank size, as Edwards should have. He made several smaller changes as well. His results were similar to Edwards.

Phillips (1967) worked with the second set of data that Flechsig had used, the Fed's quarterly survey of short-term interest rates in 19 large SMSA's, but he went far beyond what Flechsig did. For one thing, he ran regressions for one quarter of every other year from 1960 to 1966. He reported some results where an SMSA was an observation (not shown in table 12.2). Working with simple regressions only, he found positive coefficients in each year in each size class. Almost all of the *t* ratios exceeded 1.0, but only one of these 19 observation regressions yielded a coefficient that was statistically significant at the 5 percent level (for the $100,000 to $199,000 loan size group in the first quarter of 1966). However, the 16 regressions involved were based on 16 different groups of bank loan assets (loan sizes by years). The probability of getting 16 positive coefficients by chance for 16 independent draws from different but related data sets is minuscule. I conclude that he found strong evidence of a tendency for prices to rise with concentration, even with only one *t* ratio over 2.0.

He then shifted to regressions where an observation was one of the 73 to 75 banks located in those 19 SMSAs that were in the Fed's sample. Since the experience of banks in a metropolitan area was probably correlated, he was involved in a problem of serial correlation for which he did not correct. It did not bias his estimates, but he probably exaggerated their accuracy. He controlled for bank size, and again got positive effects for concentration in all 16 year-size class regressions. Those are the results shown in table 12.2. Eleven of the 16 regression coefficients had significant positive signs, so even ignoring the interclass consistency of his results, he can reasonably conclude that concentration raises interest rates. In three of the four years the largest loan size class shows the least relationship between concentration and interest rates, but in 1960, the year Flechsig used, it had the closest fit. All 19 of these SMSAs have well over a million in population.

Finally, he introduced a regional dummy, separating out the East and South from the Midwest and West. There isn't a great deal of logic to this subdivision, either, but even though it has a significant effect, it did not destroy the relationship the way Flechsig's regions did. My view is that in an interregional cross section with only a few observations, the need for regional dummies must be very strong to justify their use. I presume that Phillips introduced his mainly to show that a reasonable regional dummy need not destroy the effects of concentration and bank size on interest rates.

Jacobs (1971) sent questionnaires to 600 banks to get data on large numbers of small to medium commercial loans in 1966. His main concern was about who got hurt in periods of tight money, a major issue at that time. He ultimately was able to get data on 7,614 customers. Because he was concerned about the interest rates charged and the deposits required, he used conventional models to predict these two performance variables.

He got a strong, positive effect for concentration on interest rates. It was strongest for small borrowers (less than $500,000 assets), especially when loans were not fully collateralized.

To test for the effect of market structure on reciprocal balances, he made average deposit dependent. The effect of concentration was positive in some cases and negative in others. It's effect came closest to being significant in his largest borrower assets class ($1,000,000–5,000,000) where it had a positive coefficient ($t = 1.79$). Distinguishing between collateralized and noncollateralized loans makes the coefficient for noncollateralized loans to large borrowers positive and reduces all the coefficients to nonsignificance.

At one point Jacobs inserts six regional dummies. The effect of concentration increased in statistical significance. This is consistent with the weakening effect of Flechsig's procedure because interregional differences were the only way interest rates could differ in Flechsig's data, but for Jacobs, a borrower was an observation. When he eliminated much of the interregional variation, he still had thousands of individual borrowers with varying experience to report. Concentration is a characteristic of SMSAs and is the same for every observation in a city. As a result Jacobs may have exaggerated the accuracy of his estimates, but his problem is surely very small. He had 112 SMSAs and the t ratio on $CR3$ is huge.

Scott (1977), working at the Federal Reserve Bank of Boston, did a number of studies including one using data collected monthly for two years from 70 banks in 29 metropolitan areas in the New England and Middle Atlantic states plus Delaware in 1972 to 1974. We will limit ourselves to a set of regressions using averages of the 24 months, and these are what we report in table 12.2.

He worked with business loans of $10,000 to $25,000, so most borrowers were probably limited to individual SMSA markets. Compensating balances were reported in the surveys, so he was able to correct for them. They increased the effect of concentration. It is still significant, and it is still small.

He used three concentration measures. The first, $CR3$, yielded almost exactly the effect it did in 1955 and more effect than in 1957, even though 1972 to 1974 was a very different period. The second, the Herfindahl index, yielded a mildly better fit than $CR3$. But the most striking result was with his third concentration index, $H - 1/N$. Since $1/N$ is the value of the Herfindahl index with equal-sized lenders, $H - 1/N$ is an index inequality of bank size. It yields the best fit of the three measures used. He suggested that the good fit of the inequality variable was evidence that the effect of concentration worked mainly through price leadership.

Scott worked with data from a period of transition in small business loans. The year 1972 was as close to an easy money period as you can find after 1965, but 1973 saw very high interest rates and in 1974 interest rates reached levels never previously reported in the United States. The prime rate went from 5.25 in 1972 to 8.03 in 1973 to 10.81 in 1974, our tightest money year to that date. The traditional ceiling interest rates on small loans gave way, and interest rates at "the prime plus x percent" came into existence. If those data still exist, it would be fascinating to trace the effect of the change on small loan interest rates and on the availability of credit to small borrowers.

In general, the debate that Edwards began in 1964 was pretty much finished by 1977, and I believe Edwards clearly won. Banks in concentrated markets did charge higher interest rates, and the tendency was strongest on small loans and especially to small borrowers. It was greatest in easy money periods. Even the coefficients were remarkably consistent once general credit conditions are taken into consideration. As far as I know, there have been no further studies based on small borrower or small loan survey data since then.

Mortgage Interest Rates

We have a few other interest rates that are paid primarily by small borrowers and that are at least partially local in nature, especially residential mortgages.

The first mortgage study was Aspinwall's (1970). He worked with conventional, as opposed to FHA and VA insured mortgages, since 93.4 percent of conventional mortgages are financed in the same SMSA. A third of the insured FHA and VA mortgages are financed in other SMSAs. His two concentration measures, $CR3$ based on time deposits and N, used data from all of the major local mortgage lending institutions: commercial banks, savings and loan associations (SLAs), and mutual savings banks (MSBKs). Log N yielded a slightly better fit than $CR3$. Both coefficients were highly significant. It should be pointed out that of his 31 SMSA's, all but Denver and Pueblo, Colorado, and Tulsa, Oklahoma, were in the Northeast quadrant of the country. Concentration on his markets is a good deal lower than in commercial loan markets.

The only other mortgage rate study I know is that of Marlow which used data a decade after Aspinwall's. He used the same dependent variable but had 111 SMSAs. He had some control variables that Aspinwall did not have and worked with N rather than log N. The year 1965 differed in many respects from 1975. The later year combined a serious recession with rapid inflation; 1965 came after five years of recovery when inflation and unemployment were both fairly low. Interest rates were low in 1965 and wildly high in 1975. The theory that we started out with in the 1950s would predict that concentration should raise interest rates more in 1965 than in 1975, and wonder of wonders it did. The coefficient of $CR3$ was 0.0053 in 1965 and 0.003 in 1975. In view of the strangeness of 1975, I am surprised they are of the same order of magnitude.

As in the case of commercial loans, mortgage borrowers who are limited to local markets (for conventional as opposed to insured FHA and VA mortgages) pay higher interest rates the more concentrated the lending market, the effect is more severe in easy money periods, and it is never large.

Chicago Banking

"Chicago Banking" certainly belongs in this chapter, but it is hard to classify. It was a major study done by University of Chicago Business School faculty (Irving Schweiger and John McGee) in response to a request by the Chicago Association of Commerce and Industry. The work was done in 1959 and 1960 when computers were new and multiple regressions, difficult. Most of their statistical work was comparisons of means. Many of them involved comparisons between Chicago (usually six countries centered in Chicago) with ten other metropolitan areas. Their main concern was with the effects of unit banking. At that time Illinois was a devotedly unit banking state. In addition three-quarters of the area's banks had failed in the early 1930s, and entry was very difficult.

They put their main emphasis on loan-asset ratios and the adequacy of banking facilities in the area. These are very important, and their criticism of unit banking is quite convincing, but it goes beyond the issues to be covered by this chapter. We will limit our discussion of that massive paper (135 pages in the *Journal of Business*) to the interest rate studies.

Their data source was at least diligent. They negotiated 112 auto loans for identical new cars and 142 unsecured $500 personal loans with identical terms at banks in the six countries in the Chicago area and in ten other metropolitan areas. They reported their results in tabular form, and although they mentioned concentration as important, they did not introduce it as a variable. One striking result was that about a third of the Chicago

Table 12.3

Variable	Consumer loans	Auto loans
Constant	8.89	9.71
	(1.26)	(0.81)
	[7.04]	[11.58]
CR3	0.072	0.020
	(0.019)	(0.013)
	[3.80]	[1.58]
Unit banking dummy	2.65	−0.50
	(0.65)	(0.43)
	[4.59]	[−1.15]
Bank assets sizes		
$10−100 million	−0.92	−0.18
	(0.85)	(0.57)
	[−1.08]	[−0.33]
$100−500 million	−0.96	−0.75
	(0.75)	(0.50)
	[−1.28]	[−1.51]
More than $500 million	−0.98	−0.62
	(0.79)	(0.52)
	[−1.24]	[−1.18]
$\bar{R}^2$	0.459	0.196

area banks and similar shares in the two other unit banking states in their sample refused to make the $500 personal loans at all, while all the banks sampled in the branch banking states were willing to do so. They reported their results by city and size of bank.

I limit the analysis to the 11 metropolitan area data because I don't know how to divide the six Chicago countries into markets. I used a size class in a city as an observation. Thirty-seven of the 44 possible cells contained data. I was able to get CR3 for all 11 SMSAs for 1966 but for only 8 of them in 1960, so I used the 1966 ratios. The results are shown in table 12.3.

Concentration raised monthly payments on consumer loans significantly but had only a weak positive effect on them for auto loans. About the same applied to unit banking. Large banks tended to charge less than small ones, but that tendency was never significant.

Data from Statements of Condition

The variable based on the statement of condition that comes closest to the interest rates discussed so far is interest and other charges on loans divided by total value of loans (*IL/TL*), but it contains two possible biases that will be discussed below. Two other ratios from the same source come closer to being prices, if anything. They are service charges on checking accounts divided by the value of demand deposits (*SC/DD*), and interest paid on time deposits divided by the value of those deposits (*ITD/TD*). Many of the studies that used the statement of condition as their source worked with all three price variables.

There are two possible biases in regression estimates of the coefficients of *IL/TL*. The natural one is that the coefficient will understate the effect of concentration on interest rates paid by to locally limited borrowers because of loans to borrowers with ready access to money market sources. If half the loans at all banks were money market loans, the coefficient of *IL/TL* would be roughly half of the true effect of concentration on the price of credit for borrowers who are actually limited to the local sources.

There is an opposite source of bias, however. There is no doubt that a disproportionate share of the large, money market loans are made by large banks in large SMSAs, especially New York, which tend also to be the least concentrated markets. As a result a study that merely regresses *IL/TL* on concentration is apt to overstate the effect of concentration on these grounds and thus to offset in whole or in part the understatement mentioned above. Obviously, at least a partial correction might be to control for bank size and SMSA size. Beyond that, we can only compare the coefficients of *CR3* in studies controlling for loan or borrower sizes with those that result from *IL/TL* without any such controls.

There was one study (Taylor 1968) that attempted to correct for loan mix. He worked with 1,315 banks in the sixth Federal Reserve District (Atlanta). He introduced the percentage of loans in each of six categories as well as bank size as independent variables and then analyzed the residuals. Unfortunately, he was unable to distinguish large and small commercial loans, which is where the main problem lay.

His measure of concentration is number of banks which he classifies into one, two, and three or more banks. He reports the mean of *IL/TL* for each number-of-banks class, which we have reproduced in table 12.2, and then the mean deviations due to difference in loan mix. I subtract these from the original means to get means adjusted for loan mix.

The differences are still quite large compared with those that have appeared in other studies we have reviewed here. Moreover the mean deviations he reports are small. Interest rates are overstated by 0.045 percentage points or by 0.59 percent, in one-bank towns understated by 0.0551 percentage points or by 0.75 percent in two-bank towns, and understated by only 0.016 percentage points or 0.22 percent in towns with three or more banks. This is apt to understate the bias because commercial loans are not subdivided by size and because the banks with many money market customers are probably in a few cities with more than three banks.

He reports the differences among his number of banks categories to be "not significant at the 25 percent level." Yet the differences turn out to be quite large and highly significant. It is a problem in analysis of variance. He has 1,315 observations and three means, so our comparison is among means where $n = 1,315$, $m = 3$, $n - m = 1,312$, and $m - 1 = 2$. He reports the overall standard deviation, so we can compute variance as

$$(1.215)^2 = 1.476 = \frac{S}{n - 1},$$

so $S = 1,939.76$. He reports the means and the numbers of observations in the three groups as one bank: 7.592 (616), two banks: 7.331 (426), and three or more banks: 7.150 (217). His overall mean is 7.415. So the variance among the means is 41.35. This implies that the variance within the three categories is 1,898.41.

The F statistic is thus $(41.35/2)/(1,898.41/1,312) = 14.29$. An F ratio that large would occur by chance with 2 and 1,312 degrees of freedom far less often as once in 100. That was with the uncorrected means. Making his adjustments, the three means become for one bank 7.547, for two banks 7.386, and for three or more banks 7.168. The F ratio is reduced to 10.87, but it is still more than would occur by chance as often at once in 100. This understates the significance of the relationship because it does not take into account the fact that interest rate is higher with one bank than with two and higher with two than with three or more. It isn't just a matter of variance being greater than would have occurred by chance. The IL/TL also varied in the expected direction.

How could Taylor have read his numbers so badly? There is one hint. He "confirms" his finding by saying that in a stepwise least squares regression analysis of the same data, his concentration variables came in last and did not reduce the unexplained variance at all. But look at his other variables. He Included 34 regional variables: one for each state in the district and 28 for every significant city. After that, a variable that could only vary over space such as number of banks in town could not possibly explain anything at all! It is Flechsig run wild!

Altogether, then, we will have to judge the possible biases in IL/TL by comparing the results using that variable with those using coefficients for the same year based on data for individuals borrower size or loan size class. I know of three such comparisons.

The first involved a second Edwards article (1965). He was working with 1962 data and so the natural comparison is with Almarin Phillips' 1962 figures. Unfortunately, Edwards used $CR2$ and Phillips used $CR3$, so a direct comparison is imperfect. If $CR2$ runs about 0.75 $CR3$, then a coefficient of 0.0095 $CR2$ will be equivalent to 0.0071 $CR3$. This is very close to Phillips' estimated coefficient (0.0075) for loans in the range \$1 to \$10,000. It is less than his slope for loans in the range \$10,000 to \$99,000 and more than his slopes for loans in the ranges \$100,000 to \$199,999 (0.0062) and \$200,000 and more (0.0059).

I presume that most of the loans in the two largest loan size classes were to borrowers with access to many money market sources. If so, the estimate using IL/TL was biased downward, if anything.

In the late 1970s Stephen Rhoades at the Federal Reserve Board developed a data file designed to facilitate studies relevant to bank mergers and related subjects. It covered every other year from 1966 to 1972 and every year from 1972 to the end of the file. It reported on 167 SMSAs which had the same definition over the whole period. The bank data for each SMSA was based on the reports of condition of all banks that derived 75 percent or more of their deposits from the SMSA involved. However, concentration was based on deposits of all banks in the SMSA regardless of whether they were included in the averages. The data base was used to test various hypotheses about IL/TL, SC/DD, ITD/TD, various portfolio ratios, and a few profit measures. It has been the basis for many studies of bank structure and its effects.

It provides two other tests of bias in IL/TL. Unfortunately, it appears that IT/TL must have been expressed in terms of basis points in the initial research with the file. At least Rhoades, in describing the results, says that a coefficient of 0.0001 $CR3$ implies that ten-point rise in concentration would raise loan rates by 0.1 percentage points—for instance, from 7.0 to 7.1 percent (Rhoades 1981, 168). As a result all of the coefficients for $CR3$ in the IL/TL equations in 1966, 1968, 1970, and 1972 were reported to be 0.0001. That may be a suitably modest statement of what the researchers think they know, but it does make it difficult to compare results with other studies that controlled for size of loan.

The obvious comparison is with Phillips who also studied 1966. He reports that for the first quarter of 1966, the coefficients for $CR3$ were 0.0069 for loans under \$10,000, 0.0076 for loans in the range \$10,000 to \$99,999, 0.0105 in the range \$100,000 to \$199,999, and 0.0054 on loans of $200,000 or more. Technically, the published coefficient for 1966 from the new data set exceeds all but one of these, but with the usual rounding rule, it could coincide with any of Phillips' coefficients. That is, a little more detail could yeild a coefficient anywhere from 0.0051 to 0.0149 using Phillips' placement of decimal points. The most we can say is that the new data at the Fed yields a coefficient in the same order of magnitude.

Finally, Scott (1972) offers another point for comparison with data from Rhoades' file. For the period July 1972 to June 1974 the coefficient relating interest rates on loans of $10,000 to $25,000 to CR3 was 1.0. Assuming, as we did earlier, that Scott measured his interest rates as ratios, Phillips as percentages, and Rhoades as basis points, the comparable figure from Rhoades' article would be the numbers in parentheses shown below. They are multiplied by weights proportional to the number of months in the year that Scott used. The weights were set so that they would have a total of 1.0. In effect, this assumes that Rhoades' coefficients applied equally through-out the year:

$$0.25(0.0001) + 0.5(0.00004) + 0.25(0.00001) = 0.0000475$$

($= 0.475$ in Scott's dimensions).

This seems much less than Scott's actual coefficient of 1.00. In this case it seems that Rhoades' data, which includes many large loans, yielded a good deal lower coefficient than Scott got on small loans in the same period. Far from overstating the relationship because small loans are an increasing part of the total as concentration rises, the aggregate figures probably under-stated it, at least in the early 1970s, by including many loans to large borrowers whose credit supply markets extend far beyond the SMSA.

In general our few studies where Rhoades' data base overlaps the period when small loan interest rates studies were made suggest that the bias in the IL/TL figure from reports of condition could work in either direction.

The other ratios from the statement of condition that have often been treated as prices in statistical studies are the interest on time deposits divided by total time deposits (ITD/TD) and the service charges on de-mand deposits divided by demand deposits (SC/DD). During the period covered by most of the studies, these were probably closer to prices than IL/TL was.

The ceiling on time deposit interest rates set by the Fed during the years of most of the studies must have capped increases in time deposit interest rates during most of our tight money periods. In view of this I would expect the relationship between concentration and ITD/TD to weaken or disappear during tight money periods.

The third price, SC/DD, had no upper limit, but the Fed's rules kept it from falling below zero (banks could not pay interest on demand deposits) during the period in which the concentration-price studies that included it were made.

Rhoades' banking markets data base was extended over time so that by 1981 it was possible to run regressions covering the whole of the 1970s. I have included the Rhoades and Rutz (1982) paper in the table to show the effect of average concentration on average IL/TL, ITD/TD, and SC/DD for the entire decade. A small but happy change is that this interest variable seems now to be measured as a percentage, so the coefficient has become readable. The effect of $CR3$ is by now very significant statistically but almost negligible economically. Recall that the late 1970s was a period of wildly high and very unstable interest rates. It was the sort of period when concentration would not have made much difference in earlier studies. However, it was also the period when interest rates on small loans were beginning to be expressed as "the prime plus X percent" which would have made them more flexible. It would be interesting to know the effect of that change on the concentration-price relationship on a year by year basis. I have not been able to find such regressions after 1975. The Rhoades' data base was used for many other purposes besides testing the concentration-price hypothesis. A large proportion of the issues of industrial organization have been studied using this rich data set.

It is essential that I cover David Whitehead's study of Florida banking because it is the one banking study that yields a significant negative effect of concentration on IL/TL. His main concern in the study is the effect of intermarket relationships due to holding companies that meet in more than one market. His measure of "competitiveness" is market share instability $= [\sum (\Delta MS\ 70 - 74)/MS\ 70]$ aggregated across the top three firms in a market. He tries 11 different multimarket linkage variables and generally gets positive signs though only a couple are even marginally significant. He was testing the theory of linked oligopoly and found it unconfirmed.

He also included $CR3$ and found a negative, usually significant relationship throughout. The same was true using the Herfindahl index. Market shares were relatively stable in the more concentrated markets.

For the purposes of this book, the most important result is that IL/TL rises with his measure of multimarket linkages but falls significantly as concentration rises regardless of which of his market linkage variables are used. He also measures their effect on ITD/TD and gets conventional results. It falls as concentration rises. I can't find any serious errors in this study. I presume his result has something special to do with Florida or with the relationship between concentration and multimarket interdependence.

Rural Banking

Another approach has been to examine the relationship between concentration and price in non-SMSAs. Presumably the money market influences will be weak in such markets, so the effect of concentration on local prices will not be diluted when the researcher studies variables like IL/TL.

The first such study (Kaufman 1968) took each of the 99 counties of Iowa as markets. My initial reaction is that Iowa is not all rural. The largest SMSAs are Omaha–Council Bluffs, Des Moines, and Davenport–Moline–Rock Island, and there are several other important cities. Although none of the banks in those SMSAs are likely to be thought of as money market banks, large loans to large customers with money market options are apt to be important for banks in quite a number of Iowa counties. Kaufman controlled for this in part by including figures for county population and distance from the nearest financial center as independent variables. His concentration variables were N and $CR1$. Some rural counties have only one or two banks. In such cases $CR3$ would throw away information. Assuming that the largest bank has about 40 percent of the share of the top three banks, where there are three, then a coefficient of 0.0124 for $CR1$ would correspond to one of 0.0050 for $CR3$. This is moderately less than with Phillips' coefficients for the same year. As always, it is statistically significant but economically small.

Kaufman was also one of the first to examine time deposit interest rates as prices. The coefficient of $CR1$ was -0.018. This is close to the midpoint of such coefficients in other nonrural studies.

There followed a series of inciteful and original studies of towns or counties in Texas for the 11th Federal Reserve District (Dallas) by Fraser and Rose. In one (Fraser and Rose 1972a) they selected a sample of one, two, and three bank towns from the 11th District that were not in SMSAs and were more than five miles from the nearest other community with a bank. They computed means for the one-bank towns and for the two- and three-bank towns lumped together, of 11 balance sheet ratios 5 profit measures, and the 3 standard bank "prices": IL/TL, ITD/TD, and SC/DD. For the first two of these prices, the monopoly banks charged more for loans and paid less on time and savings deposits than the banks in two- or three-bank towns; but SC/DD were lower for the monopoly banks. In regression form, loan interest rates fell and time deposit interest rates rose as the number of banks increase, but neither relationship was significant. Demand deposit service charges fell as a number of banks rose in 1965, but that expected relationship was reversed in 1966, and neither differed significantly from zero. The presence of a savings and loan had the expected effect on all three prices in 1965, and on loan rates and service charges in 1966, but, again, none of the relationships were statistically significant. They did not find the lack of price competition in isolated, highly concentrated markets like these surprising. They came away advocating a less rigid rule on mergers in such markets because of expected economies of scale.

Their second paper (Fraser and Rose 1972b) compared banks in towns where entry occurred (but not the entering banks) with banks where no entry occurred, again in relatively isolated, non-SMSA towns with one, two, or three banks. Although their emphasis was on entry, it necessarily involved an increase in number of banks in the affected towns. The results were exactly as one would expect from such a change in concentration— interest rates on loans and service charges on demand deposits fell and interest rates on time deposits rose in the towns experiencing entry and increased numbers of banks compared with those of banks in nonentry towns, though only the relative rise in time deposit rates was statistically significant. They emphasized the change in portfolio and could point to a number of significant shifts in the makeup of loans and deposits which they characterized as "profound." They thought we were unlikely to see the full impact of monopoly, at least in the small, isolated markets of the sort they we were analyzing, looking at prices. I thoroughly agree.

In a third study (Fraser, Phillips, and Rose 1974) they created a weighted combination of performance variables (prices, profit rates, and loans-deposits) and regressed the resulting, combined variable on several other "causal" varibles formed in the same way: a market structure variable that was a weighted combination of $CR1$, N, and a dummy if a SLA was present, and five other such variables based on labor costs, on the composition of deposits, on the composition of loans, on demographic factors, and on local economic conditions. All 18 variables together (the six weighted combinations) explained 49 percent of the variability of the weighted combination of performance variables in 1969 and 54 percent in 1970. The weighted combination of the three market structure variables ranked fifth among their six weighted groups in explanatory value. By itself it could "explain" only 14 percent of the performance variability across counties in 1969 and 16 percent in 1970. With costs, composition of bank credit, composition of deposits, and demographic factors already in the regression, the market structure variable added only 1.26 percent to the explanatory value of the regression in 1969 and 2.33 percent in 1970, though the combined effect of the three structural variables was still statistically significant.

But prices (interest rates on loans and especially time deposit interest rates) are among the banks' main handles for controlling these balance sheet variables. Presumably this fact accounts for 14 to 16 percent of performance variability explained by the market structure group, and at least in part, why it falls to 1.26 to 2.33 percent once those balance sheet ratios are also in the regression. The combined effects of the three structural variables was still statistically significant, but only "economic factors" had less explanatory power. Economic factors comprised such things as deposit growth rates and nonfarm payroll.

These results have a familiar ring. Market structure (mainly concentration here) had a significant but not very large effect on performance. The really big items are internal bank policy with respect to loans, investments, and types of deposits.

At least part of this conclusion is due to the importance of the variables. The absolute value of the increase in the share of assets invested in loans just had to be more important than the rise in service charges on demand deposits because the base values of the two ratios were 34.5 and 0.5 percent, respectively.

Which is more important? If we are concerned about the direct impact of bank policies, surely the large absolute rise in loans as a percentage of total portfolios must be our main focus. Small new businesses especially have always been very much affected by their ability to borrow, and a 9.5 percent increase in the availability of credit in a town that went from two to three banks would probably have a noticeable effect on the credit prospects for new firms in town. At the same time it seems unlikely that any customer had ever been seriously disadvantaged by check charges even where they are 24 percent too high.

But if we are looking for evidence of monopoly pricing, the fact that banks in one- or two-bank towns charge prices 24 percent higher for a service with less elastic demand (because those charges are so minor) and take much smaller margins on more noticeable prices seems altogether worth noting. There is nothing like systematic price discrimination as evidence of monopoly pricing.

There are several other studies of rural markets which we will merely summarize briefly. James Harvey (1982) worked with 430 rural counties in Missouri, the plains states, and three of the Rocky Mountain states as observations. He emphasized the simultaneous aspect of the banking business, in that concentration is likely to depress the interest rates on deposits at the same time it increased loan interest rates. It is the difference between the two that counts.

He then says he would love to run a simultaneous equation model, but his two equations aren't identified. So he reports, on two OLS regressions, one explaining loan interest rates and the other, explaining cost of capital to the bank as estimated by him. Using the one-firm concentration ratio he got the expected signs but only the cost of capital to the bank yielded a significant coefficient. However, when he substituted the number of banks in the county (really number of affiliated organizations), he got a significant negative effect for N on IL/TL and a significant positive effect of N on the cost of capital.

Robert F. Ware (1972) worked with 57 non-SMSA counties of Ohio. He studied all the standard variables plus price spread (the difference between average loan rate and savings deposit rates) for 1969 and 1970. They were regressed on nine explanatory variables. His regression coefficients were not published—just the significance levels of his coefficients. There was a significant tendency for the price spread to rise with $CR2$ in 1970. Check charges, profit rates, loan rates, and deposit rates were not significantly affected in either 1969 or 1970, and price spread was not in 1969. In general, he found next to no effect for market structure in small-town Ohio banking.

There are more studies of small-town banking that I have not been able to track down. The general conclusion is that it's hard to find evidence of price competition between two or three banks that have faced each other across the main square of town for the last 50 or 100 years. I'm not amazed. There is still some point in preserving alternatives to the businessmen in town, even if it doesn't save them much money.

Winning Depositors

Finally, there are several studies that deal with interest payments and all of the other things done to win depositors.

First in time is Bell and Murphy (1969) who regressed service charges on checking deposits in New England cities on $CR3$ suppressing the constant term. A "significant" positive effect was virtually inevitable because check charges are always positive. In fact "negative check charges" were illegal at the time. Banks were prohibited at law from paying interest on checking deposits. A slope that starts at zero and minimizes its squared distance from a set of positive numbers has to be positive. Actually, there was a bit of a relationship there, which we all missed at the time. Service charges did have a tendency to rise with concentration when we re-ran their regression in a more conventional form, though it was nonsignificant by most standards ($t = 1.39$). But they only had 11 degrees of freedom.

Another, less statistical tale on the same subject deals with the coming of "free checking" to New England in the late 1960s by Steven J. Weiss (1970). Checking accounts with no service charges came first in Boston which has the least-concentrated banking market in New England. It had 72 banks, a CR3 of 33, and a Herfindahl index of 620. By the time he did his paper, it had spread to 7 other New England SMSAs with 4 to 18 banks (mean or 9.7) CR3 of 66 to 99 (mean of 81) Herfindahl Indexes of 1770 to 3690 (mean of 2,750). It had not yet been offered in 11 other metropolitan areas with 4 to 11 banks (mean of 5.0), CR3 of 81 to 99 (mean of 90.4) and Herfindahl indexes of 2,540 to 6,300 (mean of 3,190). In other words, the cities with "free checking" before mid-1968 were considerably less concentrated than those where it came later. But his main point was that most of the banks that introduced "free checking" were small and, generally, new banks. By and large they gained a lot from their new accounts. Those who followed said they gained very little from the no-service-charge policy.

A bit further down the same road, Heggested and Mingo (1976) set out to use a general set of multiple regressions to see what banks used to attract "customers" who are apt to be depositors of several sorts, borrowers, and users of various other services. They included a series of variables that characterized the bank and the city, among which were H and $-1/H$ introduced alternatively. Presumably, they used the negative sign on $1/H$ so that it would increase with concentration. They used data from 332 banks in 69 metropolitan areas surveyed by the Fed in connection with mergers in 1970.

The performance variables and the coefficients for H or $-1/H$, whichever yields the better fit, are listed below in order of their t ratios.

Dummy = 1 if bank offers trust services	$-0.7521H$
	(0.1297)
	$[-5.80]$
Interest rate on new car loans	$0.00060(-1/H)$
	(0.00014)
	$[4.15]$
Dummy = 1 if 24 hour banking service	$-0.497H$
	(0.195)
	$[-2.550]$
Hours bank office is open (per week)	$-20.067H$
	(10.506)
	$[-1.91]$

Dummy = 1 if bank offers safe deposit boxes $-0.001548(-1/H)$
                                                    (0.00886)
                                                    $[-1.75]$

Service charge on a hypothetical demand deposit $0.02242(-1/H)$
                                                    (0.01401)
                                                    $[1.60]$

Interest rate on a one-year CD $-0.000069(-1/H)$
                                                    (0.000046)
                                                    $[-1.51]$

Passbook interest rate on savings deposits $-0.000055(-1/H)$
                                                    (0.000042)
                                                    $[-1.31]$

Three other variables that had t ratios of less than 1.00 were the charge for checks returned because of insufficient funds, dummy with a value of one if the bank offers an overdraft-line of credit service, and minimum yearly charge for a safe deposit box.

Timothy Hannan (1979) set out to do something no one else had done before in any industry—to test the "limit pricing" model of Joe Bain. This seemed possible in banking in Pennsylvania because the branching laws limited entry by branching to banks with head offices in the same or adjacent counties. Beyond that he knew from other studies that such entry by branching is largely the work of banks with assets in excess of $300 million (in 1970). His measure of potential entry threat was therefore the number of banks of such size or larger with home offices in the same or adjacent counties that were not yet doing business in the market under consideration. He subdivided Pennsylvania into 53 banking markets and took a bank in a market as an observation. He controlled for several relevant variables plus concentration, his potential entrants variable, and, in some regressions, an interaction between the two. His dependent variable was the common passbook interest rates on savings deposits throughout. His study applied to 1970 only, so there was a ceiling of 4.5 percent on such interest rates, and the great blossoming of CD's had yet to occur. He tells us that about half of the rates observed were at the ceiling.

Concentration always had the expected effect on time deposit interest rates, and it was usually significant. Number of banks in the market consistently worked better than CR3 or the Herfindahl index. The coefficient of the number of potential entrants (NPE) was always positive, as expected, and generally significantly so. With both variables and an interaction in the regression, the result was

Passbook = $0.062N + 0.22NPE - 0.0062N \times NPE$.

| Interest | (0.014) | (0.07) | (0.0024) |
| Rate | [4.24] | [3.24] | [-2.58] |

Potential entrants do seem to make a difference, but quite plausibly their effect falls off as numbers of banks already in the market grows. Only when N reaches 35 does potential entry lose all of its competitive effect. N's own competitive effect disappears when there are ten potential entrants. Recall that a potential entrant had to have $300 million in assets in 1970 (maybe $1 billion 1989 dollars). Ten is a lot of big banks. It may lie beyond the range of observation.

So a directly measurable threat of potential entry affects price. It's not a surprise, but it's been awfully hard to demonstrate with the usual data.

It does not do what Hannan claimed, however. Bain's limit pricing occurred when the firms already in the market set price so low that no entry occurred. Evidence of literal limit pricing would have to show that no entry occurred. Nevertheless, Hannan should be congratulated in getting much farther down that road than anyone else had at the time of his study.

Allen Berger and Timothy Hannan (1989) have recently published another study involving the interest rates paid on money market deposit accounts. The Fed collected the data in a survey of 470 banks in 195 banking markets for ten quarters beginning September 1985. The authors worked largely with pooled cross-sectional time series. But unlike the others who have done this, they included a slope and intercept variables for each quarter, so the only thing pooled was the effect of their general control variables such as the bank branching rules. Not only were all ten slopes negative, they were all significantly so. The authors introduced market share in one formulation in an attempt to deal with the Demsetz-Peltzman formulation. Market share was significantly associated with high MMDA interest rates. And the slopes relating concentration to price became *more* negative and yielded higher t ratios in each of the ten quarters when market share was in the model.

I felt that the recent and broad application of their data made it ideal for a series of runs on alternative concentration indexes. The following note is their response to my request.

Deposit Interest Rates and Local Market Concentration
Allen N. Berger and Timothy H. Hannan[2]

In this paper we seek to examine the relationship between local market concentration and pricing behavior in the banking industry. Since the market for most of the products offered by commercial banks are geographically limited, commercial banking is one of a few industries that allows researchers the luxury of conducting within-industry cross-sectional estimations of the relationship between local market concentration and observed prices.

For the purpose of this paper, we focus on the rates offered by banks for Money Market Deposit Accounts (MMDAs). Because of regulatory constraints, these accounts are relatively uniform across banking institutions. In December 1985, the period examined here, a maximum of three checks per month could be written on these accounts, and $1,000 minimum balance was required. Results similar to those reported here for MMDA rates were also obtained for other time periods and for other types of deposit accounts and are reported in Berger and Hannan (1988).

Note that in this empirical application the prices at issue (deposit interest rates) are paid to consumers rather than by consumers. The existence of noncompetitive pricing behavior in more concentrated markets, as suggested by the structure-performance hypothesis, implies in this case a negative (rather than positive) relationship between market concentration and observed prices. Since theory provides little guidance in suggesting which measure of concentration to employ when the type of noncompetitive behavior at issue is studied, we report results obtained using several different measures of concentration. These are the one- to five-firm concentration ratios, the Herfindahl index, the square root of the Herfindahl index, and two dichotomous measures of concentration.

The Data

The data employed in this study are quite extensive. The refined sample upon which reported results are based contains 399 banks located in 177 different local banking markets. Data on MMDA rates are obtained from the Federal Reserve's Monthly Survey of Selected Deposits and Other Accounts, and they refer to the rates offered for deposits issued during the seven-day period ending on December 25, 1985.

Banks in the sample are assigned to local markets, using FDIC Summary of Deposits data for 1985. Following previous research (see Rhoades 1982), local banking markets are defined as Metropolitan Statistical Areas (MSAs) or non-MSA counties. Banks that do not have at least 75 percent of their deposits in one local market are omitted from the sample to ensure a close correspondence between the deposit rates banks offer and the characteristics of the markets in which they operate. This refinement of the sample turns out to be qualitatively unimportant since equivalent results (not reported) are obtained in the absence of this restriction.

Empirical Results

The definitions of all variables employed in the analysis are listed in table 12.4. Table 12.5 presents the results of nine OLS regressions that differ from each other only with respect to the measure of concentration employed. In the interest of brevity, the rationale for and the coefficients of

Table 12.4
Variable definitions for table 12.5

Dependent variable	
	Money Market Deposit Account rate paid on the largest dollar volume of deposits issued during the seven-day period ending on December 25, 1985 (basis points)
Independent variables	
CRi	The i firm deposit concentration ratio, defined as the proportion of total commercial banking deposits in a local banking market (MSA or non-MSA country) accounted for by the largest i firms (percent)
H	Herfindahl index of bank concentration, defined as the sum of squared market shares (sum of percent squared)
RTH	Square root of the Herfindahl index
$CCR2(47)$	Dummy variable set equal to one if the two-firm concentration ratio is greater than 47 percent (the level that maximizes adjusted R^2 and zero otherwise)
$CCR4(71)$	Dummy variable set equal to 1 if the four-firm concentration ratio is greater than 71 percent (the level that maximizes adjusted R^2) and zero otherwise.
1YRGROW	one year growth in market deposits (proportion)
BANKPROP	(Number of bank branches)/(number of bank branches + number of S&L branches) in the market
WAGE	Index of local banking wage rate ($000/quarter)
PCINCOME	Per-capita disposable income in local market ($/year)
MSA	Dummy variable indicating location in a Metropolitan Statistical Area
UNIT, LIMIT	Dummy variables indicating location in a unit banking or limited branching state, respectively

Table 12.5
MMDA rate regressed on various measures of concentration

Exogenous variables	Concentration measures								
	CR1	CR2	CR3	CR4	CR5	H	RTH	CCR2(47)	CCR4(71)
CONSTANT	689.6**	707.6**	709.0	725.3**	735.9**	690.0**	725.3**	670.0**	652.3**
	(23.8)	(24.4)	(23.7)	(23.7)	(23.1)	(24.3)	(23.3)	(27.0)	(26.0)
CONCENTRATION	−0.77**	−0.70**	−0.60**	−0.70**	−0.74**	−0.11**	−1.13**	−28.41**	−22.03**
	(−3.31)	(−4.46)	(−4.08)	(−4.67)	(−4.69)	(−3.63)	(−4.48)	(−6.59)	(−4.97)
1YRGROW	38.57**	38.29**	40.18**	42.30**	42.62**	39.55**	39.17**	41.11**	44.86**
	(2.77)	(2.78)	(2.91)	(3.08)	(3.11)	(2.85)	(2.85)	(3.07)	(3.28)
BANKPROP	1.61	2.86	5.21	6.26	5.89	5.76	3.38	20.32	26.68
	(0.77)	(0.14)	(0.25)	(0.31)	(0.29)	(0.28)	(0.16)	(1.01)	(1.29)
WAGE	3.00	2.92	2.48	2.33	1.87	2.71	2.05	3.43	3.90
	(1.26)	(1.24)	(1.05)	(0.99)	(0.79)	(1.15)	(0.87)	(1.51)	(1.67)
PCINCOME	−0.0004	−0.001	−0.0008	−0.001	−0.001	−0.0007	−0.001	−0.0007	−0.0003
	(−0.33)	(−0.78)	(−0.70)	(−0.95)	(−1.00)	(−0.55)	(−0.88)	(−0.62)	(−0.24)
MSA	−9.36	−11.00	−10.78	−12.53	−12.81	−11.32	−12.02	−10.82	−7.82
	(−1.43)	(−1.70)	(−1.66)	(−1.93)	(−1.96)	(−1.71)	(−1.85)	(−1.75)	(−1.24)
UNIT	7.64	8.75	9.34	9.99	9.34	7.21	7.88	6.33	8.54
	(1.38)	(1.59)	(1.69)	(1.82)	(1.70)	(1.30)	(1.44)	(1.19)	(1.57)
LIMIT	−6.57	−4.65	−4.52	−3.21	−3.72	−6.73	−4.68	−3.94	−4.57
	(−1.399)	(−0.99)	(−0.95)	(−0.67)	(−0.78)	(−1.44)	(−0.99)	(−0.87)	(−0.89)
$\bar{R}^2$	0.075	0.095	0.088	0.100	0.100	0.080	0.095	0.144	0.100

Note: Dependent variable is MMDA rate in basis points, December 1985 data. t ratios in parentheses. The symbol ** indicates significance of the 1 percent level.

the various control variables are not discussed here. The reader is referred to Berger and Hannan (1988) for such a discussion.

Note first that the coefficients of all nine measures of concentration in table 12.5 are negative, as implied by the structure-performance hypothesis, and all are significant at the 1 percent level. The general magnitude of this relationship may be seen by noting, for example, that the coefficient of $CR2$ implies a predicted 49 basis point difference in the MMDA rate between a bank in the most-concentrated market in the sample ($CR2 = 89$) and a bank in the least-concentrated market in the sample ($CR2 = 19$), *ceteris paribus*. Similar computations using the other concentration measures shown in table 12.5 yield 38 to 51 basis point differences between the most- and least-concentrated markets.

The two dichotomous measures of concentration, $CCR2(47)$ and $CCR4(71)$ DUM, are set equal to one when $CR2$ and $CR4$ are greater than 47 and 71 percent, respectively, and zero otherwise. These cutoff values maximize the adjusted R^2's for the regression equations. The coefficient magnitudes of $CCR2(47)$ and $CCR4(71)$ indicate predicted 28 and 22 basis point differences between banks above and below the 47 and 71 percent cutoffs, respectively.

In general, these results suggest a strong, statistically significant relationship between market structure and bank prices that is consistent with the implications of the structure-performance hypothesis. They have also been found to be robust with respect to the inclusion of additional (and potentially endogenous) variables, such as measures of bank size, bank market share, and the number of bank branches (not reported).[3]

The nine measures of bank market concentration employed here differ somewhat in their explanatory power and in their quantitative effects on deposit rates. The two dichotomous measures have the highest adjusted R^2's but give smaller predictions for the maximum effect of concentration than any other concentration variable shown. The five CRs, the Herfindahl index, and square root of the Herfindahl index are similar in both adjusted R^2's and predicted quantitative effects of concentration, although it is noticeable that the equation with $\sqrt{H}$ has more explanatory power than the H equation. Similarly, replacing each of the five concentration ratios with its square (not reported) reduces the adjusted R^2 of the equation, suggesting that measures involving the squares of market shares may have slightly less explanatory power than the square roots of these measures.[4]

Although the comparison across these measures is of descriptive interest, we cannot claim in any rigorous fashion which measure is best. What we can claim, however, is that the results of using all nine measures give statistically significant results that are consistent with the implications of the structure-performance hypothesis.

Conclusions

The general conclusion seems obvious to me. Selling prices rise with concentration, and buying prices fall with concentration. The banking industry, which has produced about as many concentration-price studies as all other industries put together, yields massive support for the prediction of conventional oligopoly theory.

The most widely studied prices are loan interest rates. I tentatively counted 47 separate loan interest rate data bases in the accompanying table counting a year or a region or a separate set of customers as a separate data base. The 47 counts the duplicates of the same data bases of Edwards, Flechsig, Murphy, and Phillips only once each and it counts the many studies based on Rhoades' banking market data base only once for each year. Of those in the table, 40 yield positive effects (for CR or H, negative for N) on loan interest rates, 21 of which are significant (by a two-tail 5 percent test). Seven yielded negative effects, one of which was significant. I am not including Flechsig in this count. He reported four nonsignificant negative and two nonsignificant positive slopes, but everyone else who worked with the same data (Edwards, Murphy, and Phillips) got positive effects in most of these cases. I am counting Taylor as yielding a significant positive effect, even though he said the relationship was not significant. His results clearly contradict his statement.

Most of the nonsignificant relationships were where they should be in theory. Borrowers with ready access to the money markets should not pay more on concentrated local markets, because they can readily borrow elsewhere, especially in New York. Four of the nonsignificant positive and two of the nonsignificant negative relationships are such cases. They do not contradict theory at all. A second group of nonsignificant coefficients appeared in the tight money years of the 1950s and 1960s, and were what was generally expected when the studies were run.

There is one more source of weak relationships that I am less certain about. That is in rural banking. To catch the effects of fewness in isolated rural setting, it won't do to include billion dollar banks, as Fraser and Rose did in two of their four studies, nor substantial cities as Kaufman did in his Iowa study. Such studies are worth making, but they don't test the hypothesis that rural banks don't compete on price. Two of the Fraser and Rose papers, one by Ware in Ohio, and at least one more limit themselves to non-SMSAs. The typical result seems to be a weak negative effect of numbers of banks on loan interest rates. I am inclined to agree with Fraser and Rose. I would not be surprised to find that the two banks that have faced each other on opposite corners in some small town in Ohio or Texas for the last century or so are unlikely to compete hard on price. But I'd much rather that problem were solved by easy entry, which one of their papers shows can have strong effects, than by horizontal merger as they propose in another paper.

The results for time deposit interest rates are weaker, but the amazing thing to me is that they worked at all. There was a ceiling on them through the period covered by the most of studies reviewed in this chapter. In fact, in the years when the ceiling was really tight, there was no relationship, but at other times concentration tended often to reduce time deposit interest rates.

In a sense the most surprising concentration-price relationship was concentration and demand deposit service charges. This turns out to be where the effect of concentration on price is strongest. Looking back on it, the strong effect makes reasonable sense. Banks discriminated when they are few enough to control their prices, and that means they raise prices most where customers resist least—on check charges, of all things!

The effect of concentration on these three prices is important for the purposes of this book. Here is an industry which has been studied again and again and concentration raises price in most of the situations where theory says it should.

But is it important for society? It's hard to imagine that check charges are. The Fed's lid on time deposit interest rates probably shifted money out of the banks and into money funds when open market interest rates were towering, but it is hard to imagine practical bankers keeping interest rates low if they were losing saving deposits in great quantities as a result. High loan interest rates have been subjects of major controversy and some government intervention—most effectively in the form of FHA and VA mortgage insurance that permitted small borrower access to the national market.

In the case of small commercial loans, however, I doubt that the interest rate has ever been the main issue. I think I agree with Fraser and Rose, again, that the main issue is the bank's portfolio. How willing are the banks to lend, especially to new, small business borrowers? They certainly shouldn't lend to all of them—just those with good prospects. Hopefully

competition will induce bankers to extend such efforts to get those customers. The studies that emphasize balance sheet ratios suggest that it does.

The other feature of the concentration—interest rate relationship in banking is that it almost always seems to turn out to be economically small.
How can a relationship that is almost always of the right sign and is
significant much of the time be so unimportant. I think there are several
ways it is often understated, but even allowing for them, the effect still
does not seem to be great.

First, interest rates rose and credit conditions tightened over the period
to which these studies applied. Edward's first year was 1955 when the
prime rate was 3.16 percent. It reached 10.81 percent in 1974. At least the
theory, when we started these studies, was that the effect of concentration
on interest rates was weak in times of credit shortages. Part of the reason
for the very small effects in the later part of the period was probably this.
It seems premature to call the change in the effect of concentration on
interest rates of the early 1970s permanent. I would guess from past
experience that a concentration—interest rate relationship in the mid-1980s
would look more like those of the 1960s than the results based on the
mid-1970s when the studies end.

Second, the banks have to take the money market rates they are given.
Only for the borrowers dependent on local markets can bankers control
interest rates. If we average the loans to large borrowers with many
alternatives with the local borrowers, as we do when we use IL/TL, we
probably understate the relationship.

Third, the nominal interest rate may understate the effective rate paid by
many small business borrowers because of the compensating balances they
must maintain. Scott found that it understated the effect of concentration
on interest rates by about 30 percent, but Jacobs found no systematic
tendency.

Fourth, banks offer local deposit services as well as local loans, and in
normal years concentration is apt to raise check charges and reduce time
deposit interest rates. To a considerable extent the borrowers are also
the depositors—partly because of the compensating balances just mentioned. A few researchers have studied the spread between IL/TL and
ITD/TD. It may be a bit more responsive to concentration than either of
its components.

Now put them all together. Imagine that in the 1990s conditions like
those of the early 1960s reappear so that a ten-point rise in $CR3$ raises
interest rates by 2.0 percent. At 1988 interest rates this would mean about
0.2 percentage points. Add a third for compensating balances, and it rises
to about 2.6 percent. Perhaps with no ceiling on time deposit interest rates

the slope of the concentration–*ITD/TD* relationship falls below any previous level, to −0.2 percent. All of these are at or beyond the outer fringe of what such studies have yielded since they began. Yet the combined effect of a ten-point rise in concentration does not add up to even 5 percent, which would be less than half a percentage point of interest if it all fell on the borrower.

Is it worth all the fuss? People who say yes are apt to be thinking more of bankers' willingness to lend locally and of his ability to be arbitrary. The concentration-price relationship may be a symptom of monopoly power that can have more serious effects in other dimensions.

Americans have worried about monopoly in banking almost since the nation began and, I have no doubt, will continue to do so. I would much rather that concern be oriented toward promoting competition in banking than toward regulatory restrictions a it did so often in the past.

We seem to be moving quite rapidly toward nationwide or at least regional branch banking, mainly by means of the holding company device. That seems fine with me. I hope we wind up with one or two hundred banks instead of 10 or 15 nationwide branch systems such as most countries have now. My way of ensuring that is to prohibit the ten largest banking organizations from acquiring the *leading* bank in any SMSA. This is a small restriction. They can acquire other banks, and smaller organizations can acquire the leading bank. But this should ensure that we still have a hundred or more major banks when it is all over and that a variety of banks exist in most SMSAs.

Two or three or even four branches of national banking organizations facing each other in downtown Centerville may not compete very hard either. I liked the Weiss paper on "free checking" (and not just because of the author's name—no relation). To go by that paper, the way to have competition in a town with room for only three banks is for one of them to be a branch of a regional holding company, one to be a branch of Citycorp, one to be a local unit bank, and the fourth to be a savings and loan association with NOW accounts. Add to that no legal restrictions on entry, and Centerville could have a fairly competitive banking market even with $CR3 = 100$.

Notes

Leonard Weiss is indebted to Kenji Nishida, a student at Keio University, Tokyo, for help on the statistical work done in connection with this chapter.

1. The last column of table 12.2 reports the percentage effect of a ten-point increase in $CR3$. Ideally this should be calculated at the point of means. That is, the percentage increase (or decrease) in interest rate, say, from the mean interest rate. This was done when the author reported mean interest rates, but only a small minority did so in the published material. In other cases we used rough estimates. For the years 1955 to 1965 we assumed that small borrowers or small loans paid 6 percent and that large borrowers paid the prime rate as reported in 1985 *Economic Report of the President*. In later years we based our percentage increases on the prime for IL/TL and on the prime plus 1 percent for small loans. Only one study with small loans after 1965 (Scott 1977).

The meaning of a ten-point increase in $CR3$ also required some assumptions when concentration was measured by some other index. We assumed ten-bank market with market shares as follows:

20   17   13   12   9   8   7   6   5   4

After a ten-point increase in concentration, we pictured an eight bank market with the following market shares:

24   20   18   12   10   7   5   4

This implies that a ten-point rise in $CR3$ would mean a 4-point rise in $CR1$, a 7-point rise in $CR2$, a 12-point rise in $CR4$, a 13-point increase in $CR5$, a two-firm decline in N, an increase in $1/N$ of 0.0250 (0.1000 to 0.1250), an increase in the Herfindahl index of 0.0360 (0.1250 to 0.1610). If readers find this fiction unreasonable, they may try other changes where $CR3$ is not the measure of concentration. Most of these numbers are the result of trial and error and are merely plausible, but the relationship between $CR4$ and H was derived from a regression of $CR4$ on H and H^2 for a random sample from the 1982 census concentration volume for manufacturing. The numbers in that case were chosen to fit together where $CR4$ was near 60 and H rounded to 0.1000.

2. Allen N. Berger and Timothy H. Hannan, economists, Board of Governors of the Federal Reserve System. The opinions expressed here are those of authors and do not necessarily reflect the opinions of the Board of Governors or its staff.

3. See Berger and Hannan (1989) for a detailed discussion of these and other robustness tests conducted.

4. The Herfindahl index and the squares of the concentration ratios have been derived as the appropriate measures of concentration in *nonlinear* relationships between price and concentration under varying assumptions concerning the nature of the noncompetitive behavior at issue. See Yamawaki (1984) for a concise exposition. However, theory provides little guidance in this regard in the case of *linear* equations.

References

Aspinwall, R. C. 1970. "Market Structure and Commercial Bank Mortgage Interest Rates." *Southern Economic Journal* 36 (April), 376–384.

Bell, F., and N. Murphy. 1969. "Impact of Market Structure on the Price of a Commercial Banks Service." *Review of Economics and Statistics* 51 (May), 210–213.

Edwards, F. R. 1964. "Concentration in Banking and Its Effect on Business Loan Rates." *Review of Economics and Statistics* 46 (August), 294–300.

Berger, A., and T. Hannan. 1989. "The Price-Concentration Relationship in Banking." *Review of Economics and Statistics* 71:2 (May), 291–299.

Edwards, F. R. 1965. "The Banking Competition Controversy." *National Banking Review* 3 (September), 1–34.

Flechsig, T. 1965. "The Effect of Concentration on Bank Loan Rates." *Journal of Finance* 20 (May), 298–311.

Fraser, D., and P. Rose. 1972. "Banking Structure and Performance in Isolated Markets: The Implications for Public Policy." *Antitrust Bulletin* 17 (Fall), 927–947.

Frazer, D., and P. Rose. 1976. "Static and Dynamic Measures of Market Structure and the Performance of Commercial Banks." *Journal of Economics and Business* 28 (Winter), 79–87.

Hannan, T. 1979. "Limit Pricing and the Banking Industry." *Journal of Money, Credit, and Banking* 11 (November), 438–446.

Heggestad, A., and J. Mingo. 1976. "Prices, Nonprices, and Concentration in Commercial Banking." *Journal of Money, Credit and Banking* 8 (February), 107–117.

Jacobs, D. B. 1971. *Business Loan Costs and Bank Market Structure*. NBER Occasional Paper 115. New York: Columbia University Press.

Kaufmann, G. G. 1966. "Bank Market Structure and Performance: The Evidence from Iowa." *Southern Economic Journal* 32 (April), 429–439.

Marlow, M. 1982. "Bank Structure and Mortgage Rates: Implications for Interstate Banking." *Journal of Economics and Business* 34 (Spring), 135–142.

Marvel, H. P. 1976. "The Economics of Information and Retail Gasoline Price Behavior: An Empirical Analysis." *Journal of Political Economy* 84:5 (October), 1033–1060.

Marvel, H. P. 1978. "Competition and Price Levels in the Retail Gasoline Market." *Review of Economics and Statistics* 60:2 (May), 252–258.

Murphy, N. 1968. "A Study of Wholesale Banking Behavior." Ph.D Thesis, University of Illinois.

Phillips, A. 1967. "Evidence on Concentration in Banking Markets and Interest Rates." *Federal Reserve Bulletin* 6 (June), 916–926.

Rhoades, S. 1981. "Does Market Structure Matter in Commercial Banking?" *Antitrust Bulletin* 26 (Spring), 155–181.

Rhoades, S. 1982. "Structure—Performance Studies in Banking, An Updated Summary and Evaluation." Staff Study 119. Board of Governors of the Federal Reserve System.

Rhoades, S., and R. Rutz. 1979. *Impact of Bank Holding Companies on Competition and Performance in Banking Markets."* Staff Studies 107. Washington DC: Board of Governors of the Federal Reserve System.

Schweiger, I., and J. McGee. "Chicago Banking." *Journal of Business* 34 (July), 203–366.

Scott, J. 1977. Price and Non Price Competition in Banking Federal Reserve Bank of Boston.

Taylor, C. 1968. "Average Interest Charges, the Loan Mix, and Measures of Competition: Sixth Federal Reserve District Experience." *Journal of Finance* 23 (December), 793–804.

Ware, R. 1972. "Banking Structure and Performance: Some Evidence From Ohio." *Federal Reserve Bank of Cleveland Economic Review* (March), 3–14.

Whitehead, D. 1978. "An Empirical Test of the Linked Oligopoly Theory: An Analysis of Florida Holding Companies." Working Paper Series, Federal Reserve Bank of Atlanta (June).

Yamawaki, H. 1984. "Market Structure, Capital Expansion and Pricing." *International Journal of Industrial Organization* 2, 29–62.

13   Conclusions

This project has been long and varied and needs a summary more than most. The first section will deal with the basic question, does price rise with concentration? The second will examine the evidence available on functional form. The third addresses the question, What difference does it make?

Does Concentration Raise Price?

Our first step is simply to classify the results and sum them up. This is done in tables 13.1 and 13.2. In table 13.1 a data set is an observation. Data on the same markets for different periods were treated as different tests. In one set of cases in banking one author found nothing, but the three others who worked with the same data found quite a lot. The nonresults seemed easily explainable by the dummy variables used. At any rate the data sets involved were assigned the conclusions of the other scholars.

There are many cases in banking, mainly because there were many studies, but Phillips (1967) studied four borrower-size classes in four periods and thereby presented us with 16 similar data sets. In the gas stations case Howard Marvel ran the same regression in 24 months in 1973 to 1975. His purpose was not to accumulate points for this book but to test whether and when prices were set by price controls rather than market forces. At any rate, gas stations got over weighted in table 13.1.

Table 13.2 attempts to remedy this by letting an industry be an observation. That is, the results of one data set or of many on the same industry are reported in percentage terms. So for cement, where seven different years are studied, each year is reported as 14 percent of the results. Banking and gas stations play a much larger role in table 13.1 than in table 13.2.

Which is right? Probably the correct answer falls somewhere in between. Successive months' results for gas stations seem bound to be correlated,

Table 13.1
Effect of concentration in price

Industry or study	Number of data sets	Number of Data Sets with:			
		Significant positive effects	Non-significant positive effects	Non-significant negative effects	Significant negative effects
Cement	7	5			2
Change in concentration	3	2	1		
Auctions	6	6			
Unions	2	2			
Change in CR Germany (prices)	1		1		
EEC (margins)	5[a]	3[a]	1[a]	1[a]	
Advertising space and time	7	2	2	2	1
Airlines	9	9			
Gas stations	26	20	5	1	
Supermarkets	2	2			
Rail freight rates	3	3			
Banking	49	21	20	7	1
Beef purchases	1[b]	1[b]			
Total	121	76	30	11	4
Percentage of total		62.8	24.8	9.1	3.3

a. Change in price-cost margin dependent.
b. Buying price so negative coefficient expected and found.

Table 13.2
Percentage of studies that yielded various results

Industry or study	Percent significant positive	Percent non-significant positive	Percent non-significant negative	Percent significant negative
Cement	71			29
Change in CR—change in price	67	33		
Auctions	100			
Unions	100			
EEC (margins)	60	20	20	
Germany—change in CR—change in price		100		
Airlines	100			
Advertising space and time	28	28	28	14
Gas stations	77	19	4	
Supermarkets	100			
Rail freight rates	100			
Banking	43	41	14	2
Slaughter house beef	100			
Mean	72.8	18.6	5.1	3.5

but time series on rail grain shipments in the nineteenth century seem so different from a cross section on unit train freight rates for grain in 1982 to justify their treatment as different "industries," though that was not done. And the single result for slaughter house beef purchase price is actually a pooled cross-sectional time series of ten successive years. The author ran each year separately at one point and got negative coefficients for each of them, but they were statistically significant in only eight years—which is pretty good with nine degrees of freedom. Reporting it as one sure thing reenforced the results in table 13.2. Reporting them as ten different regressions would have had the effect of shifting too much of our information into the "perhaps negative" category where it distinctly does not belong. In other words, even tables 13.1 and 13.2 are subject to judgment. The reader can remake those tables, if he wishes, since they are based entirely on the material reported in this book.

The results in tables 13.1 and 13.2, whichever one chooses, seem to give overwhelming support to the concentration-price hypothesis. If you could take the 121 data sets analyzed as independent random draws, then a finding that *either* 61 or 73 percent of them yield significantly positive effects and that only 3 percent of them had significantly negative effects would tell you to accept the hypothesis. Using a 5 percent two-tailed test standard, we should see several data bases that yield "significant" negative effects by pure chance. Using the same approach, we can guess that several of the positive tests are the result of chance also, but we have more than half of the total sample left in the statistically significant group. Moreover there are far more nonsignificant positive than negative results. And I believe that a number of these actually represent very significant positive results when taken altogether.

The four significant negative effects should be examined more closely. Two of them are essentially the same case. The first significant negative effect in cement, found for 1961, seemed so strange that I was sure it was due to a large error we couldn't find. So I asked my coauthor to run it over for a similar nearby year. He tried 1959, calculated all of the variables over going back to the original sources, and got essentially the same result. What did it mean? After thinking about it for two years I now believe that it probably reflects the previously collusive character of cement markets. The positive effect of concentration on price in 1948 and 1953 was due primarily to a few extremely concentrated markets mainly in the West. With the basing point system in tact in 1948 and effectively so in 1953, it didn't make much difference within the range of observation now concentrated the market was.

That doesn't say why the industry yielded a negative effect of concentration on price in 1959 to 1961. I think this was largely an historical accident. The least-concentrated markets were the ones centered in eastern Pennsylvania and the Hudson Valley. Until 1961 they had many small, old plants and hardly any large ones by national standards. The small firms that owned these small plants account for the low concentration. Cement has one of the steepest long-run average curves in modern industry. When the basing point system died in the late 1950s, prices fell to levels reflecting the costs of the low-cost producers that already owned quite large kilns in the Midwest and California, but not in the East at first. This could not last, and with the opening of the Ravena plant near Albany, low prices came to the East with a vengeance. Even that does not interpret the finding as the obvious result of oligopoly pricing but rather as the result of a large, high-priced market attracting a firm with huge economies of scale. It was at least partly historical accident still. By 1973 and 1980, when there were huge kilns selling cement in most large markets and when rising energy costs had reduced their advantage, the standard positive concentration-price relationship began to represent the normal prediction of oligopoly theory.

Newspapers are clearly a special case. Huge economies of long production runs, the role of circulation in selling advertising, and the importance
of at least local ads in selling papers all point to low monopoly prices!
All of the coefficients of local newspaper competition are negative, but
only the Sunday competition coefficient is significantly so. I don't know of
any other unregulated industry that yields anything like this result.

I know much less about the other significant negative relationships that
were found by David Whitehead (1978) in Florida banking. His main
concern was with the effect of multimarket holding companies on interest
rates. I really have no explanation for his unusual result. I presume it had
something to do with Florida or the period or both. It should be pointed
out that he got the usual significant negative effect of concentration on
ITD/TD.

Others read some of the 11 nonsignificant negative coefficients and the
30 nonsignificant positive coefficients in table 13.1 differently also. The
author of the gas station studies, Howard Marvel, interprets the significant
effect of concentration as indicating that gasoline prices are determined by
market forces. During the winter and spring of 1974 which he feels was the
one period when oil price controls really worked, concentration had no
significant effect. These account for one nonsignificant negative and five
nonsignificant positive coefficients in table 13.1.

Quite a lot of the banking studies that yielded nonsignificant results
should have done so according to standard analysis. Large loans to large
borrowers were distinguished in a number of the early studies. These
borrowers have access to national credit markets, and local concentration
should have little or no influence on the interest rates such borrowers must
pay. Some of the early banking studies were also expected to show little
effect on even small loan interest rates in tight money periods in those
days, because small loan interest rates seemed to be pegged at a rough
ceiling not very different from the interest rates charged large borrowers
when credit was tight.

It is time to stop trying to explain outliers. They will occur in any review
of 121 data sets. Every case is a special case. The point to statistics is to
identify and characterize the general leaving the special features of each
case to random residuals. Taking this approach, we have found what I feel
is very strong evidence that concentration raises price.

Is it correct to take 121 data sets or 70 or so studies or even a dozen or
so categories of studies as independent random draws from nature? Is there
a bias in favor of positive, or even more, significant results? I doubt it,
considering some of the stuff that has been published in banking in par-

ticular. In any case, if bias toward significant results exists, it would follow from the presence of only three of four significant negative findings that the exceptions where prices fall systematically as concentration rises must be very few. A bias in favor of positive effects is conceivable, but I should think the opposite bias is more likely. A well-done study yielding a clear-cut negative effect is certainly unusual, whereas well-done positive effects are all about us. Ultimately, the reader will have to draw his own conclusion. At least it is not obvious.

In tables 13.1 and 13.2 a data set was judged to support the positive concentration-price relationship if it yielded at least one significant coefficient with the expected sign for a concentration index, even if it also yielded nonsignificant coefficients for others. It seems excessive to demand that all formulations have significant coefficients. The Cournot relationship seems to imply that price should rise with $1/N$ or H. If it does not also rise significantly with CRi, that prediction is not hurt.

A significant negative relationship in a well-done study must be taken as evidence against a tendency for price to rise with concentration, of course. Happily, we never found a case where concentration significantly raised prices in one formulation and significantly lowered them in another. The closest we came was in cement in 1959 where the coefficient of $CR4$ had a t ratio of -1.89 and that for $CCR2(90)$ had a t ratio of $+1.70$. We concluded that the general relationship was negative in that year and the $CCR2(90)$ reflected the special conditions in a few very concentrated markets, mainly in the West.

Did we rig it? One economist told me after a seminar in which I had summarized the material in part I of this book that he would have gotten similar results some times but that he felt certain they would not have been so consistently positive. I certainly did not intentionally distort the studies in part I or select only positive results in part II. Indeed, when I learned of the Whitehead study and did not have a copy, I made considerable effort to get one and include it. And when Ferguson sent me a draft of his summary of his newspaper advertising paper in which emphasized the nonsignificant results, I revised it myself to include the significant negative effects for Sunday papers.

At the same time, however, there is no doubt that my reaction to the significant negative result found in 1961 for cement was different from my response to the many significant positive results that flowed in. I never responded merely because of the result with "That is impossible. Look hard for a big error." When I thought I saw a big or small error, I called for more work, but not merely because of a "wrong" sign on concentration.

Functional Form

The main difference among the great oligopoly theories is a matter of functional form. Cournot ([1838] 1963) implies that price should rise with $1/N$ or, according to Stigler, with the Herfindahl index if costs differ (Stigler 1968). Chamberlin (1983, 1948) expected a critical concentration ratio. Stigler's theory pointed to H again. Auction theory pointed to the maximum or second-order statistic. I don't know of any theory that points to a linear relationship as is implied with the i-firm concentration ratio, but it is used widely, so we will see how well it stacks up with other indexes. One fault with the concentration ratio is that it derives from only one point on the concentration curve, whereas H reflects the entire curve, but H puts a great deal of emphasis on the shares of the top firms. An alternative that rises more slowly with CR is the square root of the Herfindahl index.

Ideally, we should run a series of regressions using alternative concentration indexes but keeping the other explanatory variables the same and choose among them on the basis of goodness of fit. This was only possible in a few cases. For the most part I had to work with what was available.

Table 13.3 reports the t ratio for each of variables outlined in the next to last paragraph. In the cases of CRi and $CCRj$ only the best fits are reported. The estimated best fitting CRi's and $CCRj$'s are identified along with the t ratios. The best-fitting functional form where goodness of fit was based on R^2 was the same as that based on t ratios. Unfortunately, most studies used only one or a few indexes of concentration. When only one is reported, we skip it, but when two or more appear, we report them. In cement, airlines, and money market deposit accounts, we were able to introduce many of these functional forms.

In cement $CR1$ yielded the best fit in 1948 and 1953, and a $CCR2$ of 90 yielded the only positive effects worth mentioning in 1959 and 1961. For the record, the largest negative t ratios were for $CR6$ in 1959 and $CR5$ in 1961, and both were highly significant. The ordinary continuous $CR3$ fit best in 1965, $CCR2$ of 40 and $CCR4$ of 70 tie in 1973 and $CCR2$ of 50 and $CCR4$ of 80 tie in 1980. These ties may look suspicious but recall that there were only 24 observations. $CCR2$ of 40 and $CCR4$ of 70 split the industry into the same set of markets and therefore yielded the same set of residual variances.

In auctions where all three measures are available the maximum-order statistic fits best in five of the six classes of autions and is barely nosed out by the second-order statistic in the last. Both fit much better than $1/N$ in those regressions. Where the single-bidder case is included, which means

Table 13.3
t Ratios relating alternative concentration indexes to price concentration index

Industry and date	CR4	Best-fitting CRn	H	$\sqrt{H}$	N	1/N	Best-fitting CCR2	Best-fitting CCR4
Cement								
1948	3.56	CR1 5.52	4.96	4.48			50 4.10	90 3.53
1953	2.12	CR1 5.58	5.12	5.22			90 3.61	90 5.01
1959	−2.59	CR1[a] −0.76	−0.36	−1.10			90 1.37	90 −1.25[a]
1961	−2.89	CR1[a] −0.13	0.06	−0.74			90 1.70	40 −0.05[a]
1965	4.11	CR3 4.18	3.05	3.71			30 2.60	50 3.24
1973	4.40	CR5 4.53	3.45	3.85			40 3.68	70 3.68
1980	2.58	CR2 2.64	2.38	2.46			50 2.94	80 2.94

	For 2−11 bidders				For 1−11 bidders	
	Maximum-order statistics	Second-order statistics	1/N		Maximum-order statistics	1/N
Underwriting						
General obligation Bonds	−12.86	−10.75	8.70		−18.24	14.13
Revenue bonds	−10.73	−10.53	9.00		−12.33	19.91
Offshore oil tracts						
1954−1971	21.54	15.00	−9.88		16.83	−7.02
1972−1975	8.59	7.08	−6.01		12.09	−6.59
National forest timber						
Oral bids	5.61	5.37	−4.85		6.94	−4.80
Sealed bids	7.51	7.54	−7.26		11.61	−7.67

Industry and Date	CR4	Best-fitting CRn	H	$\sqrt{H}$	N	1/N	Best-fitting CCR1	Best-fitting CCR2	Best-fitting CCR3
Air fares									
Lowest unrestricted daytime fare		CR1 3.69	4.09	3.76	−2.58	2.58	54 4.38	71 2.11	93 1.62
Average unrestricted daytime fare		CR3 2.94	1.38	1.18	−1.94	1.33	35 3.11	60 3.11	93 3.41

Table 13.3 (continued)

Industry and date	CR4	Best-fitting CRn	H	$\sqrt{H}$	N	1/N	Best-fitting CCR2	Best-fitting CCR4
Gas stations			4.84				CCR4 of 50[b]	
Super-markets	4.044	CR3 4.825	3.323	3.396			Not as good a fit as CR4[b]	
Freight rates Grain								
1969–1898					−1.07	2.73		
1877–1886		CR2 1.76	2.07	2.22	−2.40	2.08		
Banking								
Scott (1977) small business loans		CR3 2.3	2.6					
Aspinwall (1970) mortgages		CR3 2.71				Log N −3.88		
Marlow (1982) mortgages		CR5 2.44			−2.17			
Kaufmann (1966) Iowa banks 1959								
IL/TL		3.96			2.85			
ITD/TL		−5.15			−4.28			
1970								
IL/TL		4.59			2.82			
ITD/TL		−5.83			−3.36			
Berger and Hannan (1987) interest rate on MMDA December 1985	−4.67	CR2 −4.69	−3.63	−4.48			47 −6.59	71 −4.97

a. Least negative.
b. *t* ratios not comparable with those shown here.

that the second-order statistic does not exist, the first-order statistic yields the better fit in five of the six auction classes, but $1/N$ fits better for underwriting spreads on revenue bonds.

In airlines the best fit in terms of the t ratio is for $CCR1$ of 54 for the minimum unrestricted daytime fare and for $CCR3$ of 93 for the average unrestricted daytime fare. There is ambiguity in the first result, however, because of colinearity between $CCR1$ and entry. If we use R^2 as a criterion, H is a better explainer of average unrestricted daytime fares. This result persists when distance and distance squared are included in the model (not shown). We conclude that H yields the best fit for the minimum but $CCR3$ of 93 yields the best fit for the average unrestricted daylight fare.

Howard Marvel used only H in the original form of both of his gas station studies (1976, 1978), but he found a distinct $CCR4$ of 50 when he ran his earlier study over in a paper searching for CCR's using dummy variables (Geithman, Marvel, and Weiss 1981). Muller, Marion, et al. used several concentration indexes. Their best fit was for $CR3$. In the same subsequent study in which Marvel participated, Geithman searched their data for a critical concentration ratio and found none (Geithman, Marvel, and Weiss 1981).

For rail freight rates when we tried to characterize the entire period 1869 to 1898, the only concentration variables available for all years were N and $1/N$. It is not surprising that $1/N$ won. In the period 1879 to 1886, when we had the data to construct most of the standard concentration indexes, H yielded the best fit. MacDonald used H exclusively in his study of unit train rates, so we cannot compare them with other indexes.

Most of the banking studies used only one concentration index. The few that tried two or three appear in table 13.3. The most common comparison was between CRi and N, and CRi won. But log N did better in the one case where it was the alternative, and H did better in another. At my request, Berger and Hannan, in a brief section of chapter 12, tried almost all the concentration indexes we have used working with their study of December 1985 MMDA interest rate. They found that a $CCR2$ of 47 offered a much better fit than any other index they examined.

To summarize, some simple CRi fit best in three years in cement (five if you think in terms of maximizing negative coefficients in 1959 and 1961). CRi did better than N in two banking studies, but worse than log N or H in two others. Many CRi's were used by themselves in other studies and yielded significant coefficients quite often. They should not be written off, especially if the researchers have no alternative. H fit best for minimum unrestricted airline fares and the rail freight cartel when it was available, and again did well in a number of other cases where no alternative was tried. $1/N$ worked better for the longer-period nineteenth-century freight rates when we had only N and $1/N$.

But the most unexpected result was that $CCRj$ fit best at least once in four cases where we could compute or at least approximate it. This was true of four of the seven cement years, average but not minimum unrestricted daytime airfares, retail gasoline, and MMDA interest rates. It only missed for food retailing. What the four cases where CCR worked best have in common is that the dependent variable is the price of a single well-defined product. This makes some sense. In the supermarket case the dependent variable was a price index covering 94 products. It seems probable that retail concentration will affect the prices of some of these products differently from others.

Our form of CCR was merely a dummy variable for cases where some CRi exceeded a specified level. We tried a variety of alternative $CCRj$'s and reported the value of j that fit best. Early in the history of the project, we took steps of five and ten points each. In banking and airlines we took one-point steps in the area where the CCR seemed to lie. In two respects our measure was undountedly too restrictive. No change in concentration above or below CCR was considered, and when CCR was reached, it was abrupt. Chamberlin had pictured a more gradual transition (1933, 1948, 52–53). It is all the more surprising, then, that CCR was the best-fitting index in so many cases.

The CCR was certainly predicted in advance—by 60 years. The first concentration profits studies gave it mild support (Bain 1951; Stigler 1963), but it has simply dropped out of fashion. To the extent that we are able to estimate it, at least for well-defined prices, we are probably seeing something real. When working with broad averages or some indirect measures such as profits or margins in many different industries, we are less likely to spot it—perhaps it deserves resuscitation.

One thing that all the functional forms discussed so far imply is that the effects of concentration seem to be minor at levels below $CR4$ of 50. This is true with respect to $1/N$, H, and all of our $CCRj$s. Something like it is true of all of the auctions we studied. By the time there are eight bidders, most of the effect of numbers on winning bids has been attained. It therefore is true of all the auctions studied, minimum restricted air fares, gas stations, nineteenth-century freight rates, and bank MMDA interest rates. It is doubtless true of some of the other cases where H fit well but where no comparison with other indexes was presented.

The suggestion that concentration below $CR4 = 50$ makes little difference for many of our concentration indexes would not necessarily apply is the best fit involved CRi or N or $\sqrt{H}$. $CR3$ fit best in cement in 1965 and in supermarkets. These cases might conceivably imply that concentration has a significant effect on price well below $CR4 = 50$. Extensions of the effects of concentration below $CR4 = 50$ are limited to cement, where the minimum $CR4$ after 1961 is 33, and supermarkets, where the sample included two SMSAs where $30 < CR4 < 35$. The power of $CR1$ in the early days of cement offers no help at the low end of the distribution.

We can hardly claim to have exhausted the possibilities. We have tested $CCRs$ with a few data sources we could readily manipulate. Many other people have the data that can be used to test the appropriateness of $CCRs$. And we haven't even tried all the viable concentration measures. Some very reputable economists believe that entropy or a variant of it offers information not available in the indexes we have used.[1] This is one more reason for us to limit our enthusiasm when drawing conclusions from this section.

In view of the policy implications of a possible finding that concentration makes little difference below $CR4 = 50$, our suggested results seem to call for a great deal more careful research.

What Difference Does It Make?

The last step is to try to work out how much prices are likely to be raised by concentration. Our criterion will be the percentage rise in price associated with a ten percentage point rise in $CR3$. Table 13.4 contains our estimates.

We adopt the $CR3$ standard for consistency with chapter 12 and, in the process, adopt the series of arbitrary equivalents used there. We assume that a 10 point rise in $CR3$ implies a 4 point rise in $CR1$, a 7-point rise in $CR2$, a 12-point rise in $CR4$ and a 13-point rise in $CR5$. We also assume it will ordinarily imply a 2-firm fall in N, a rise in H of 360, and a rise in $1/N$ of 0.025. This was all a matter of plausible guesswork except for H which was derived from a rounded version of a regression of H on $CR4$ and $(CR4)^2$ squared using a random sample from the 1982 concentration data.

A problem arises when we examine markets with few sellers. What is a 10 percent increase in concentration when we have only two sellers in the market? We will interpret it to mean that in a sample of ten markets all with two sellers to start with, one of the ten has only one seller at the end while

Table 13.4
Effects of a 10 percentage point rise in CR3 on price

Study	Percentage change in price with a 10 Percentage Point in CR3
Cement	
1948	1.12
1953	0.88
1959	−0.36
1961	0.12
1965	2.32
1973	7.85
1980	3.98
Airlines	
Call and Keeler 1980, minimum trunk fare	0.9
minimum unrestricted daytime fare	2.4
average passenger yield	0.9
Bailey, Graham and Kaplan, Q3 1980	2.5
Q4 1980	2.4
Q1 1981	3.4
Q2	2.7
Town and Milliman, Q3 1980	
Minimum unrestricted daytime fare (using H)	2.6
Average unrestricted daytime fare (using $CR3$)	4.3
(using $CCR1(39)$ one route in 10)	1.6 (16.3 on that route)
Change in concentration, change in price	
Consumer goods	5.8
Materials	5.7
Captial goods	1.7
Auctions (going from 5.5 to 5 bidders)	
Underwriting general obligation bonds	4.5
Underwriting revenue bonds	4.3
Offshore oil tracts, 1954–1971	8.6
Offshore oil tracts, 1972–1975	7.2
Sealed-bid timber auctions	13.9
Oral timber auctions	9.6
Effect of $CR4$ on	
Wages of nonunion workers	4.2
Implied effect on price if labor is 30 percent of price	1.2
Collective bargaining coverage	19.6
Wages of union workers	10.5
Implied effect on price if labor is 30 percent of price	3.1
Effect of change in $CR4$ by 0.12	
on price in Germany	3.3

Table 13.4 (continued)

Study	Percentage change in price with		
	10 point rise in CR3	In one town	In one town out of 10
Advertising rates			
Stigler, milline rates			
Going from 2 evening papers to 1 evening paper		4.2	0.4
From evening and morning papers to 1 evening paper.		6.8	0.7
Going from 10 to 8 or 20 to 16 or 50 to 40 stations on commercial rates (elasticity of −0.07)	1.6		
Ferguson, milinch rates			
Going from 2 to 1 daily paper.			
national rates		−5.9	−0.6
retail rates		−1.8	−0.2
Sunday papers:			
national rates		−12.2	−1.2
retail rates		−13.3	−1.3
Bloch and Wirth:			
Going from 2 to 3 stations in 1 city out of 10	3.4		
Going from 3 to 2 stations in 1 city out of 10	3.9		
Retailing			
Gas stations			
1964−1971			
High prices	Premium 2.6 Regular 2.6		
Low prices	Premium 10.8 Regular 11.2		
1973−1975			
Overall mean	4.9		
Supermarkets			
In 32 large SMSAs	1.7		
In 35 towns in Vermont		4.8	0.5
Railroad freight rates			
1871−1898 average rates	1.62		
1878−1886 rates	0.6		
1982 unit trains:			
wheat	1.3		
corn, soybeans	2.3		
Slaughter house beef purchase prices	−2.6		
Banking			
Edwards, Murphy, and Phillips			
Loans to borrowers with less than 100,000 assets	1.1−3.0		
Mortgages	0.3−2.2		
Chicago banking:			
auto loans	0.2		
personal loans	0.7		

Table 13.4 (continued)

Study	Percentage change in price with		
	10 point rise in CR3	In one town	In one town out of 10
Reports of condition			
IT/TL:			
1962–1972	0.7–1.7		
1973–1975	0.1–0.4		
1978 Florida	−1.0		
Rural banking			
Iowa 1959–1960 means	IL/TL	1.7	0.2
	ITD/TD	−5.2	−0.5
Texas, means for	IL/TL	3.4	0.3
1960, 1961, 1965, and 1966	ITD/TD	−6.7	−0.7
	SC/DD	16.5	1.6
ITD/TD:			
1959–1962	−1.1 to −4.8		
1966–1975	−0.07 to +1.0		
SC/DD:			
1966–1975	6.0–12.0		
MMAD interest rates:			
1983–1985	−1.3		

the other nine have two. This of course implies that the effect of concentration on price is linear, which is not at all necessary, especially at the monopoly-duopoly level, but it seems the best we can do. The alternatives are much less comparable with a 10 percent change in concentration in other industries. One of the alternatives is to stick to the smallest direct observation available—which might mean a 50 percent drop in numbers of sellers or a 100 percent increase in $CR1$ for newspapers, for instance. Both are far greater than we will see in most industries with a true rise in $CR3$ of 10 percentage points. The other alternative is to project the change from one and two newspapers out to ten, which seems absolutely insane. It is several miles beyond the range of observation.

The results of table 13.4 are striking primarily because they are small. The increase in price is much less than proportional with the decrease in concentration in almost every case.

Is this really small? How big is a 10 percentage point increase in $CR3$? It depends on where you start. Our main public policy with respect to concentration today has to do with mergers. Two mergers that raised $CR4$ from 20 to 32 (no one merger could do it) might go unchallenged in 1989, but one that increased $CR4$ from 60 to 72 probably would be sued. Such mergers are rare. They are surely significant in most people's eyes when they occur. The point is not to comment on merger policy but rather to say that at least within the industries where $CR4$ is high, perhaps more than 50, many observers count a 12 percentage point increase in $CR4$ as important. The small effect of concentration change is not due to a small change in concentration.

If all the effect of increasing concentration went into profits, the effect on profits might be quite large. For instance, if profit were 10 percent of price in a competitive market, 12-point rise in $CR4$ might raise price by only 1 percent, say, but this could double total profits before taxes. There are several potential slips between the rise in $CR4$ and the rise in profits, but assuming it did work out that way, the main result would be almost entirely a matter of income distribution. Even a series of changes that raise concentration from 20 to 70 would raise price by only 5 percent. The direct welfare loss due to a 5 percent rise in price is pretty small, though the rise in profits could be huge.

Of course it doesn't all go into profits. One of the main papers in this book concludes that concentration raises wages either directly for non-union workers or indirectly for union workers in the sense that it encourages unionism, which raises wages. But even this does not lead to a large price concentration if wages are only a third of total receipts.

The largest expense for most manufacturing is materials. We have not emphasized this, but the clearest case we covered, beef purchases by meat packers, yielded a significant negative effect of concentration. The same applied to interest on time deposits. Might the tendency for high concentration to yield low purchase prices offset the tendency for high seller concentration to increase price? In meat packing, which has been extremely competitive on the selling side, I would expect sellers to take every advantage they can find. This would imply that most of any monopsony gains there reach the consumers. This argument seems less compelling in the case of small-town banking, especially if many of the deposits are required as compensating balance.

What about the auctions? Why do they yield such large price effects of concentration? Some auction theorists tell us it is because high value assets attract more buyers in auctions, and that we are making a mistake in assigning the entire effect to the numbers of bidders. We should estimate a two-equation model with value attracting bidders as well as many bidders forcing up winning bids. I have resisted this argument, largely because our results fit so well to the theoretically predicted functional form. We were not just testing the hypothesis that winning buying bid rises with number of bidders. We were fitting the values to the maximum and the second-order statistics. We got remarkably close fits—better than with a quite similar functional form $(1/N)$ for things as diverse as offshore oil tracts, underwriters' fees on municipal bond issues, and National Forest timber. There just has to be something there.

Is there something we are missing? Is the tendency for prices to rise with concentration merely a symptom of monopoly power? Does monopoly yield other changes that may be much more costly to society than a small percentage rise in price? Where it is a matter of merger to monopoly or at least market dominance, I think, the nonprice effects can dominate. So far, at least, mergers to monopoly on national markets subject to ordinary antitrust are still out of the question, but there are two places where they have often occurred locally in recent years. One is in small-town banks where monopolies or duopolies have been created by mergers approved by the banking authorities. I have no doubt that the effect of concentration on various bank prices is minor compared with the possibility of arbitrary treatment of individual borrowers. Even if such behavior is rare, there is good evidence that concentration permits small-town banks to keep the percentage of their assets in the form of local loans low, which has the effect of limiting credit to small borrowers.

The other place where merger to near monopoly was often permitted has been in the airlines. The Department of Transportation rather than the Anti-trust Division was responsible for mergers in the unregulated airline industry during the first decade after deregulation (through 1988). A number of the major airlines were permitted to merge with other airlines with the same hubs. As a result competition in service to small cities using those hubs was largely eliminated. As a resident of Madison, Wisconsin, which depends primarily on Detroit and Minneapolis hubs for most destinations, I can report on the effect of the Northwest-Republic merger.

Announced prices did not change, but I feel certain that the availability of "special deals" is reduced. Before the merger there were four morning departures for Detroit. Now there are two, and if you expect to get to New York or Washington in time to do anything the day you arrive you have to get up at 5 am for a flight at 7. Northwest also laid off about half of the airport staff of the two airlines. As a result you could count on standing in a long line at any popular hour. Northwest undoubtedly saw these changes as cost reductions. I have no doubt that this was highly exploitative behavior which an economist looking at prices would not detect.

So there may be more cost than higher prices when concentration reaches very high levels. It is not at all clear, however, that these nonprice elements of monopoly appear at the same rate that prices rise short of near monopoly.

Summary

I believe that our evidence that concentration is correlated with price is overwhelming. I also believe that contestable markets is a largely empty box and that until someone provides us with clear evidence that it exists somewhere, it should play no role in public policy. Our evidence on functional form is so diverse that we cannot justify any one oligopoly theory over the others. It does look as if concentration makes little difference below $CR4 = 50$, but our evidence below that level is limited to cement and supermarkets. Evidence on functional form is still spotty. Future studies of the effects of concentration should try a variety of concentration indexes and not just $CR4$ or H. A functional form that has been slighted in the past has been the critical concentration ratio. Yet one of the main oligopoly theories points to it, and it fits better than any other transformation in three of the five prices where we used that index, and in several years in cement as well. In a world of cheap and easy computers, I see little reason not to search for a CCR in future studies of concentration.

Finally, I must admit that the results to date, though much more consistent than I expected in advance, do tell us that monopoly is not our most serious economic problem. It is a problem, but it does not compare with even small wars or recessions, and it probably does less harm than unequal access to education or distortions introduced by the tax system. But this conclusion is reached by an inhabitant of the largest economy in the world, a country that has taken antitrust more seriously than any other country for close to a century. In smaller lands and/or in nations with less enthusiasm for antitrust, the problem must surely be greater.

References

Bain, J. 1951. "Relation of Profit Rates to Industry Concentration in American Manufacturing 1936–1940." *Quarterly Journal of Economics* 65 : 3 (August).

Chamberlin E. 1933. *The Theory of Monopolistic Competition.* Cambridge, MA: Harvard University Press.

Cournot, A. 1838. *Researches into the Mathematical Principles of the Theory of Wealth, 1938.* Reprint 1963. Homewood, IL: Irwin.

Ferguson, J. 1983. "Daily Newspaper Advertising Rates, Local Media Cross-ownership, Newspaper chains, and Media competition." *Journal of Law and Economic* 26 : 3 (October).

Geithman, F., H. Marvel, and L. Weiss. 1981. "Concentration, Price, and Critical Concentration Ratios." *Review of Economics and Statistics* (August), 346–353.

MacDonald, J. M. 1987. "Competition and Rail Rates for the Shipment of Corn, Soybeans, and Wheat." *RAND Journal of Economics*, 151–163.

Marion, B., W. Mueller, R. Cotterill, F. Geithman, and J. Schmelzer. 1979. *The Food Retailing Industry Market Structure, Profits, and Prices*. New York: Praeger.

Marfels, C. 1971. "The Consistancy of Concentration Measures: A Mathematical Evaluation." *Business and Economics Section Proceeding*, American Statistical Association, 143–151.

Marfels, C. 1971. "Absolute and Relative Measures of Concentration Reconsidered." *Kyklos* 24:4, 753–766.

Marfels, C. 1972. "On Testing Concentration Measures." *Zeitschrift fur Nationalokonomie* 32, 461–486.

Marvel, H. P. 1976. "The Economies of Information and Retail Gasoline Price Behavior: A Empirical Analysis." *Journal of Political Economy* 84:5 (October), 1033–1060.

Marvel, H. 1978. "Competition and Price Levels in the Retail Gasoline Market." *Review of Economics and Statistics* (May).

Phillips, A. 1967. "Evidence on Concentration in Banking Markets and Interest Rates." *Federal Reserve Bulletin* 6 (June), 916–926.

Stigler, G. 1963. *Capital and Rates of Return in Manufacturing Industries*. Princeton: Princeton University Press.

Stigler, G. 1968. *The Organization of Industry*. Homewood, IL: Irwin.

Theil, H., 1967, *Economics and Information Theory*, Amsterdam: North Holland, Chapter 8.

Whitehead, D. 1978. "An Empirical Test of the Linked Oligoply Theory: An Analysis of Florida Holding Companies." Federal Reserve Bank of Atlanta Working Paper Series (June).

Index